INAPPROPRIATION

INAPPROPRIATION

The Contested Legacy of Y-Indian Guides

PAUL HILLMER AND RYAN BEAN

UNIVERSITY OF MISSOURI PRESS

COLUMBIA

Copyright © 2023 by
The Curators of the University of Missouri
University of Missouri Press, Columbia, Missouri 65211
Printed and bound in the United States of America
All rights reserved. First printing, 2023.

Library of Congress Cataloging-in-Publication Data

Names: Hillmer, Paul, 1960- author. | Bean, Ryan, 1980- author.
Title: Inappropriation : the contested legacy of Y-Indian Guides / Paul
    Hillmer and Ryan Bean.
Description: Columbia : University of Missouri Press, 2023. | Includes
    bibliographical references and index.
Identifiers: LCCN 2022047676 (print) | LCCN 2022047677 (ebook) | ISBN
    9780826222794 (hardcover) | ISBN 9780826274847 (ebook)
Subjects: LCSH: Y-Indian Guides--History. | Fathers and sons--United
    States--Societies and clubs. | Parent and child--United
    States--Societies and clubs. | Children--Societies and clubs. | Cultural
    appropriation--United States. | Ethnocentrism--United States.
Classification: LCC BV1172 .H55 2023 (print) | LCC BV1172 (ebook) | DDC
    267/.3973--dc23/eng/20221207
LC record available at https://lccn.loc.gov/2022047676
LC ebook record available at https://lccn.loc.gov/2022047677

∞™ This paper meets the requirements of the
American National Standard for Permanence of Paper
for Printed Library Materials, Z39.48, 1984.

Typefaces: Adobe Garamond and Museo Sans

Frontispiece: From the cover image of the first printed issue of *Long House News*, January
10, 1935. All issues housed at the Kautz Family YMCA Archives, University of Minnesota
Libraries.

CONTENTS

ILLUSTRATIONS

ACKNOWLEDGMENTS

The authors listed on the cover of this book did not accomplish this project alone. We are indebted to many people who have inspired and informed us over the years as we continued to study, write and see our views about this topic evolve.

First and foremost, we thank Pam Atkins, Gene Keltner Cannon, Bob Eilenfeldt, Carmelita Gallo, Stephen Hanpeter, Bruce Klingman, Peggy Larney, Dave Lehleitner, Norris Lineweaver, Greg Measor, Les Neal Jr., Greg Norman, Larry Rosen, Thomas Saylor, Mel Shelby, Barbara Taylor, Shiloh Thurman, Ronn Wilson, and Jim Wotruba. Your generous sharing of time and experience added to our understanding and appreciation of the complex and nuanced narratives that shaped this project.

We also thank those who read all or parts of our manuscript and gave substantive feedback. These gracious individuals include Colleen Arendt, Eric Dregni, Katie Johnston-Goodstar, Don Kodluboy, Norris Lineweaver, Denis O'Pray, Debbie Redmond, Larry Rosen, Debbi Snook, and our two anonymous reviewers. We hope you see that we took your comments to heart.

We are grateful for the wonderful people at the University of Missouri Press; specifically Gary Kass, who took the time to send an encouraging reply to our proposal so many years ago; Mary Conley, for expertly guiding this project to conclusion, and our copy editor, Miranda Ottewell, who polished the text in a way only a stickler could. Kudos also to Robin Rennison for marketing expertise and Drew Griffith for overseeing production.

We offer sincere thanks as well to Greg Measor, a cofounder of National Longhouse, who shared numerous resources with us, including accounts and records from Joe Friday's descendants that we would not have otherwise seen. His generosity is greatly appreciated.

The efforts of those who helped us search for documents, photographs, and other historical artifacts must be recognized, especially: the staff and student workers at the Kautz Family YMCA Archives, University of Minnesota Libraries; the late Gene Keltner Cannon, who was the steward of her father's Indian Guides effects until her death; the late Zelli Fischetti at the Thomas Jefferson Library, University of Missouri–St. Louis; Renée N. Godinez at the YMCA Trout Lodge and Camp Lakewood; Debbie Redmond from the Gateway Region YMCA; and Ann Sindelar at Western Reserve Historical Society, Cleveland, Ohio.

We tried to include as many Native American perspectives as possible in this book, and we respect those who chose to decline or not reply to our inquiries.

We acknowledge the limitations placed on this study because two white males authored it. We studied, accumulated knowledge, developed informed perspectives, and endeavored with sincere and well-intentioned hearts and minds, but we admit nonetheless that our identities bind us and limit our ability to understand the full complexity of this topic. Though we have striven to rise above our limitations, we claim no infallibility. We have done the best we could with the resources we found.

Finally, we remember that during the course of writing this book, one of us lost his father, father-in-law, and last two uncles. The other came close to losing his father, said goodbye to his last grandfather, and, proudly, became a father. Fatherhood is not only a strong motif in this book, it has been a recurring area of reflection for both of us these last several years. What did our fathers and other male role models do for us? What do we owe them? What did we learn from them, both as examples and warnings? What, looking back years later, might they have done differently? Do our disagreements with them in any way diminish our love, gratitude, and respect for them? How might parental love override or ignore broader societal concerns and obligations? Our hope for the father figures (and mothers, too) who read this book is that, like us, they take an opportunity to reflect on their relationships with their children and how they develop and nurture those relationships. Do parents need a co-opted persona to tell their children they love them, to convey the values they hold dear, to have an excuse to go hiking or camping or build something together? We hope not.

Individually, Ryan Bean would like to thank Jessica Ayers-Bean for her love, patient listening, engaging conversation, and witness through this journey and others. My mother, Ellen Corsiglia, for always being my champion; yours is a strong example of unconditional love. Scott Bean and John Corsiglia, father and stepfather, for showing me the many ways of being a father. This book would not exist without my coauthor Paul Hillmer, who took a wayward transfer student so many years ago and pointed him toward the archives for an internship; one can only wonder how things would have turned out minus your practically divine intervention and years of friendship. Lastly, I want to thank Miles Bean for inspiring and challenging me to be a loving and intentional father each and every day; I love you, buddy.

As for Paul Hillmer, I thank my beloved partner Janet Starn Hillmer, who makes all my life's endeavors more bearable, joyous, and worthwhile. I remember and honor my father, Stan Hillmer, my father-in-law, Roger Starn, but also my mother, Ann Hillmer, who was my real "guide" as a boy. I thank Drs. Fred Bartling, Robert Kolb, Paul Marschke, and Richard Cushing, father figures to me in different stages of my life. I thank Concordia University-St. Paul for giving me time away to finish this manuscript. I may have helped Ryan Bean get his start, but he has become a highly respected and widely consulted individual within the YMCA movement and to the many scholars who study it. His knowledge as an archivist has been indispensable. I could not have asked for a better partner and friend on this journey. Finally, I dedicate my work on this book to our late daughter, Julianna Marie.

To anyone we've neglected to mention, we hope you see your contributions. We may have lost the thread, but your impact is nonetheless real. Thank you.

INAPPROPRIATION

INTRODUCTION

THIS BOOK ISN'T about Indians. We will, of course, discuss Indigenous peoples, and given the subject, one should be prepared to see the word *Indian* throughout this book. What we mean is that this book is not centered on the rich and varied cultures that comprise the peoples collectively known as Indigenous, Native American, American Indian, First Nation, and Indian.[1] This book is about mostly white middle- and upper-middle-class fathers and sons (and later fathers and daughters and mothers and daughters) who participated in a program first developed by Harold Keltner, a YMCA boys' work secretary from St. Louis, Missouri, and Joe Friday, an Ojibwe Indian and member of the Temagami First Nation in Lake Temagami, Ontario.

Y-Indian Guides grew both out of Keltner's desire to replace old, moribund annual father-son banquets with something more sustained and effective, and Friday's critique of white urban fathers who, in his opinion, foisted their child-rearing responsibilities onto mothers, teachers, scout leaders, and pastors. Y-Indian Guides insisted that fathers and sons—never one without the other—gather twice a month in the homes of fellow members, adopt "Indian" names, and sit together in a circle. They pledged to be "Pals Forever," to be clean in body and pure in heart, to love the sacred circle of their families, be attentive when others spoke, love their neighbors as themselves, and seek and preserve the beauty of the Creator's work in forest, field, and stream.

Like many other institutions in and occasions on which white people seek to imitate and/or emulate Native Americans, Y-Indian Guides (and later Y-Indian Princesses for fathers and daughters and Y-Indian Maidens for mothers and daughters) provided a kind of remedy or palliative to the ills of an industrialized, corporate postwar America. In an era when the melting pot was the ideal, they sought guidance not

Figure 1. Y-Indian Guides fathers leg-wrestle at a "tribe" meeting in Flint, Michigan, fall 1948. Y-Indian Guides created an environment that encouraged fathers to be more playful with their sons, and at least occasionally with each other. Kautz Family YMCA Archives, University of Minnesota Libraries.

in the traditions of the country's white forebears but in what was seen increasingly, through the eyes of regret, nostalgia, and romanticism, as quintessentially American cultures: those of Indigenous peoples.

In 1968 over 500,000 members participated in Y-Indian Guides in the United States. In January of that year, the program's leaders were so convinced of its power to transform relationships that they described it as "one of the most productive avenues of positive advance" for the YMCA and society as a whole. It not only strengthened families but became a force for "constructive interracial advance," facilitating integration both nationally and in the South.[2] It received endorsements or attention from celebrities and local, state, and federal officials. But most importantly for its adherents, it fostered warm and lasting relationships between fathers and sons. Participation in the program was often multigenerational, with fathers enthusiastically bringing their sons into the program because of the ways it enhanced relationships with their own fathers. Stories abound of men being buried in their Indian Guides vests or a father walking his daughter down the aisle, both in their Indian Princess vests. Seasonal rituals forged durable bonds that stood the test of time. Boys too shy to speak drew comfort and strength from their "tribe," learning to embrace the talking stick and the opportunity to converse with their fellow "braves." A father, until his dying day, closed his letters to his son with "Pals Forever."

Joe Friday's role not only in developing Y-Indian Guides but also in traveling the country recruiting new participants and establishing new "tribes" seems in the minds of many to inoculate the program against charges of insensitivity or cultural misappropriation. After all, a real Indian, born in a wigwam and living in the wilds of Lake Temagami, Ontario, helped bring it to life. To this day, tens of thousands of alumni cannot understand how anyone could find fault with the Y-Indian Guides program. Their intention was to honor those who first occupied this continent. From the accounts of the many former participants the authors of this book have interviewed, this confusion is often sincere, not merely defensive. But things are rarely that simple.

Participants in Indian Guides sought to step into spaces they deemed American Indian, co-opting what they believed were the best cultural traits of our nation's original inhabitants. The frequently claimed "permission" of Joe Friday was wielded as what Danielle Endress calls a trump card, shutting down any question of appropriation.[3]

The origin story for Indian Guides centers on how Keltner was inspired by Friday's lectures and conversations about growing up in the woods and being raised into manhood by his uncles. Even the most superficial examination of the program, however, reveals that it was designed to nurture an idealized white, Christian YMCA father-son relationship and had little to do with actual Native Americans. For instance, the "sacred circle" of family was a space not for matrilineal or extended family structures but rather for the prototypical American nuclear family: a mother who managed the home, a father provider, and children. Anything "Indian" was not only filtered through that lens but was and remains foundationally white, with a faux Indian motif added for self-serving theatrics. When, therefore, we say this book is not about Indians, it is because Indian Guides rarely surpassed a superficial and largely transactional relationship with Indian cultures.

Another frequently employed justification for the program is the countless families strengthened through participation. While we are not seeking to throw millions of participants under the bus or engage in blanket condemnation, one must understand that programs like Indian Guides have been harmful. By advancing narratives of Native Americans as a people of the past, they perpetuate colonialism, presenting no resistance to the appropriation of cultural heritage and, importantly, denying Native people's agency and identity in the present.[4] No amount of good can justify that truth. We shall see examples of colonialist thinking and practice throughout this book, alongside well-intentioned, sometimes even effective attempts to understand Indigenous peoples in their own context. Most notably, the YMCA used Christianity as a means of describing white political, cultural, and social dominance over Native Americans. In one case it went so far as to call Jesus, depicted in the New Testament not only as the Son of God but the son of Jewish parents raised in Egypt and Israel, as a "Great White Chief," more a personification of political subjugation or military conquest than universal, unconditional love (see chapter 5). And Harold Keltner, self-professedly "nuts about Indians" and Joe Friday's dear friend, could not help but publicly ascribe a negative attribute to Friday, not because of who he was as an individual, but because "he is Indian" (see chapter 4).

Organizations like the YMCA are an enterprise of white privilege at their foundation. In the United States, though serving a broad constituency, YMCAs have been predominantly white middle-class institutions that focus on and respond to the hopes and needs of that demographic group. This dynamic of centering whiteness gives insight into the construction of race through "everyday performances of White privilege."[5] In spite of Joe Friday's hand in founding the program, it was largely white fathers, and to a lesser extent YMCA professionals, who decided and implemented what was Indian. Though participants professed admiration for Indigenous peoples, as stated, their engagement rarely went beyond the superficial. What was truly "Indian," if anything, about the program, was usually lost in translation. The centering of the program on the needs of its white middle-class base meant that any attempts at legitimacy would miss the mark in every regard. "Authenticity," no matter how ardently sought, would prove perpetually elusive.

Those appropriating Native American culture rarely stop to contemplate how it would feel to have their own culture and values used in a similar way. Dr. Steve Long-Nguyen Robbins did exactly that in a 2002 essay. Imagine being a Christian, he wrote, living in a community founded by Christians but where currently only a small percentage of residents adhere to the Christian faith. Non-Christians start a school, and in homage to the city's founders, their athletic teams are called "the Christians." Since they have heard that nearly all Christians engage in something called "Communion," they decide that their mascot should ritualize the eating of bread and wine at games and school functions. Not only will it build school pride, they reason, it will also show that while they are non-Christians, they value the Christians in the community. Though Christians insist that the ritual actually dishonors Christians and is blasphemous, the majority takes offense and insists Christians should be grateful that non-Christians want to be like them. Their intentions are good, and Christians need to "lighten up."

> By this time, the re-enactment of Communion has become a regular part of half-time activities at basketball and football games. They've even added a life-sized cross with a real student on it for "effect." . . . When their team needs support they put their hands to their mouth twice, once to signify the eating of the bread and the other to show the drinking of wine. Non-Christians . . . are full of school and community pride when they see it.
>
> You and others in the Christian community continue to object. But since there aren't many of you and you are thought of as the "minority," no one listens. They tell you that you are wrong to take offense to such a wonderful display. . . . They continue their

insistence that there's nothing wrong with what they are doing. They tell you they won't be bullied by what they call "political correctness."[6]

We don't believe that the actions of Y-Indian Guides participants were malicious; rather we see in the program evidence of the ways in which whiteness, privilege, and colonial mindsets became reinforced over time. Of course, one can find evidence of such developments in many places.

In the spring of 2019, Republican Minnesota state senator Mary Kiffmeyer was so outraged and angry with her state's historical society that she sponsored a bill to cut $4 million from its $11 million budget. What egregious deed had the Minnesota Historical Society (MHS) perpetrated? On a sign welcoming people to Historic Fort Snelling, MHS added a Dakota place name, Bdote, meaning the confluence of two rivers (the Mississippi and Minnesota in this case). As *Minneapolis Star Tribune* columnist Jennifer Brooks described it, "Tribes and traders gathered [at Fort Snelling]. Zebulon Pike staked out the site of a future fort. Dred Scott dreamed of freedom. Soldiers served their country here. . . . The fort's language school taught Japanese to scores of soldiers during World War II. Sakpedan and Wakan Ozanzan—Little Six and Medicine Bottle—were hanged here. As many as 300 men, women and children died here during the Dakota War, killed by disease and exposure." MHS did not erase the name of Fort Snelling, but simply added, in smaller print, the phrase "at Bdote." According to Republican state senator Scott Newman, "The controversy revolves around whether or not the Historical Society is involved in revisionist history. I do not agree with what the Historical Society is engaged in doing. I believe it to be revisionist history." Longtime Democratic state senator John Marty replied, "I think that what you're calling revisionist history might be more accurate history. . . . Some people don't like that, because they like what we were told in [school]."

Senator Kiffmeyer later explained her actions: "It is the history of Minnesota. It is military appreciation. Minnesota's history all the way back to the Civil War and the very first regiments . . . is deep and strong and long. . . . Fort Snelling is about military history and we should be very careful to make sure that we keep that. It's the only real military history in a very unifying way amongst all Minnesotans."[7]

What Kiffmeyer meant by "unifying" or "all Minnesotans" may be open to interpretation, but few would doubt that she excluded the vast majority of Indigenous peoples in her definitions. But why? Scholars like Philip Deloria, Shari Huhndorf, and David Treuer would suggest that attitudes like Newman's and Kiffmeyer's are consistent with long-standing social and political practice in the United States. "That we [Native Americans] even *have* lives—that Indians have been living in, have been shaped by, and in turn have shaped the modern world—is news to most people," writes Treuer in *The Heartbeat of Wounded Knee*. "The usual story told . . . about 'the Indian' is one of diminution and death, beginning in untrammeled freedom and communion with the earth and ending on reservations, which are seen as nothing more than basins of perpetual suffering. Wounded Knee has come to stand in for most of that history. . . . It neatly symbolized the accepted version of reality—of an Indian past and an American present, begun in barbarism but realized as a state of democratic idealism." Even histories written by Indigenous peoples, says Treuer, most notably Dee Brown's classic *Bury My Heart at Wounded Knee*, can provide "the same old sad story of the 'dead Indian.'"[8] Efforts like Kiffmeyer's, then, continue the process of colonization that seeks to keep Native Americans limited by "the ghost of [their] modern afterlife," telling them that they who "were once great people are great no more."[9] Part of the anger over the "revisionist history" perpetrated by the Minnesota Historical Society seems to be a kind of frustration that Native Americans refuse to stay "dead." Triumphant white culture and history, this view implies, should remain dominant. As most college freshmen can recite, "History is written by the winners," and Indians were not the winners.

Yet before the massacre at Wounded Knee, even before the United States came into existence, writes Deloria, white people were already seeking to use Native American trappings for their own purposes by "playing Indian."

In the beginning, British colonists who contemplated revolution dressed as Indians and threw tea into Boston Harbor. When they consolidated power and established the government of the early republic, former revolutionaries displayed their ideological proclivities in Indian clothing. In the antebellum United States, would-be national poets donned Indian garb and read their lyrics to each other around midnight backwoods campfires.

At the turn of the twentieth century, the thoroughly modern children of angst-ridden upper- and middle-class parents wore feathers and slept in tipis and wigwams at camps with multisyllabic Indian names. Their equally nervous post–World War II descendants made Indian dress and powwow-going into a hobby, with formal newsletters and regular monthly meetings. Over the past thirty years [Deloria's book was first published in 1998] the counterculture, the New Age, the men's movement, and a host of other Indian performance options have given meaning to Americans lost in a (post)modern freefall. In each of these historical moments, Americans have returned to the Indian, reinterpreting the intuitive dilemmas surrounding Indianness to meet the circumstances of their times.[10]

In Deloria's view, then, European Americans seeking to emulate Native Americans, whether sincerely or opportunistically, are not honoring Indians but serving their own needs and desires. Non-Native people "playing Indian," even out of a stated love for Indians, he insists, cannot occur without committing a kind of reenactment of genocide against Indigenous peoples as well.[11] Non-Natives want to "re-create" cultures that once dominated the continent without coming to grips with the myriad misdeeds that led to their near extermination. As we shall see, even as Indian Guides leaders and participants sought to emulate Indigenous peoples, they rarely attempted to wrestle with the causes of the devastation visited on them. It is as if, inexplicably, Native American people all but vanished from the landscape, leaving their history and culture behind for non-Natives to use as they saw fit.

In her 2001 book *Going Native*, Shari Huhndorf explored the ways European Americans appropriated Indigenous cultures by "temporarily donning native costume and emulating native practices (real or invented)" as part of a quest for identity or authenticity. For Huhndorf, "going native" was a response to the late nineteenth-century military conquest of Native American people and land, which, when complete, brought about "widespread ambivalence about modernity" and created a sense of nostalgia for older, simpler, more "primitive" times. This coincided with Americans' attempts to "resolve . . . anxieties about the terrible violence marking the nation's origins. . . . Going native has thus been most widespread during moments of social crisis, moments that give rise to collective doubts about the nature of progress and its attendant values and practices."[12]

Harold Keltner certainly saw what became the Y-Indian Guides as a solution to a great social crisis. With hundreds of thousands of individuals migrating from farm to city in the late nineteenth and early twentieth centuries, Keltner asserted, fathers left home to earn their incomes elsewhere, severing the ties between themselves and their wives and, especially, their children. The father meant to do better, he insisted, but "instead he saw them less and left the job of training his son to the church, school, YMCA, and later [Boy S]couts and of course the good mother of the family." When these individuals and institutions failed to produce a responsible, dutiful son, wrote Keltner, "the father believed that these institutions were falling down on the job rather than himself."[13] Y-Indian Guides, coformulated with his able and enthusiastic partner, Joe Friday, became a way to avert juvenile delinquency and the breakdown of the family by focusing the father's energies on something he meant to do but didn't: spending time with his son (and later his daughter as well). Huhndorf's definition of "going native" thus describes the impetus for the Indian Guides' creation very well. By the late nineteenth century, many Americans came to believe that "adopting some vision of native life in a more permanent way [was] necessary to regenerate and to maintain European-American racial and national identities. Going native as a collective phenomenon . . . expressed a widespread ambivalence about modernity, and it is in relation to modernity's ills that these Native relationships took shape."[14]

But how did a people and culture once seen as inferior, even deemed by some as worthy of complete erasure, become so widely imitated and exploited? Huhndorf points first to the country's growing desire to focus on and interpret its own history. In 1895, for example, a government report entitled *What the United States Government Has Done for History* asserted that "it was not until about 1875 that the Government and the people of the United States [clearly a reference that excluded all Native

Americans] seemed to realize that our country had a history."[15] In order
to rectify this deficit, civic leaders and scholars created ever greater numbers of "public historical displays" and "large-scale commemorations of
the white man's foundational events." Examining the full history of the
United States, however, raised a significant quandary: "The history of
America, a nation born from the genocide of Native peoples and built
on slave labor, undermined the values of liberty and equality the nation
claimed to hold dear. . . . Native America challenged Europeans' occu-
pancy of the continent and thus, threatened the legitimacy of the nation
itself."[16] Historians of the period, then, sought to explain the slaughter
of American Indians in a way that justified white Americans' possession
of and their place and privilege in the country.

To show the origins of this process, Huhndorf studies nineteenth-
century world's fairs, the country's "first mass cultural events." As such,
"their influence was monumental, and they both shaped and reflected a
white, middle class ethos." The 1876 Philadelphia Exposition, attended
by ten million people (nearly a fifth of the nation's population at that
time), "commemorated the birth of the white nation, while its vision of a
unified America hid the massive racial and class conflicts which plagued
the nation during the late nineteenth century." Since the thirteen colonies
formally declared their independence from England in Philadelphia, one
hundred years prior, exhibits had understandably used this event to mark
the nation's origin. The exposition's all-white planners settled on three
ideas that they claimed had "already been identified with the national
character: the Pioneer Spirit, Republicanism (incorporating democracy)
and Progress." Given expositions' focus on national self-promotion and
technological innovation, progress was the most dominant theme. Yet
innovations like the Corliss steam engine, telephone, telegraph, and
sewing machine needed a point of comparison to illustrate just how important they were and how they demonstrated America's superiority over
other cultures. Hence the Philadelphia Exposition also created displays
of "primitive" cultures, such as those of Indigenous peoples, to show
just how far American technology had come. Weapons dominated the
Native American exhibits, which portrayed "primitive, weapon-making
Indians as inevitably vanishing peoples whose significance and fate lay
in their obvious inferiority to (white) civilization."[17] In fact, the secretary

of the Smithsonian and organizer of the exhibit announced that within a century Indians would cease to exist in their pre-Columbian state and "be merged in the general population."[18] While some displays depicted the Indian as primitive but harmless, many others were meant to shock or frighten. The message sent by this juxtaposition of white American technological progress with Native American primitivism and savagery was clear: though the military subjugation of Indians was not yet complete (the Battle of Little Bighorn occurred only a few weeks after the exposition), it was inevitable.

When the World's Columbian Exposition opened in May 1893 in Chicago, Native Americans had been militarily subdued and consigned to reservations, no longer posing the threat depicted in Philadelphia. But the technological innovations of white America had not wrought the unmitigated progress suggested there. The Panic of 1893 sent stock prices tumbling only a few days prior to the exposition's opening, exacerbating already festering social and economic problems unleashed by the Industrial Revolution. Millions of poorly paid immigrant workers labored in dangerous and/or demoralizing conditions, increasingly resorting to strikes that had often turned violent (1886's Haymarket Riots would have been a still-painful memory in Chicago). Working-class living conditions—crowded, unsanitary, and often unsafe—further stoked discontent. Unchained from the restrictions of Reconstruction, white supremacy once again reigned in the South, enforced through a series of legal and extralegal practices known as Jim Crow. White middle-class Protestants who felt the country belonged to them (or at least more to them than others) felt overwhelmed, threatened by the influx of Catholic and Jewish immigrants who came from different parts of Europe than they had and who often could not speak English. European Americans on the West Coast did their best to limit immigration and opportunities for Asian Americans. Significant technological and economic shifts, coming on top of these upheavals, "wrenched American society from the moorings of traditional values."[19] Popular notions of what America stood for were complicated by changing notions of class and "race," the latter an even more complicated and diverse word then than now. (Italians, Irish, Jews, and other immigrants were initially not considered "white.")

Chicago's exposition, therefore, spoke to a starkly different reality than Philadelphia's. Yet its promise of continued progress was, like that of its predecessor, linked to the idea of America's superiority, built primarily on the notion of race. Beginning with Columbus, the figure chiefly responsible for bringing Italian Americans higher social status, the exposition's planners created a vision of a nation "born in imperial conquest . . . Nativism and imperialism depended to some degree on particular conceptions of the white nation's 'superiority,'" which were built on assumptions of the close relationship between "race and social progress."[20] This was established in significant part by illustrating that those who occupied the continent prior to Columbus's arrival (though he never set foot on the continent) were inferior. As Frederick Putnam, director of Harvard's Peabody Museum and the man in charge of the exposition's Department of Ethnology and Archaeology, asked, "What . . . is more appropriate . . . than to show in their natural conditions of life the different types of peoples who were here when Columbus was crossing the Atlantic Ocean and leading the way for the great wave of humanity that was soon to spread over the continent and forced those unsuspecting peoples to give way before a mighty power, to resign their inherited rights, and take their chances for existence under the laws governing a strange people?" These Native peoples, he continued, "have about vanished into history, and now is the last opportunity for the world to see them and to realize what their condition, their life, their customs, their arts were four centuries ago. . . . Without them, the Exposition will have no base."[21]

While the exhibits in Philadelphia and Chicago did not differ a great deal, Huhndorf suggests that the displays sometimes communicated the message that "natives welcomed Western dominance, or at least tolerated it." Borrowing from the work of Tony Bennett, author of *The Birth of the Museum: History, Theory, Politics*, she further asserts that through the very act of organizing and making public various displays of the "vanishing" native and his/her culture, white spectators were given an "intoxicating illusion that positioned [them] as the subjects rather than the objects of state power." Non-white peoples were subjugated, vanishing or melting into the dominant white culture that defined American identity.[22]

But the centerpiece of the World's Columbian Exposition's role in re-defining the relationship between Native peoples and European settlers was historian Frederick Jackson Turner's speech "The Significance of the Frontier in American History." The frontier, argued Turner, stripped the European immigrant of his civilization:

> It takes him from the railroad car and puts him in the birch ca-noe. It strips off the garments of civilization and arrays him in the hunting shirt and moccasin. It puts him in the log cabin of the Cherokee and Iroquois and runs an Indian palisade around him. Before long he has gone to planting Indian corn and plowing with a sharp stick; he shouts the war cry and takes the scalp in orthodox Indian fashion. In short, at the frontier the environment is at first too strong for the man . . . so he fits himself into the Indian clear-ings and follows the Indian trails. . . . Here is a new product that is American.[23]

In Huhndorf's view, Jackson was essentially arguing that Europeans who arrived in North America needed to go native, "in a limited way and for a limited time," in order to become a new, unique "American" character. Only in going native could white settlers transcend their "savagery" and attain dominion over Indigenous peoples and the land on which they lived. White settlers then underwent a kind of "social evolution" from hunting to trading, ranching, and farming before arriv-ing at the then ultimate state of urban manufacturing. In other words, Jackson depicted Native Americans not as obstacles to progress but as the necessary first step in the "civilization" of the United States.

In his *City of God*, Saint Augustine proclaimed that Rome had col-lapsed once it fulfilled its essential mission of providing a stable environ-ment through which the Christian faith could be spread from one end of the empire to the other. Now Jackson suggested that American Indians, having served their primary purpose—giving birth to a superior form of human culture—were necessarily vanishing from the landscape. As whites moved farther west, Turner asserted, "the frontier became more and more American. . . . Thus the advance of the frontier has meant a steady movement away from the influence of Europe, a steady growth of independence on American lines. And to study this advance . . . is to study the really American part of our history.[24]

Once militarily subdued beyond any hope of resurgence, Indigenous peoples were redefined not as savages and obstacles but as proto-Americans. Buffalo Bill's Wild West Show, which held court at the Chicago exposition, described Indians for the first time as "The Former Foe—Present Friend—the *American.*" During this period some professional baseball teams began adopting Indian names, and a generic Indian began appearing on US currency. Yet even as Native Americans captured the popular imagination, the federal government was forcing Native children into schools to purge them of their language, culture, and identity, and the Dawes Act imposed Western constructs of private property and social structure. Even as historical First People identities were being obliterated, "Indianness" was being celebrated as "unquestionably American." Not only were the winners writing their own history, they were destroying and rewriting others'. "Despite the shifting nature of individual, social, and national identities," writes Philip Deloria, "Indianness has made them seem fixed and final. . . . For those who came here from other countries, the ultimate truths of America's physical nature—rocks, water, sky—were intimately linked to a *metaphysical* American nature that would always be bound up with mythic identities. The secrets of both natures lay in Indianness."[25]

The process by which European America transformed "Indian" identity as it saw fit was facilitated, says Scott B. Vickers, not just through military and political dominance and historical prestidigitation but through the written word, which the former possessed, and the latter often did not. Language, especially religious language, Vickers asserts, became "both a destroyer and a creator of identity. . . . In collusion with the political imperatives of colonialism, Christians and Christian societies have created numerous self-perpetuating stereotypes of Indians that . . . have sought both to void Indians of any viable sense of identity with their own cultures, mythologies, or even individuals, and also inject in their stead the 'whiteness' endemic to Christian culture and identity." Indigenous peoples' own history has been written by outsiders for most of the past five hundred years, obscuring oral and pictorial histories by which Native people understood themselves.[26] What we must remember, as we examine the relationship between Joe Friday, Harold Keltner, and the formation of Y-Indian Guides, is that both men shared a Christian worldview that would limit the degree to which, even under the best of circumstances, Indigenous peoples' identities would be studied or accepted on their own terms.

The "mascotting" of Indigenous peoples continues to the present day, though some changes already under way were significantly accelerated and more widely understood after May 2020, when a video circulated of a Minneapolis police officer kneeling on the neck of George Floyd, an African American alleged to have passed a counterfeit $20 bill. As Floyd begged for his life and called out for his mother, and as bystanders pleaded with the officer to release him, Mr. Floyd stopped breathing and was later pronounced dead. The apparently callous stare and intransigence of the officer, the speed with which the video went viral, the partisan animosity already at work in the country, the intensity of the pandemic the world was facing, and the social, economic, and psychological damage it wrought served to galvanize the reaction to this police killing of an unarmed African American man in ways that the scores before it had not. One response to this new consciousness has been a movement, after decades of resistance, to remove "Indian" names from professional sports franchises. The Major League Baseball club in Cleveland, Ohio, unveiled its new name, the Guardians, in July 2021. The National Football League team in Washington, DC, followed suit with its new sobriquet, the Commanders, in February 2022. But numerous holdouts at the professional, collegiate, and K-12 levels remain. These entities, assert Jason Edward Black, "claim authenticity in justifying the appropriation of American Indian culture as a truly admirable synecdoche for what remains 'good' in society and on the playing field: strength, determination, obstinacy, and courage."[27]

This facile and one-sided recategorization of Native Americans from inferior savages to exemplars of virtue is at the heart of what is problematic with using Indians as mascots, advertising tools, or yes, role models for youth development programs, of which Y-Indian Guides is only one example. The problem is not the virtue of the people who participate(d) in the program, though in fact participants and alumni often feel personally impugned when criticism regarding Indian Guides arises.

A refrain they have frequently articulated is that their activities were designed to honor Indigenous peoples. After all, Joe Friday established the model, and they were just following in his footsteps. The story of Joe Friday, written into every edition of the Y-Indian Guides handbook, was fundamental to its appeal, its sense of legitimacy, and its longevity. So too were other Native Americans who worked with local Y-Indian Guides "tribes" to enhance their experience and provide deeper insight into their own cultural practices and beliefs.

In 2015, twelve years after the national YMCA had abandoned the Indian Guides program in favor of its more generic replacement, Y-Adventure Guides, the LaGrange, Illinois, YMCA still retained the original programs. When Andrea Barnwell, a woman of Ojibwe descent, saw a flyer about an informational "powwow" to recruit fathers and daughters into Indian Princesses, she sent Y officials a concerned email. "I find it to be extremely racist and offensive. The participants dress in Native American regalia, call themselves names based on real tribes, and drum and [chant] in a style they deem to be Native American. . . . I think this sets a bad precedent for what kids learn about Native American culture, and it makes me sad to think that dads are teaching their children it's OK to patronize and [caricature] other cultures." It turned out that the YMCA of Metro Chicago had been trying to convince LaGrange's twenty-five hundred Indian Guide and Princess participants to adopt the new Y-Adventure Guides model, but to no avail. LaGrange Indian Guides leader Tyler Jeffrey explained that it worked closely with "American Indian educators to provide accurate historical and cultural information to parents and their children." "It's in no way any kind of disrespect," Jeffrey argued. "It seems to be a hot button at times, but I honestly believe if people understood the program and what we do at our meetings and ceremonies, they would be in support of it." According to Bruce Sirchio, who led the LaGrange program in the 1990s, "We tried to do everything we could to teach them about Native Americans, that we were supportive of Native Americans and the culture, and I think our kids became more aware of the Native Americans' plight and how they were treated." Bob Carlsen, who led a thirteen-hundred-member "Algonquin Longhouse" in Chicago's northwestern suburbs, added, "Given the length of time and tradition and the amount of good [the program] has done for so many people, I would be really shocked if it changes," he said. "We're not trying to be in anybody's face; we're just trying to do our own thing."

But the Indian Guides in question were not just doing "their own thing." They were asserting that they had the right to use—or misuse— Native American names, symbols, words, and other cultural elements any way they wished, regardless of their impact on others. Brian Howard, a legislative assistant with the National Congress of American Indians and a member of Arizona's Akimel O'odham tribe, asserted that despite their intent, Indian Guides' activities were insulting. "When you bring in this outside group that's essentially mocking your religious practices, it does affect not only your self-perception but the perception of others." Barnwell, who grew up in Minnesota with strong ties to her culture, observed, "I can't even understand why someone would want to put on a headdress and mimic another culture. I can't understand their point of view. They think maybe they're educating about it, but they don't know about it."[28]

Though always a minority, numerous Indigenous peoples have support-ed Indian Guides. When, for example, the Seattle YMCA phased out Indian Guides' Lummi "tribe" in 2003, Ronn Wilson, a member of the Kwaquilth (or Kwakiutl) tribe, said that if done appropriately, the use of Indian themes could actually be valuable in spreading cultural awareness. [29]

Wilson grew up in Milwaukie, Oregon, "as an All-American, everyday kid, nothing unique or exclusively tribal in that sense." But his grandfa-ther took him to ceremonial dinners where "people I didn't know spoke a language I could not understand," read him books, and told him legends and stories that captured his imagination. While visiting the Portland Zoo, Wilson saw a story pole crafted by the widely respected Chief Lelooska. "Something triggered inside of me . . . I was just drawn to it." During his junior year, Wilson's high school art teacher, John Checkis, took him to a ceremonial potlatch, where he met Chief Lelooska and many of his relatives. "I felt the conviction of where my life would go." Checkis used his influence to secure a two-year full scholarship for Wilson at Clackamas Community College, where he studied under another Native American artist, Norman Bursheim. There he crafted his own monumental story pole, placing him in the middle of a controversy between those who thought he was creating "a religious symbol" with public money and others claiming American Indian lineage who felt he had no right to create it.

Wilson moved on to the University of Washington, studying under Bill Holm, whom he called "the Moses of Northwest Native Art and Culture." Area educators began asking him to speak to their students. With their guidance, he developed a curriculum discussing Northwest Coastal Indian culture and history, including projects where students colored, cut out, and assembled ceremonial masks and headdresses and played games to learn their significance. "We'd teach dancing and drumming and the kids performed right along with me." A gymnasium became a longhouse with an electrical firepit, a sixteen-foot-long drum, and a vast array of culturally significant props. "I tried to embellish an authentic experience for these kids about what Northwest Coastal potlatching ceremonies would really be like and the lifestyle of doing everything by hand."

As demand for his services increased, Wilson made it his full-time job in 1986. The following year he incorporated into a nonprofit educational organization, affiliating with the state art commission and its artist-in-residence program. For more than forty years, relying on his formal and informal training, as well as advice and donations from "different cultural elders and chiefs," Wilson provided a wide variety of educational experiences for schoolchildren and also became involved with Y-Indian Guides in the early 1980s. At campouts he "brought in animal pelts for the kids and parents to touch and handle and we'd talk about the Native traditions and the culture that surrounds it. . . . In the evenings I would dress up in my button robe and tell stories and legends. We'd silk screen T-shirts, pillowcases and posters with a Native design on it." When his own children were of age, he brought them into Y-Indian Guides, creating his own tribe, braiding cedar bark headbands trimmed with white rabbit (instead of ermine), and carving amulets for each member.

Wilson assumed a unique role of mediator, standing between the Y-Indian Guides program and any "tribal person, chief, or elder who was there to either file a complaint or had a problem with what was being done or how it was being done." He recruited numerous chiefs and elders to help him create a robust program, though he recalled, "in some cases they took offense because it's one more thing you want to manipulate and use our cultures for your own profit margin." Through it all, Wilson, insists, his objective was clear: "to keep the organization above reproach. If you're going to do it, do it right." In his view, the Y-Indian Guides and Y-Indian Princesses programs in his area did this in the vast majority of cases. "And it is incredibly sad that because of one or two negatives, the entire program was scrapped, because the YMCA didn't want to cope with the negative PR."

We started by asserting that this book is not about Indians. Yet we must account for the history of this continent and the peoples who call it home, as well as the colonialism that deemed the conferring of Christianity and Western civilization to be compensation for stolen land and cultural eradication. We must note the *survivance* of Native peoples—that is, their ability, despite history and continued colonization, to do much more than persist but claim, reclaim, shape, and reshape their cultural heritage, demonstrating an active continuity between past, present, and future.[30] And in so doing, we must recognize that this book *is* about Indians.[31] All of the ideas and activities described here had and continue to have an impact on Native Americans, and that impact is by and large negative. A clearer statement, then, is that this book is not concerned with what Indigenous peoples like Ronn Wilson do with their own culture or with whom they choose to share it. Our concern is what non-Indigenous people choose to do with Indigenous culture, and how they seek to control and own it. The process of taking Native American culture in an "extractive" way and putting it under the control of non-Indigenous, mostly white people is the source of the problem we will explore.

As with Joe Friday and Ronn Wilson, the Indian Guides newsletter, *Long House News*, chronicles numerous occasions when Native Americans attended events, told stories, spoke at banquets, and provided training at state or regional workshops. But receiving approval from an individual is not the same as an endorsement from an entire group, which begs the question: Is there an appropriate way to appropriate?

When history, power dynamics, and ignorance are factored in, it seems a dubious proposition. And so this is a book about aspirational Indians who, in their desire to build character in their children and strengthen familial bonds, participated in the quintessential American tradition of co-opting American Indian culture, of "going native."

For good and for ill, a kind of mystique remains over Y-Indian Guides, primarily related to the lasting parent-child bonds it helped produce, a tragic irony when one considers the tens of thousands of Native American children forcibly separated from their parents and placed into government boarding schools where thousands died. While it has inspired little scholarship, the Indian Guides program appears in numerous memoirs and websites of members who include participation as part of their biography. Some recall it with great fondness, if perhaps at times a kind of guilty reverence. Others include their affiliation as a footnote of childhood. Many who still treasure their memories of participating in Indian Guides insist that the new "Adventure Guides" program is simply not as effective or attractive because it has been stripped of all its "Indian" trappings. They argue that Native American values of honoring nature, family, and community were central to the success of the program. Perhaps they simply wish to pass on to their children the kind of experiences they enjoyed with their own fathers. In more recent years, websites and blogs from former participants, and critical articles from Native American authors, have unleashed a sharper attack on the program and its legacy.

A close examination of the long history of Y-Indian Guides yields two irreconcilable yet irrefutable truths: it strengthened innumerable families through its emphasis on close, warm, and playful bonds between parent and child. And it contributed incalculably, through the hundreds of thousands who participated in the program, to a gross mischaracterization, oversimplification, and marginalization of Native American identities; it was complicit in the continued colonization of those identities.

We understand that in articulating this twofold thesis, we risk angering all and pleasing none, but we see no alternative. The mountain of testimony from Indian Guides participants makes the former statement self-evident; numerous studies from cultural anthropologists, child psychologists, and testimonies from a wide cross-section of Indigenous peoples make the latter no less persuasive. In a diverse country, however, where power is often race- and class-based, these two truths do not balance; one cannot condone the other. Through Y-Indian Guides, non-natives had the power to decide for themselves what it meant to honor or depict Native Americans. The program ignored the bloody history that separated Indigenous peoples from their lands and their way of life, and the harm their depictions could cause in the present. No matter how good-hearted and well-intentioned its participants were (and in most cases they were both), and regardless of the contributions of its Ojibwe cofounder, Joe Friday, we conclude that the YMCA, at both local and national levels, should have more quickly addressed the ills increasingly associated with Y-Indian Guides and ended the program well before 2003.

For institutions like the YMCA, programs like Indian Guides beg the question, What if one of your most successful programs was also its worst? Can the ends justify the means? An examination of Indian Guides, beyond demonstrating the harms that flow from unchecked privilege and appropriation, points toward a wounded identity within white American culture. Why did so many of these fathers need to be a mascot to love their children? Though we will not be able to answer that question, we hope this text will be of service to those exploring the topic.

We want to make it clear, however, that we have no intention of depicting those who participated in any of the Indian Guides programs as hateful racists. We take pains to depict the program as it was, not as residents of the early twenty-first century imagine it to be. Some critics of Indian Guides and its various spin-off iterations, for example, go so far as to suggest that Joe Friday is a myth. And of course anyone who grew up watching the television show *Dragnet* in the 1950s and '60s or who saw the film spoofing it in 1987 knows Joe Friday as a fictional detective who wants "just the facts." But the real-life Joe Friday was indeed a Canadian Ojibwe Indian born in the northern Canadian forest of Matagami in Ontario. As we shall see, he was not just an Indian "born in a wigwam" who lived his life in the pristine wilderness of northeastern Canada. He was an entrepreneur who traveled widely promoting tourism to Bear Island. He was a sportsman, a guide who interacted regularly with white hunters and fishermen. He became an influential advocate for the rights of Canadian First People. And he also dedicated himself for several years to the promotion and expansion of Y-Indian Guides in the United States. While one should question whether the blessing of one Indian makes all that followed in the establishment of Indian Guides appropriate, one should also get to know Joe Friday and understand him and his times in their own context.

In the early chapters of this book, we introduce the reader to the origins of the YMCA and its work with boys before turning our attention to the cofounders of Indian Guides. We discuss the times in which the program was founded, as well as other figures and movements who appropriated Native American culture and imagery at the time. In addition, we try to define just who the "Indian" in Indian Guides really was.

Another core thesis of this book is that the relationship between Y-Indian Guides and the YMCA at large was problematic from the beginning. A program involving play between fathers and sons did not, in the minds of most YMCA professionals, measure up to the expectations that YMCA activities should mold boys and young men into serious-minded, responsible adults. Indian Guides surmounted the hesitancy, even derision, it received, first through the dedication of YMCA staff who were themselves participants. The zeal they displayed in supporting its elevation to national status is a clear testament to the benefit they believed they and their sons derived from the program. In addition, the YMCA noticed that middle- and upper-middle-class fathers were joining "tribes" and devoting themselves to twice-a-month meetings. For decades they hoped these fathers would insist that their sons continue through the entire continuum of YMCA youth development programs, ultimately graduating from high school as disciplined, devout, useful citizens. They further anticipated fathers, out of gratitude for all that Indian Guides and the YMCA had done to build strong relationships with their sons, would serve as faithful Y volunteers and board members. These expectations, especially the former, were never satisfactorily realized.

As years went by with little reward for their efforts, the Y began working harder to strengthen its ties with (many "tribes" would have said "control over") Indian Guides. When this proved unsuccessful, it set out to make the program pay for itself. Through it all, most "tribes" remained far more loyal to themselves and each other than they ever were to the YMCA. The later chapters of this book trace this devolving relationship, even as Y-Indian Guides became more and more popular in the 1950s, '60s, and '70s. The demise of Indian Guides came not just from increasing external pressure, which expressed itself in numerous ways and for numerous reasons, but from a growing sense that the program was not just a public relations liability and a poor embodiment of the Y's growing commitment to diversity but had also always been inexplicably popular and insufficiently beneficial to the YMCA.

Before the era of political correctness, fake news, and Facebook algorithms, Y-Indian Guides was already a controversial entity, employed largely by well-intentioned white families who could essentially ignore the bloody events that killed, dispossessed, and sought to erase the cultures of the very people they aspired to emulate. This book, admittedly authored by two white males, seeks to depict the program as fairly but as unstintingly as possible.

Y-Indian Guides strengthened innumerable families and contributed incalculably to a gross mischaracterization, oversimplification, and marginalization of Native American identities. Together, these two trails of truth both soothe and rub raw the continuing definition of our American identity.

CHAPTER ONE

The YMCA and Social Change, 1844–1925

THE Y-INDIAN GUIDES program, which remains active on a limited scale to this day, was in many ways a response to social change and the crises that accompanied it. A growing middle class and professional workforce created a generation of men who could provide an improved quality of life for their families. Many of these men, who recently returned from World War I and/or had moved from a rural setting to an urban one, set out to start families but found making time for their children difficult. A solution was found in camaraderie with other fathers and sons, nurtured through childish games, stories, and pageantry that helped bind the generations together in mutual understanding and affection.

Social change also proved the demise of the program (or at least the YMCA's support for it) three-quarters of a century later. The women's rights movement fostered an increase in the number of mothers entering the workforce. The civil rights movement and the rise of the American Indian Movement (AIM) exposed the YMCA's inherent whiteness in an increasingly ethnically diverse society. Together they exposed the trappings and methods of Indian Guides for what they were—a gross mischaracterization and invention of Native American cultures for the benefit of a predominantly white middle class. To appreciate this history and understand why the YMCA would have created and nurtured the program, we must first understand the origins of the YMCA, which was itself a response to social change.

The Young Men's Christian Association was a child of the Industrial Revolution. The booming industrial economy, massive shifts in populations through migration, and the accompanying growth of urban centers in Europe and the United States led both to calls for reform and to a yearning for a simpler, cleaner, and kinder environment. Fueling this narrative were the tens of thousands of religious young men raised on farms and in small towns who migrated to the city and found in the YMCA a refuge of sorts. Many of them noticed that the hard work and "rugged individualism" exemplified by their rural parents were not necessarily rewarded with reasonable success or comfort. Individual skilled jobs were being replaced by mechanized, unskilled ones requiring little if any proprietary knowledge. The wealth produced by farmers seemed increasingly controlled by middlemen. In the United States, many feared that the new economy was undermining traditional American values of self-reliance, delayed gratification, and self-control.[1] These crises of identity, in their earliest forms, inspired the creation of the YMCA in London.

ORIGINS OF THE YOUNG MEN'S CHRISTIAN ASSOCIATION

In 1844 a young man named George Williams, fueled by a desire to create a safe harbor from temptation and vice for the young men of Victorian London, gathered a group of like-minded individuals for fellowship and spiritual reflection. This meeting was the genesis of the Young Men's Christian Association. Williams and his colleagues were concerned that the nation's young men, who were moving into urban environments from the countryside in large numbers to search for work, were leaving behind their traditional safety nets of family, community, and church. They created the Young Men's Christian Association in London to organize and provide morning prayer groups and Bible study within various houses of business. Their hope was that these Christian activities would re-create some of the lost social structures members had left behind, and in the process keep them on the path of righteousness.

Williams's journey began nine years before these programs were organized. The tale recounted by an early biographer places Williams and his father on a slow trek from the countryside to the town of Bridgwater. "As they turned the corner and the spire of Bridgwater Church rose into view against the evening sky, the boy's heart beat fast."[2] The young boy was going out into the world and leaving behind all that he knew. The youngest of eight sons, Williams would not be expected to inherit the placid, bucolic farm life of his parents. His world was changing, and his father, desiring to see his son succeed in this new urban and industrialized world, apprenticed him to a draper at the age of fifteen.[3]

Reflecting on his apprenticeship, Williams is recorded as saying, "I entered Bridgwater a careless, thoughtless, godless, swearing young fellow."[4] But he left a changed man, gaining far more than a trade. He had become a converted Congregationalist, likely due to the influence of his employer, Mr. Holmes. Fortified by his newfound faith and ambitions of succeeding in his newly earned trade, George Williams found himself setting off to London at the age of twenty.

Once in London, Williams deepened his evangelical faith at King's Weigh House Chapel. Biographer Clyde Binfield comments that the personal nature of Williams's evangelical faith meant that "the individual was at once a worm in the presence of God and yet, by total reliance on the merits of his Saviour, there was nothing that he could not do."[5] This belief created a worldview where personal faith was paramount and constructed a paradigm where once saved, one had the responsibility to fulfill the duties of the Christian faith in addition to enjoying its privileges.

For Williams, his duty was to bring like-minded men together for the purpose of improving their spiritual condition. To accomplish this, he frequently attended other houses of worship, where he would come into contact with men of similar (but not identical) religious persuasions and professions. Fellowship with familiar but different faiths allowed the YMCA founder to create (within the context of his time) an ecumenical institution focused on tackling the major social issues of his age. In a rapidly changing world, the YMCA seemed to provide the means to have a hand in shaping or at least managing that change.

Initially, the YMCA's goal was not the reformation of the soul but rather its preservation. Young men who wanted to join were scrutinized and their close associates questioned to determine the makeup of their character. Only once he was judged a convert or member of an evangelical Christian church and a possessor of strong moral fiber was a young man admitted into membership. This practice of emphasizing the character of an individual rather than alignment with a particular denomination established within the YMCA the foundation for its future work with youth. While the first members had to demonstrate their character, it would not take long for the YMCA to contemplate shaping character. Character in young men could be reformed, but in youth, it could be developed from the ground up.

During London's Great Exhibition in 1851, under the majestic edifice of the Crystal Palace, the Western world was introduced to the Young

Men's Christian Association. George Williams and his fellow volunteers extolled the virtues of the member-driven organization, holding prayer groups and Bible studies, and demonstrating the vigor of the nascent movement. The concept of the YMCA spread like wildfire. As they left the exhibition, many introduced to the YMCA were inspired by Williams's vision. As soon as they returned to their respective nations, they set about organizing associations of their own. While YMCAs in every country agreed that evangelical Christianity was the core belief of their organization, each association operated independently and could choose the religious and/or social aspects it wished to emphasize.

THE YMCA IN THE UNITED STATES

In the United States, a former sea captain named Thomas Sullivan learned of the YMCA from newspaper reports of the London Exhibition. In 1833 hardships associated with life at sea, including a shipwreck in the Antarctic and an attack by pirates off the coast of Brazil, combined with the effects of a chronic illness, led Sullivan to reflect on his life and dedicate himself to a more active Christianity. Sullivan began a "marine mission at large," performing works similar to those of the London YMCA. He boarded ships to preach and distribute tracts. He called his work "social religion," and when he read about the London YMCA, it resonated so strongly with him that he wasted no time in expressing his enthusiasm for establishing one in Boston.

Once on American soil, the YMCA expanded ferociously. Within three years there were twenty-six YMCAs that met for the first time to discuss the nature of their work. Like its English counterpart, the American YMCA was very clear that it was not seeking to form a new denomination but rather to more fully engage Christians in public acts of faith and in more meaningful roles in their own congregations.

One explanation for the early and rapid success of the YMCA is the active nature of its work. This new form of dynamic Christianity gave members and volunteers the tools to live out their values. The individuals who gravitated to the YMCA (often in lieu of joining the ranks of the ministry) used these tools not only to evangelize but also to tackle injustice and advocate for a more egalitarian and compassionate society.[6] The YMCA in the United States, for example, was experiencing dramatic social change resulting from immigration, industrialization, and urbanization. YMCAs in other countries were experiencing not only similar issues but also war, colonization, and new forms of government. They were attracted to the YMCA's capacity to rally communities to temper the effects of modernity through individual and collective improvement.[7]

The YMCA's collective perspective was shaped by a white Anglo-Saxon Protestant Weltanschauung reflecting its political and social hegemony in mid-nineteenth-century Europe and the United States. Progressive reformers within and outside of the YMCA noted that immigration patterns that had previously ushered large numbers of northern and western Protestant Europeans onto the eastern shores of America were shifting. By the 1880s, larger and larger numbers of immigrants came from southern and eastern Europe, as well as Ireland. Many were Catholic or Jewish and brought (as far as the Protestant majority was concerned) strange languages, customs, styles, religious practices, and behaviors with them. Many came with whole or even extended families whose women understood that they would not be sitting at home taking care of the children, but working just as hard as their male counterparts.

From the perspective of the Progressive Era reformers who by the 1890s populated the Y in ever greater numbers, the Industrial Revolution led to the concentration of wealth in the hands of a disproportionately powerful few; debased vulnerable working families who constantly struggled to live and work in safe, clean, and dignified surroundings, to say nothing of making ends meet; corrupted politics by allowing political machines to buy the votes of immigrants; and left the children of immigrant parents to fend for themselves in the filthy streets until they joined the workforce, all too often at age ten or earlier.

These conditions left the late nineteenth-century YMCA in a quandary. As an organization primarily dedicated to the promotion and preservation of young men's religious faith and virtue, how could it hope to succeed when many boys were already being subjected to harmful conditions unimagined only a decade or two earlier? How could it answer to the community—to God—if it did nothing to address these critical social problems? In rising to answer this calling, the YMCA added an important new mission: caring deeply for the welfare of the less

fortunate, especially boys. Urban YMCAs became increasingly diverse as
they offered associate (nonvoting) memberships to Catholics and Jews
who appreciated the programs the association brought to their communities. Their increasing participation and enthusiasm, in turn, continued
to expand the scale and sophistication of youth programs focused on the
development of the whole person.

It is no exaggeration to say that in the last two decades of the nineteenth
century and well beyond the first half of the twentieth, the YMCA
became obsessed with turning boys (and ultimately girls as well) into
spiritually, intellectually, civically, and physically upright adults. Not
surprisingly, early attempts to work with boys were relatively simplistic:
lowering the age of participation at Bible study meetings or holding special Sunday schools for them. After all, the reasoning of the time went,
a boy's character was a reflection—perhaps even a manifestation—of
his soul. If a boy's character could be molded or reformed, then his soul
could be redeemed. But soon it became clear that Bible study, prayer,
and moral suasion were not addressing boys' most immediate needs.
After all, if a boy went to work at age nine, ten, or eleven, he was losing out on the opportunity to become properly educated. In response,
many urban Ys opened night schools for boys who worked during the
day. Much of this work actually started not with male Y staff but with
women from the YMCA auxiliaries.[8] "As the 1880s passed," writes C.
Howard Hopkins,

> the programs of boys' groups widened to include occasional use
> of the gym, outings, talks, and discussions, and an increasing par-
> ticipation in planning by the boys themselves. A great deal of the
> program was didactic and moralistic—temperance and medical
> lectures, the "cold water" pledge against intoxicating liquors and
> others against tobacco and profanity, or talks on manners, clean-
> liness, travel, science, history. Occasionally a far-sighted secretary
> introduced features more directly suited to adolescent interests
> and needs, including "magic lantern" shows, sports, excursions,
> debates, and projects furthering education.

By 1884 the number of YMCAs providing Sunday school and Bible instruction had grown to such an extent that when Robert McBurney of the New York YMCA was approached to enter into a joint operation with a proposed school for Christian workers in Springfield, Massachusetts, he enthusiastically agreed. McBurney, the first YMCA employee to hold the title of secretary, was keenly interested in recruiting and training men to conduct the growing scope of YMCA work. A year later, the Springfield Training School, at first as a department of the School for Christian Workers, was established to better equip YMCA staff for work with boys and young men.[9]

As Bible study brought more youth into contact with the Y, the staff identified needs beyond religious instruction, eventually establishing "Boys Departments" to provide extracurricular activities to meet their educational and physical needs. The first Boys Department was organized in Salem, Massachusetts, in 1869, and by 1900 the national YMCA office hired Edgar Robinson to support the work at a national level. When Robinson started, there were more than 30,000 boys benefiting from YMCA programming; twenty years later, that number had grown to 200,000.[10] A prime motivator for the YMCA to expand its work with youth was the deceptively simple insight that boys become men.

YMCA leaders made another decision in the mid-1880s, one that would trouble the Y's collective conscience for years to come. In an attempt to preserve the virtue of boys "who have had some moral training," they agreed that boys' work should be restricted to those from "better homes." Rescue missions could handle neglected and homeless boys. Some ignored this dictum, but their efforts received little attention.[11]

Another important feature of boys' work emerging by the 1880s was "rambling." By this time Americans were reading John Burroughs and John Muir. Theodore Roosevelt was in North Dakota, developing the love of nature that would inform his presidential legacy. While the records of the Vermont State YMCA show a "boy's missionary" taking "a group of boys for summer encampment on the shores of Lake Champlain" in 1867, more organized camping trips began appearing in the records of the national association in 1882. Brooklyn, New York, Detroit, and Richmond, Virginia, were among the first to announce these.[12]

Organized camping, both the overnight stay-away and relatively recent day camp, remains a cornerstone program of the YMCA to this
very day. The very first Y camp was established by Sumner F. Dudley, a
medical equipment salesman and member of the Orange, New Jersey,
YMCA, who took a group of boys fourteen years or older out to the
shores of Lake Orange near Newburgh. Each day included one to two
hours of Bible study and a religious service with prayer in the evening,
but the boys also enjoyed boating, fishing, and swimming. As photos of
the time clearly indicate, boys of a younger age were increasingly a part
of the camping, hiking ("tramping"), and cycling programs developed
by Ys across the country. The time boys spent on these excursions was
tightly organized and controlled, and its success was dependent on a
firm but benevolent and charismatic leader.[13]

Any time boys were taken out of the city and into nature—nature to
which some of them had little or no previous exposure—those in charge
of them stressed at least three ideas. First, most of the adults present had
the opportunity to hearken back to their own childhoods, which more
often than not unfolded in a more rural setting than that of their charges.
Their willingness to spend time with a group of often-unruly boys came
in no small part from their desire to reconnect with a comforting, even
nostalgic landscape and convey that experience to boys growing up in
the city. Second, as members of a Christian organization, YMCA leaders
took the opportunity to connect the boys' camping experience to discussions about God's creation and humanity's place in it. Boys were more
open to a discussion of how it all came into being, believed Y staff, while
viewing a sky undimmed by city lights or seeing birds, beasts, and plant
life in stunning variety and volume. But finally, and for our purposes
most importantly, being in an unpopulated landscape led to questions
and discussions about the people who first occupied North America. A
return to nature evoked thoughts of Native Americans. Indeed, as one
reviews old camp programs and photographs, real and invented Indian
names and images abound, and not just in the YMCA. Campers could
be organized by "tribe," be encouraged to dress up "like an Indian," or
tell fanciful tales related to the imagined lives of Native Americans who
may have occupied the area where they stood. Many camps adopted
"Indian" names. The St. Louis Y, for example, had Camp Negaunee,

Cleveland "Ta-Wa-Sen-Tha," and the Twin Cities created both Iduhapi and Menogyn.

Developments in camping coincided with the efforts of urban reformers who stressed the need for children to play and escape the crowded, unsanitary conditions of the city. By the mid-1890s playgrounds had opened in at least nine major cities. In 1900 the Cleveland, Ohio, YMCA built and supervised the city's first playground. A broad coalition of settlement house workers, educators, child psychologists, and YMCA staff advocated the construction of playgrounds where children could play under controlled, supervised conditions that promised to develop their mental, moral, and physical well-being.[14]

Figure 2. An early YMCA camp scene, date and place unknown. Note the lone feather on one boy's head. Kautz Family YMCA Archives, University of Minnesota Libraries.

For a YMCA secretary working with boys, physical activity was important in part because it occupied and (if one was lucky) exhausted boys who needed wholesome diversion. But there were also broader concerns about city life and its potential to sap one's physical vitality. In the country, boys and young men "developed healthy and vigorous bodies by an active outdoor life."[15] In the city, work was done with the brain while sitting at a desk or by standing relatively still in front of a machine. Youthful, masculine vitality might slip away if the Y didn't

keep its members physically active. Such concerns gave rise to the
Muscular Christianity movement, which chastised men for becoming
weak and passive, emphasized the "masculine" attributes of Jesus Christ,
and promoted physical vitality as an essential Christian virtue.[16]

Numerous urban reformers also viewed play as the crucible of personal and civic maturation. By their way of thinking, a boy without a
playground became a man without a job. It was preferable, the more
radical of them preached, to build a playground without a school than a
school without a playground. The Y's philosophy, which never reached
that extreme, contributed significantly to the growth, supervision, and
regularization of the playground and camping movements.

By the 1900s, students of YMCA training schools frequently re-
searched the burgeoning field of youth development. A dissertation
written from George Williams College (which had been established as a
training school for YMCA staff in 1890) made the case for boys' work
in the YMCA by asking, "Do we see how essential it is that the boys of
today are trained spiritually, mentally, physically and socially, that they
may properly perform the duties of tomorrow?"[17] A slogan used some
years later got more to the point: "Building boys is better than mending
men." By the turn of the century the YMCA was an established leader in
youth development. Various clubs and groups met regularly in buildings
designed for the express purpose of producing youth fortified with a
sense of "Christian citizenship." These "manhood factories" were now
found in every urban center across the nation.[18] Yet just when it seemed
that the YMCA was perfecting the art of helping youth navigate the
treacherous paths of a modern, urban, industrialized, and impersonal
life, a new modern crisis arose that once again challenged ideas of faith,
progress, and virtuous manhood: the Great War.

THE Y TESTS ITS METTLE IN WAR

The YMCA itself had provided services to the military as early as 1856,
when the Portsmouth, Virginia, association began to hold meetings
aboard a US training vessel.[19] Work with the army and the navy slowly increased as the YMCA expanded into new territories, though the
work remained primarily religious in nature. Like the Union itself, the
YMCA's fragile peace, built on avoiding any discussion of slavery, evap-
orated with the attack on Fort Sumter in 1861.[20]

In some of the most active YMCAs in the north, men answered Lincoln's call for volunteers. These volunteer regiments of Christian soldiers, most notably the 176th of New York, rallied to both fight in the war and serve as a wholesome influence for their comrades.[21] Fifteen northern YMCAs banded together to form the US Christian Commission (USCC) in 1861. President Lincoln called their work "obviously proper and praiseworthy."[22] By war's end, five thousand men and women had volunteered through the commission to offer prayer and Bible study, teach literacy, write letters for the sick, and disperse food and clothing to those in need. Its efforts proved so successful that the YMCA was asked to respond in a similar fashion in 1898 when war broke out against Spain.

THE GREAT WAR

Chief justice and former president William Howard Taft wrote the foreword and was chairman of the editorial board that authored an impressive two-volume account of the YMCA's efforts during what came to be known as World War I. The Y, which offered its services to US president Woodrow Wilson the day the nation declared war, provided ninety percent of all welfare services to American soldiers. According to Taft, "This organization, first and last, ministered to not less than nineteen millions of the soldiers of the Allied Armies and extended its helpful activities to over five millions of prisoners of war. . . . It may be questioned whether in all time a human society has ever brought its helpful ministry to such vast numbers of men over such wide areas, under such varying conditions, and in so short a time."[23] The scope of the YMCA's contributions during the war was unprecedented and likely could not occur today. Labeled an auxiliary of modern democracy, the YMCA and other social service organizations built an "army within the army" to attack one of the greatest challenges presented by war: "the crucial problem of morale."[24]

From 1917 to 1919, nearly 26,000 men and women were dispatched by the YMCA to attend to the needs of the Allied forces both at home and abroad.[25] As in the Civil War and the Spanish–American War, educators offered literacy and English instruction, and ministers provided spiritual support. Now, however, they offered the new dimension of "physical work," developed by the YMCA after the Civil War. General

John J. Pershing, commander of the American Expeditionary Force, had witnessed firsthand the benefits of the YMCA. During the 1916 Punitive Expedition into Mexico to capture Pancho Villa, he "had come to consider the Association as much a part of army equipment as the army mule or commissary cook."[26]

On August 28, 1917, Pershing commissioned the YMCA "to provide for the amusement and recreation of the troops by means of its usual program of social, physical, and educational and religious activities."[27] He specifically asked the YMCA to organize athletic activities to help make the troops fit to fight.[28]

Unlike in previous conflicts, in 1917 the YMCA was tightly integrated into the war effort, its mission expanded to establish exchanges for the American troops and later canteens throughout the army. This work was conducted within 491 wooden huts, 1,045 tents, and 255 rented structures. The YMCA provided an assortment of athletic equipment, which it used to organize games and mass drills to the benefit of more than 37 million soldiers in the Allied Forces.[29] The YMCA also coordinated "Leave Areas for the Army," where they were asked to provide wholesome recreation such as theater, motion pictures, dances, theatricals, athletic programs, and sightseeing trips for soldiers who might otherwise be in the company of prostitutes,[30] and recommended that the great casinos and resorts be taken over to accommodate a program of mass recreation. Aix-les-Bains was the first to open as a leave area in February 1918.[31]

The work of the YMCA did not end with the armistice. Shortly after the end of hostilities, athletic director Elwood Brown organized the Inter-Allied Games, a large-scale international competition that filled the gap left by the cancellation of the 1916 Olympic Games. The games were held in Pershing Stadium, which was constructed on land donated by France. American troops provided the labor for the stadium's construction, and the YMCA paid for the design and materials. Fifteen hundred athletes from eighteen nations participated in this historic event in the summer of 1919. It was one last effort to boost morale, and a testament to the hopes for a new era of peace and prosperity.[32]

The Great War, despite its almost inconceivable scale of destruction and tragedy, seemed to justify the YMCA's confidence in its Christian mission. Amidst the most dire circumstances imaginable, it had performed admirably, addressing and ameliorating the woes of millions, and receiving numerous accolades from a variety of powerful circles. If another crisis arose, as it most assuredly would, the vast majority of leaders within the YMCA felt confident they could once again rise to the occasion.

POSTWAR CHALLENGES

Back in the United States, it seemed that in many ways Americans could justifiably breathe a collective sigh of relief in the wake of the Great War. They had been spared the massive human, material, economic, and psychological devastation visited throughout Europe. America's 114,000 deaths paled next to the roughly ten million military and seven million civilian deaths suffered throughout Europe and Western Asia. But though its physical landscape remained unscarred, tremendous challenges emerged. The roughly half million African Americans who left the South seeking jobs and a better life in the North, and the 370,000 or so who served in the war hoping to establish once and for all their common humanity and patriotism, largely met with disappointment at war's end.[33] Race riots broke out in more than thirty American communities in 1920. Postwar fears of Bolshevism and anarchism led to illegal raids, arrests, and ultimately deportation of 556 "undesirables," as well as repressive actions taken against labor unions, often depicted as havens for anti-American extremists. President Wilson's naïveté about his influence at the peace talks in Versailles, his politically unwise decision to bring no Republican advisers with him, and his take-it-or-leave-it attitude when he submitted a deeply flawed armistice treaty to the Senate doomed any hopes for a reasonable peace or a viable League of Nations.

Complaints against the YMCA's war work and charges of profiteering also reached a cacophonous state in the immediate postwar period, leading national Y leader John R. Mott to request a government investigation. Yes, it was true, said the ensuing report, that there were a few small volunteer stations set up by the Knights of Columbus, the Jewish Welfare Board, and so on giving free coffee and doughnuts to isolated groups of troops when the YMCA charged for all of its services (leading to allegations of profiteering). But, as C. Howard Hopkins put it, "The welfare organizations obtained prestige in reverse ratio to the share of service given."[34] The YMCA's much greater burden, said the study, justified the fees it charged.

The United States was also officially becoming an urban nation. In fact, reports Daniel Okrent, rural Christian forces seeking to outlaw the consumption of alcohol fought to block congressional reapportionment after the 1920 census because they knew it would shift representation toward the now-majority urban population who tended to oppose Prohibition.[35] The YMCA responded to this new urban reality in much the same way as it responded to past changes: by extending old and crafting new programs. As Hopkins framed it, the Y became driven by "new philosophies of purpose and program." One of the largest programmatic shifts the YMCA undertook following World War I was meeting the need for practical, secular education. The YMCA was a pioneer in the establishment of vocational education.[36] These schools were designed to provide the skills that were needed in the modern postwar era. This work was begun during the war with the assistance of the US Department of War. Following the war, the YMCA used remaining funds to establish a proto–GI Bill, providing scholarships for returning veterans seeking to learn a trade or pursue a degree. Demobilization was not, however, exclusively marked by progress. As the YMCA explored ways to equip the nation with the skills for the future, the vibrancy and relevance of its evangelical roots were being increasingly questioned.

The Great War helped usher in a cynical modern era and usher out a spirit of optimism, orthodoxy, and internationalism. The moralistic rhetoric that had been used to recruit American soldiers and mobilize the YMCA to support them so avidly now rang hollow to many. Many returning from war felt they had, as Ezra Pound wrote,

> walked eye-deep in hell
> believing in old men's lies, then unbelieving
> came home, home to a lie,
> home to many deceits,
> home to old lies and new infamy;
> usury age-old and age-thick

and liars in public places.
Daring as never before, wastage as never before . . .

There died a myriad,
And of the best, among them,
For an old bitch gone in the teeth,
For a botched civilization . . .
For two gross of broken statues,
For a few thousand battered books.[37]

While disenchantment and cynicism were often aimed at America as a whole, an increasing target was Christian fundamentalism and, more generally, rural life and sensibilities. Rural folk—and evangelical Christianity in general—became targets of ridicule, even contempt. While the YMCA was becoming an increasingly urban organization, its roots and those of many of its members were still decidedly rural and evangelical. Not all members of the YMCA were fundamentalists or biblical literalists by 1920, but the Y was an inclusive, ecumenical organization still tied to fundamentalism, or at the very least to a strong adherence to and reverence for scripture.

Yet in striving to compete against attractively appointed taverns, pool halls, and gambling establishments, many Ys had built worldly facilities financed with donations from wealthy, usually conservative donors. Many of its more progressive-minded secretaries began to question this alliance between the Y and businessmen. A YMCA building, they insisted, should avoid repelling the working class and "suit the financial ability, social needs and habits of the life of men in its community."[38] The best way to make the YMCA a more inclusive organization, they argued, was to refashion, or perhaps even do away with, the old evangelical test requiring full members to belong to an evangelical Christian church. (In fact most college and railroad YMCAs were already out of compliance, and even some urban Ys gave it mere lip service.) Though more conservative members howled in protest, the YMCA's 1907 national convention in Washington narrowly voted to exempt college associations from the test. The most prominent dissenting voice was that of William Jennings Bryan, who only a year later would lose a US presidential contest for a third time. "A man who has not formed an opinion as to whether he will ever join a church," he protested, "is not in a good position to join in a work that has for its expressed object the bringing of young men into the church."[39]

By the 1920s fundamentalists within and beyond the YMCA had begun to speak out and act against "modernist" theology and biblical criticism, which sought to reconcile the Bible to advances in science, most notably the theories of Charles Darwin, and interpret scripture more as a human than a divine text best understood in the light of the sensibilities of the historical cultures which had produced it.

Christian fundamentalists fought back in a number of ways, including attempts to outlaw the teaching of evolution in public schools. In a fiasco of epic proportions, William Jennings Bryan once again stepped forward to defend the teachings of the Bible and the values of rural America.[40] When the attorney for the defense, Clarence Darrow, put Bryan on the stand as an expert on the Bible, the resulting combative exchange made fundamentalists seem as backward and punitive as critics like H. L. Mencken had suggested. The trial ended in a tepid and later-overturned conviction; Bryan died five days later. While figures like Billy Sunday and Aimee Semple McPherson maintained public profiles after the Scopes Monkey Trial, many evangelicals abandoned the public arena and turned inward.

"SO GO THE YOUTH, SO GOES THE NATION"

Perhaps traumatized, most likely in some way disenchanted by war, the YMCA's top man, John R. Mott, left the organization in 1928. Speaking to a gathering of boys' workers that same year, Mott remarked that the YMCA was feeling "the effects of prevailing unfavorable economic conditions, and of the bafflingly difficult post-war psychology."[41] This new era for Mott was marked by pessimism, questioning, and criticism of the existing order and contained the demobilization and retraction of the YMCA's international work, Mott's signature initiative. Summarizing the impact some years later, Owen Pence commented: "Accustomed to working extensively rather than intensively, and relying heavily upon organization or structural strength, the post-war Association had great need to re-examine . . . objectives, methods, and structure."[42] The

YMCA now found itself a force in the community writ large rather than exclusively within mainline Protestant circles. While this softening of the Christian "C" predated the war, the new massive organizational and bureaucratic structure coupled with modern critical worldviews created the need for a YMCA pivot.

In 1927 the Association of Secretaries, a YMCA professional society, met under the theme "The YMCA as a Christian education movement." The increasingly youth-oriented work in the postwar years coupled with a rise in American "liberal" evangelical Christianity led many in the YMCA to reflect on its purpose. Aware that the organization's evangelical test had largely gone unheeded by large associations for years, they sought to reframe the nature of YMCA membership and identity to more appropriately fit the kind of work it was now doing in a society dramatically different from that of Victorian England or the antebellum United States. At the same time, they appreciated the need for their beloved association to continue focusing on basic human needs. In 1931 they forged a new identity for the YMCA as a developer of character and a builder of a Christian social order:

> The Young Men's Christian Association we regard as being, in its essential genius, a world-wide fellowship of men and boys united by a common loyalty to Jesus Christ for the purpose of building Christian personality and a Christian society.

Christian citizenship became the solution to the YMCA's question of how to graft its diverse array of programs and services onto its evangelical Christian foundation. It also became the motive force behind a nationwide program (though individual Ys could still interpret it as they thought best).

In 1920 the Association Press released *Handbook for Comrades*, a standardized and graded program of Christian citizenship training. The handbook was an amalgam of several up-and-coming programs within the YMCA sphere of work, incorporating nature and camping instruction, aquatics and games, and most importantly a chapter on "American Citizenship for Boys." The handbook describes the program as a system "point[ing] the way toward success," so that each participating boy could

THE MAKING OF
CHRISTIAN CITIZENS

The Boyhood of America
for the Boy of Galilee!

A Group of real City "Y" Boys

The appeal of consecrated leaders backed by the appeal of nature never fails to leave a deep impress. Under these conditions, enlistment for Christian service is a more likely result.

 "Ideals must begin to work in the plastic period of youth."

Figure 3. "The Making of Christian Citizens," poster from an exhibit highlighting the American Y's Christian citizenship programs at the World's Assembly of YMCAs in Portschach, Austria, 1923. Kautz Family YMCA Archives, University of Minnesota Libraries.

complete the program able to say "I can do all things well, some things better, one thing best."

The program was heavily influenced by religious educators within the YMCA, with each chapter including Bible verses and a biblical framework, but it was undogmatic and contained the latest scientific findings where relevant. For example, a section on the development of plant life opens with Genesis 1:2 and includes a lesson on geological time and fossil formation. The staff pioneering the field of youth development, however, had the strongest hand in shaping the program, which covered topics as wide-ranging as pet care, first aid, sexual education, public speaking, and community relationships. A point system was devised to measure intellectual, physical, service, and devotional development that, if attained, could help mold participants into well-rounded individuals who engaged in a wide assortment of interests and activities.

The *Handbook for Comrades* contains early clues regarding the future direction of YMCA youth work. Youth were encouraged to improve their community through service learning projects. To earn 25 points, a boy could "as an act of worship, beautify a church building by planting trees, shrubs, vines, or flowers, involving at least eight hours' service." Camping brought religion outdoors by encouraging boys to see the hand of God in nature, music, poetry, and art. Finally, a sense of ruggedness was nurtured within each boy by teaching him how to tie knots and build a variety of fires and shelters. The *Handbook* was in effect a manual on how to become a man. Perhaps it was too comprehensive in its approach, resulting in an unwieldy and unrealistic model. One possible reason the Comrades program failed to yield a core of supporters was that the burden of conducting the work was placed solely on the boy. His leader would monitor and encourage, but the boy on his own chose the activities and reported on his results.

The *Handbook*, while a noble attempt to modernize and standardize youth development, could not rise above the status quo. During this period the primary youth development strategies involved youth clubs and special events. The highlights for both were often dinners with speakers, likely modeled on the increasingly businesslike culture of the YMCA administrative offices. These dull events encouraged both the boys and the fathers to be good Christian men, but provided no ongoing mechanism through which they were encouraged to follow through.

By the end of the Roaring Twenties, the YMCA had made a name for itself as a pillar of the community. It had cultivated the support of many prominent philanthropists whose dollars allowed the Y to expand both physically and programmatically, which in turn facilitated an ongoing evolution in its services to young men and boys.

Despite its zeal and opportunity for growth, however, the YMCA struggled to keep the attention of the broader community. Its early offerings of Bible study and evangelism were perfectly suited to a largely homogenous middle-class white Protestant population, but the broad changes of the Industrial Revolution, culminating in the Great War, left a society more diverse, more secular, more jaded, and more incompatible with the founding principles of the Young Men's Christian Association. Any attempt to help boys, and especially to create lasting bonds between boys and their fathers, could not rest on a shopworn model of stolid banquets and moralistic programs where fathers and sons sat mutely in their Sunday best. Now changes in the aftermath of the Industrial Revolution were transforming the nation even further. It became less common for a boy to go to work at ten or eleven. Perhaps boys no longer needed to sprint into responsible, working-life manhood, and the pace of transition could be relaxed. Fathers too were dealing with numerous transitions: rural to urban; school, even college, to working life; bachelorhood to marriage to fatherhood; wartime to peacetime. Most were still working out their own lives, roles, and identities. Perhaps they needed just as much help as their sons. The answer, it appeared increasingly, even intuitively, was not so much to pull boys up into adulthood as to allow fathers to come down to their sons' level and use boyhood and imagination as a vehicle for mutual interest, interaction, and intimacy.

HAROLD KELTNER

One Y secretary slowly coming to this conclusion was Harold Keltner. By the time he was recognized as the father of the Y-Indian Guides, Keltner had written and been interviewed many times about the establishment of the program. One source untapped until now, however, is an undated, heavily edited manuscript of approximately fifty pages typed on onionskin paper and kept by his youngest daughter, Gene Keltner Cannon. Cannon was unsure of this document's ultimate purpose, but surmised that her father was attempting to write a biography of his friend and cofounder Joe Friday. While portions of the manuscript have been lifted, polished, and used for other occasions, it contains numerous other previously unknown stories and observations.[43]

Harold Keltner, born on May 7, 1893, in South Bend, Indiana, grew up attending First Baptist Church with his family. When asked on his application to Springfield College, "How long since you entered upon the Christian life?" he answered "1904," which most likely means he was baptized in that year. His father, a real estate developer who doubled as a building contractor, kept a busy professional schedule. "When a small boy," Harold wrote, "I [often] heard my mother say to my father, 'Arthur, you have got to do something with that boy,' meaning me. 'You must give him some of your time and thought.' When that did not seem to bring results she joined the women's Auxiliary, in those days an important part of the Y. . . . That first Y as I remember was in the basement of a laundry in South Bend." Though Keltner was not impressed with the YMCA, even when the Studebaker brothers donated "a fine new building of modern design," Keltner's mother thought otherwise and signed him up for several programs. "Before I knew what had happened I was a member and learning to swim, play basketball, and enjoy the luxuries of an athletic club of my own." South Bend's boys' work director, Frank H. Cheley, clearly played an influential role in his life. Upon graduating high school, Keltner applied (listing Cheley as a reference) to the International Young Men's Christian Association Training School in Springfield, Massachusetts (today Springfield College), to make the Y his life's work.[44]

Just as he had done on his grandfather's farm back in Indiana, Keltner searched for Indian relics along the banks of the Connecticut River in Springfield. Upon graduation, according to his hometown newspaper, "he acted as physical director of the Y. M. C. A. in Buffalo, N. Y." (In Buffalo, too, wrote Keltner, "I had put on pageants historical concerning the Iroquois. It was known that Keltner was nuts about Indians.") Later he "held down a 'Y' hut on the Mexican border in 1916, enlisted in the navy in 1917," and moved to St. Louis in 1919, where he served as an employed boys' secretary. Keltner's childhood mentor Frank Cheley had

Figure 4. Harold Keltner (standing left) with a group of boys, date unknown. Gateway Region Young Men's Christian Association (S0473).

moved from South Bend to St. Louis on January 1, 1916, helping to explain Keltner's relocation there.[45]

Just as George Williams had observed social ills growing in London in the 1800s, Harold Keltner also witnessed a disturbing shift in social dynamics, affecting not only young single men but entire families and communities. "The exodus from farm to city was in full swing," he recalled. "This made a profound change in our family life in America. On the farm a father and his family were together on almost all occasions. Around the church the family had their social life, religious life and around the school the educational and social life, too." The move into the cities separated the father and his workplace from his wife and children. "He was still a good father and really intended to get around to the job of knowing his family better as soon as he could. Instead he saw them less and left the job of training his son to the church, school, YMCA, and later [Boy S]couts and of course the good mother of the family." The fruit of such a dramatically different lifestyle, averred Keltner, "was to come later in the form of delinquency, but the father believed that these institutions were falling down on the job rather than himself."[46]

The YMCA's initial response to this problem, beginning in 1911, was the father-son banquet. "Dad came out enthusiastically to these events," wrote Keltner. "He knew he was in the red in this business. The idea spread so rapidly that soon most every church had their annual banquet. The Y acted as the clearing house for them, securing the speakers and aiding them on programs. Most of us Secretaries were used as speakers for literally scores of these banquets. It was a busy time of year for us." The movement gained momentum, first from President Theodore Roosevelt, who proclaimed a fathers and sons week, then governors, and finally mayors. Each day of the banquet week emphasized a different aspect of the father-son relationship. But the proclamations slowly died away, leaving only the banquets, "an annual habit, you might say, and meaning less as the years passed. We were bogging down," observed Keltner.

Figure 5. A father-son banquet in Harold Keltner's home town of South Bend, Indiana, c. 1912. Kautz Family YMCA Archives, University of Minnesota Libraries.

One attempt to revive father-son work was undertaken in St. Louis by Cheley and New York transplant Lansing F. Smith, who would later become a passionate advocate for Y-Indian Guides. Smith had been in the publishing business in the 1890s. After arriving in St. Louis he organized the American Educational Society, a distributor of educational books. Together with J. A. Wolf, Cheley and Smith spearheaded the creation of the twenty-volume Father and Son Library, which could be purchased by YMCAs across the country and serve as a resource for interested fathers. Published by Smith's University Society imprint and encompassing topics as broad as fathering the boy, sports and games, tools and handicraft, popular science, nature's secrets, citizenship, and the world of business, these volumes were intended to light a fire under the father-son program. The volumes were highly detailed. In describing baseball, for example, volume 3 explained equipment, field configuration, fielding and throwing, catching fly balls, fielding grounders, "playing the bounce," throwing to a "target," various pitches including different forms of the curveball, batting and baserunning, and the hook slide. Keltner called the collection "magnificent," yet he acknowledged that "home from work at night [fathers] were too tired to initiate anything from these maze of materials and the boys could not lift themselves by their bootstraps."[47] The library suffered the same fate as the *Handbook for Comrades* and father-son banquets. Smith, discouraged by its logistical and financial failure, encouraged Keltner to find another way. "While this was said only half seriously," wrote Keltner, "it sank deep into my thoughts."[48]

As Keltner and the rest of the Y slogged on with the old father-son banquets, he wrote, the "weaknesses of the . . . system were now magnified in my mind." Each banquet speech further cemented the idea that he "was wasting precious time. When parents went on vacations and often left their sons in the care of the Y camp, it seemed as if they were avoiding their responsibilities. When they brought their problems of discipline to me it was so obvious that the boy's father had been delegating his job to others."

Then, wrote Keltner, came a night in a particular autumn, when, speaking for the tenth time, he "was suddenly aware that I was not holding my audience." The blame, he decided, rested not with his audience but with himself. The situation at hand required less talk and more action.

"Gentlemen," I heard myself saying, "this is my last father and son speech." Immediately there came a deep silence in the crowd. . . .

"We all know what is coming," I continued. "Shortly when I finish you will all clap whether I have done a good job or not. Then you will have a little boy rise and tell how wonderful the fathers are, and then a father will arise and tell how wonderful the sons are. Finally you will have the ladies out from the kitchen and they will stand along the wall and we will clap and thank them for the wonderful meal. It seems to me that they are the only ones that really deserve the applause because they have been working in the kitchen to serve us. . . . We will leave here tonight and forget all about our good intentions to be pals to our sons but come back again next year for another shot in the arm at another father and son banquet. If you ever invite me again to speak to you (incidentally I never was) I will have something more than a speech."[49]

It is difficult to know if this incident actually occurred as Keltner described, or if he was using it as a narrative device to spotlight the need for a program like Indian Guides. In any event, it is clear that Keltner was indeed searching for an innovative, effective way to deepen the bonds between fathers and sons.

The solution the St. Louis YMCA ultimately developed would spark a nationwide revolution in youth development, a program that brought fathers and sons together to discuss their identities as men, as fathers, and as sons, and would become one of the most successful youth development programs ever launched by the YMCA. It captured imaginations, transformed families, and made busy fathers set aside time for their sons. And in so doing, it allowed the Y to do what Keltner believed was essential: it put fathers rather than institutions in charge of engaging, inspiring, and teaching their own boys.

But the program also granted white fathers and sons permission to appropriate, characterize, and transform for their own purposes, and often without real understanding, the cultures of many Native American tribes. It was intended to be an homage to American Indian fathers like those in Joe Friday's Canadian Ojibwe community, and the responsibility they took for raising their sons. It meant to instill in participants a love and respect for nature, all living things, and "the Great Spirit." In 1926, when Y-Indian Guides was founded, these ideas sparked no controversy, no protest. No one questioned the propriety of such actions.

Then again, few if any Native Americans had or felt they had the power to protest, and few if any white Americans would have thought to ask them.

CHAPTER TWO

"White Men Raise Cities; Red Men Raise Sons"

ON NUMEROUS OCCASIONS throughout the history of what became Y-Indian Guides, cofounder Harold Keltner reflected on how it all began. These stories always referred to a fortuitous meeting—during his honeymoon, no less—with Joe Friday, a Canadian Ojibwe who became his collaborator and chief inspiration for Y-Indian Guides. Since Friday never recorded any origin account of his own (at least none that is extant), and since Keltner was writing to an audience perhaps more interested in good storytelling than good history, it is difficult to know how to assess these narratives. It is doubtful that Keltner sought to fabricate any of the details, but the vagaries of human memory must have unconsciously encouraged him to fill in forgotten spaces, while the retrospective and celebratory nature of his topic might have encouraged, however unintentionally, a few "improvements."

One must be mindful of the same dynamic noted by Robert Tilton in an 1825 relief over the west door of Washington, DC's Capitol Rotunda, portraying Pocahontas rescuing John Smith. Comparing the Pocahontas narrative with stories of other Indians such as Squanto and Massasoit who helped whites, Tilton observed, "What tied the stories of these virtuous Indians together was that for such figures to be seen in this light they generally had to act against the best interests of their own people. . . . This elevation saw the actual histories of these figures replaced by mythic narratives depicting the crucial elements when aid was given to the whites, such as the first Thanksgiving dinner in New England and the saving of John Smith."[1] As S. Elizabeth Bird concludes, such narratives also serve to justify the white conquest of America and "help deal with lingering guilt about the displacement of the Native inhabitants—after all, the 'good' Indians helped out European settlers and recognized the inevitability of White conquest."[2]

Past Y-Indian Guides members would undoubtedly bristle at any comparisons between the establishment of their program and the forced appropriation of Indigenous peoples' lands and lives. But the basic idea of whites controlling a narrative about an Indian figure is still worth considering in the case of Keltner and Friday. Nonetheless, despite their acknowledged limitations and the care with which we must read them, Keltner's stories are the only recorded sources we have regarding the founding of Indian Guides.

THE MEETING

In Keltner's typewritten narrative, the story of his confessional address at the Father and Son Banquet (recounted in chapter 1) leads almost immediately to his story of meeting Joe Friday. Having found the father-son banquet wanting, Keltner mused, "Now bridges had to be cut." There were boys' programs in St. Louis (which we will discuss shortly) that were not affiliated with the YMCA, but "they seemed to be duplicative of other boy programs. They had to go if our time was to be used on the father and son angle. . . . As good as they were, they were sacrificed for the big gamble."

Keltner described the voyage through which he met Joe Friday in biblical terms: "Our way of life today does not provide us much time to go apart into the wilderness for contemplation. Jesus spent 40 days and nights in the wilderness renewing his spiritual strength. . . . Even a short period of prayer away from the crowds puts out of focus the trifles of life and before us we see ourselves as we actually are with all our weaknesses. This happened to me in the solitude of the Canadian wilderness. It was like being seated on a planet and looking down on the earth and seeing so many futile and useless things that I had been doing in the big city. Here is where the Indian name came in."

As he would recall time and time again, Keltner and his wife Martha met Joe Friday while canoeing in the wilds of Northern Ontario. The couple married during World War I, but their honeymoon had to wait until Keltner's return after the war's conclusion. "I had camped and fished in Canada in 1916, only a few years after the opening of the country by the railroad, in the Timagami section," wrote Keltner. The landscape clearly appealed to him, and he promised his wife that when he returned, "we would go to the wonderful country of Canada on a canoe trip among the Indians' lakes, and forests."[3]

Accompanied by Harold's father (who slept in a separate tent), the Keltners set out from their home in St. Louis in 1921 for Lake Temagami. Canoeing was a new experience for the older Keltner, a heavyset man who sat in the bow, thereby elevating Harold's position in the stern. One day as they made their way across the massive lake, a storm broke out. Martha furiously bailed water while the men struggled to make progress against the waves. As the storm subsided, the trio made for the shores of Bear Island. No doubt witnessing the spectacle from afar, a crowd of "Indians" stood onshore, ready to receive them. From within the crowd Harold heard, "Keltner, what are you doing here?" Al Sauer, a YMCA secretary turned missionary, had relocated to Temagami to establish a church. He excitedly told Keltner that he wanted to introduce him to his first convert, Joe Friday.

Friday observed that the nail on one of Keltner's fingers had been ripped off during his misadventure. "'Come up to my cabin and I will have my wife fix you up,' said the tall Ojibway. This was not what I had bargained for," recalled Keltner. "I had wanted to see the agent or factor of the Hudson Bay Company and have a qualified white person do the repair work, but as the boys say, 'the fat was on the fire now,' and I did not wish to offend my new friend. We walked up the hill to his cabin and found his wife to be a white woman and a graduate nurse at that." (One wonders, of course, what might have happened if Friday's wife had been a Native woman with traditional rather than white, professionally accredited skills.)

Keltner often reflected back to this particular historical tableau: his father, whose time and attention he had been denied as a boy; his wife, who would actually galvanize the efforts to establish the first Indian Guides tribe five years later; and "the Indian whose life and stories inspired me to use the Indian ways of life as the basis for the father and son program." God himself, Keltner believed, had worked through the storm to bring them together. It is important at this juncture to note that the bond between Keltner and Friday was established in part because Friday was an Indian, and Keltner was fascinated with Indian lore and artifacts. But the real bond that cemented the relationship was their common Christian faith. Central to that faith was the belief that Native American spirituality would inevitably be replaced by an acceptance of Jesus Christ as the Savior of all humanity.

The following year, 1922, Keltner brought his brother Bernard camping on the islands of Temagami. Friday was serving as a guide for a "party of tourists" but managed to do so while staying close to the Keltner brothers. Harold remembered catching "the biggest [trout] I had ever caught in my life." After a period of silence, Keltner could contain his enthusiasm no longer and showed Joe his fish. Though Keltner hadn't seen him catch anything, Joe reached over the side of his canoe and wordlessly held up a trout a little bigger than Keltner's. "I could never beat him at his own game," he observed.[4]

Two years later, Friday's uncle White Bear died and left him an island upon which he planned to build a cabin. Keltner, Martha, and their two young girls, ages four and nine months, traveled all the way up to Temagami in their Model T Ford to be with him. Keltner's decision to bundle up his family and drive approximately 2,500 miles round trip to see Friday—well before the days of interstate highways, in an automobile with a top speed of forty-five miles per hour, while traveling roads that often demanded lower speeds—suggests, at least on Keltner's part, a deep connection. The family camped under the pines, caught trout and bass with a copper wire, and accompanied Friday when he went canoeing and hunting for moose. When their portaging forced them to leave valuable items behind, Keltner would suggest hiding them. This was not necessary, Friday replied, since there was no white man for twenty-five miles, and the Indian "respected the property of others to a remarkable degree." On one of their trips they needed a frying pan to cook supper, and Friday "recollected he had left one in a hollow tree some years ago. Upon reaching the spot, he put his hand into the hollow tree and out came the pan." On the same trip the canoe slid over a sharp rock that tore a hole nearly half its length. As Martha furiously bailed and the four-year-old tended to her young sister, the two men paddled to shore, where Friday turned the canoe over onto a flat rock, then searched in the forest for birch bark and spruce gum. "In a few minutes he returned, made a torch of the bark, and blew all along the tear in the canoe, thoroughly drying the canvas and wood. Then he placed small lumps of the spruce gum along the tear before blowing on it again and melting these lumps into a solid mass of liquid. He spit on [his] hand and with a quick swipe of it made a clean seam along the entire rip." According to Keltner, the canoe did not leak a drop the rest of the trip. Clearly Friday was the consummate wilderness host.

Later that summer, having returned home, the St. Louis camping director told Keltner that he "wished he had an Indian to use in his program." (One wishes Keltner would have explained exactly what he meant by this.) Keltner thought of Joe Friday immediately. Somehow he persuaded Friday to relocate to St. Louis and teach woodcraft at Camp Niangua. Friday spent many nights in the Keltner home. According to both Keltner and William Hefelfinger, a St. Louis brick-company plant director who played a critical role in making Indian Guides a national program, Friday was impressed with the trappings of the modern metropolis, but took a dim view of white society and family life. As Hefelfinger recalled years later, "Joe stopped for a moment" as they walked through downtown St. Louis "and looked up at the tall buildings. 'Yes, white men have learned to grow tall buildings, but they can't even raise their own sons.'"[5] Keltner remembered a similar sentiment from Friday, perhaps from the same conversation: "[The white man] is a great worker, but I cannot understand how he can be so dumb in the raising of his children. The dangers to youth in the city are greater than in our woods and yet the white man spends far less time in teaching his sons about these dangers, and the trails he will have to travel than the savage Indian."

As described in chapter 1, Keltner had by this time grown disenchanted with the traditional, ineffectual YMCA father-son programs. Banquets highlighting a religious or civic speaker did not tend to arouse passion in boys or meaningful conversations between the generations. He had examined other programs: "The Woodcraft League of Ernest T. Seton, the Y Friendly Indians, [Boy] Scouts, but nothing would jell."

One should note, before moving further in this narrative, that all three of the programs mentioned above appropriated American Indian culture in some form. Established in 1902, Ernest Thompson Seton's Woodcraft League was originally called "The League of Woodcraft Indians." Seton himself was born in South Shields, Durham, England,

Figure 6. Joe Friday at the dedication of the South Side Y, St. Louis. The girl next to him may be one of Harold Keltner's daughters. Gateway Region Young Men's Christian Association (S0473).

though his large family (he was one of ten boys who survived infancy) migrated to Lindsay, Ontario, and later settled in Toronto. Trained as a naturalist, Seton eventually settled in Cos Cob, Connecticut. According to the institute that bears his name, Seton responded to the repeated vandalization of his gate by inviting boys from the local school to his home; "Rather than prosecuting them . . . he sat down with them and told them stories of Native Americans and nature. He adopted the 'Indian' name Black Wolf. The unique feature of his program was that the boys elected their own leaders, a Chief, a Second Chief, a Keeper of the Tally and a Keeper of the Wampum."[6] Seton, who was also a cofounder of the Boy Scouts, worked for years to temper the militaristic tendencies of Lord Robert Baden-Powell's Scouts by freely appropriating imagined Indian symbols and names for its campfire rituals. The scouting magazine *Boys' Life* provided an ideal forum for Seton's thoughts on nature and Indians and their utility in shaping youth.[7]

The Y Friendly Indians were a part of the YMCA's Christian citizenship programs of the 1920s (see chapter 1). Boys of nine to twelve were in Friendly Indians; of thirteen to fourteen, in Pioneers; and of fifteen to seventeen, in Comrades. Friendly Indians adopted "Indian" names, wore "Indian" headbands, and went on hikes and picnics to learn more about nature. In a *Long House News* essay written after Friday's death, Keltner mentioned that before the formation of Y-Indian Guides, "we had about fifteen or twenty [Woodcraft League] tribes in the St. Louis Y with perhaps thirty Friendly Indians tribes."[8] In other words, the unique characteristic of what became Y-Indian Guides was not the (mis)appropriation of American Indian identities, which was and remains rampant in and beyond American culture, but the introduction of a father-son dynamic absent in other programs.

According to Keltner, a single event ultimately coalesced these disparate programs into a new, unique form in his mind: "One evening Joe was speaking in a church to a group of fathers and sons" about growing up with his Ojibwe tribe in the wilds of Lake Temagami. "At the close of the meeting the men rushed up to the platform and packed around so closely to Joe that the little boys could not reach the Indian to ask him questions such as their fathers were doing. . . . Then it hit me. Men were just as intrigued with the Indian and all his life as little boys. In fact, men were nothing but little boys anyway. Ask the women and they will tell you the same thing."[9] What fathers saw in Friday, thought Keltner, was a vision of what they dreamed of being themselves, and perhaps on some level a memory of a simpler life they once lived, a sentimentalized relationship with their own fathers that more closely resembled the one Friday described. The Indian may have been "a creature of imagination" to those fathers, as Keltner would later write, but he also clearly evoked yearnings within them for real, if somewhat nostalgic, connections to family and to nature.

Suddenly, Keltner recalled, "the simple homely truths of the Indian's methods of training their youth began to have meaning." He began asking Friday "hundreds of questions." How, for example, did Indian fathers teach their sons about honesty? "Our fathers said very little about this," replied Friday "They *were* honest. We boys knew that without being taught." To illustrate the point, he said, "On the trail, if my uncle found an axe that had been dropped by another person, he carefully tied it by a piece of moose hide and hung it up near the center of the trail so that it could be easily found by its owner. . . . That was another person's property. We knew that." Keltner's thoughts leaped to a father in St. Louis who had allowed his son to lie about his age to get a reduced fare on the streetcar, then later complained that his son was a liar. Sons learned best, reflected Keltner, through their fathers' example.

After Friday's father died, his uncle took up the task of preparing Joe for adulthood. "He knew that the ambition of every little Indian boy was to grow up to be a famous guide for fishing and hunting now that the white man had taken over his country." Even simply living in their native landscape required learning all the skills of one's forefathers, "So uncle kept us in touch with these skills." When Joe was old enough to take on his own party of white fishermen, his uncle took him aside. "I will tell you what you will run into. This will be your first trip guiding and the lives of these people will be in your hands." He went on to describe a spot in the river they would be navigating that was about a day's paddle away. Where a white cedar tree leaned over the river, the water was deep and the current calm. On the other side the water ran fast and looked threatening. Even so, his uncle instructed, "go over to the other side. This looks bad and is, but not as bad as the good side is later on." When Friday reached the point his uncle described, he alarmed his party by paddling over to the rushing waters, eschewing the more placid side of the river. But "Uncle had never lied to me and I knew that I must do as he said." For several tense moments Friday wondered if he had done the right thing, the men in his charge tensely clutching the gunwales of their canoes. "Then as the current eased up after a hard fight I looked over to the side that we had left. It was a turmoil of rushing water ending in a whirlpool where logs were being ground to pieces by the rocks. I doubt that I would have made it had I not followed uncle's advice." As Keltner remembers, there was a long pause after Friday told the story. "The trail of life. That was it. We must put the son's small feet on the trail of life. No, not us the paid social worker, but help the father to do it. He is the one who cares most and has the most at stake. We must put the father in the saddle." With the father in the saddle, thought Keltner, "his example will count for more than words with this little boy who at the tender age of six knows that his dad is a hero." Fathers, Keltner thought, had no choice but to actually be the heroes their sons imagined them to be. "One father said to me, 'I just cannot go on doing some of the things that I am if I am to be in this tribe.'" (In other words, he would have to give up some competing commitments and perhaps some bad habits to be the father he needed to be for his son.) "This is one of the big byproducts of Indian Guides."

This relationship between white middle-class fathers and their sons, modeled insofar as it was possible on Joe Friday's observations on the way Canadian Ojibwe fathers raised their own boys, was also rooted in Keltner, Friday, and the YMCA's shared Christian identity. "If the Indian was anything," wrote Keltner, "he was religious in his own way. If the Indian Guides are to be anything, they must be this, not ostentatiously, but deeply believing in the power of prayer and the faith of our [the YMCA's] Christian founding in 1844 and the same process of the Indian Guides in 1926. Our movement was an answer to unceasing prayer, faith, and of course hard work, too. 'It had to be an answer to prayer,' said Joe to me in later years, 'or an ordinary Y secretary and a savage Indian could not have made it go.'"

Keltner and Friday spent many nights talking about what first became known as Indian Rovers after they had come home from work. As Keltner told Adele Starbird in 1963, he feared their brainchild would be a spectacular flop. "'It's too idealistic, Joe. The fathers won't go for it.' 'Well, then we must get down and pray, Harold. You tell me all things are possible to God. Let's kneel down right here.'"[10] Mrs. Keltner heard them talking over the course of many nights. "I found out later," recalled Keltner, that she "knew more than we dreamed about our plans." Keltner kept stalling, wondering if the ideas he and Friday discussed were really palatable to an adult, professional audience. When his wife finally asked him whether he was ever going to initiate the program about which he and Friday had spent so much time planning and praying, she volunteered to call a minister to gather some men together to hear him out. Keltner thought no more about it until one night she announced that a meeting had been set up at the home of Howard B. Phillips, minister of Richmond Heights Presbyterian Church, whose church had hosted a father-son banquet in 1922 (and who later, Keltner wrote, resigned from his church to become "a missionary to the Indians in Montana").[11] Shocked and perhaps more than a little irritated with his wife, Keltner arrived, he recalled, to find "the leading men of the community" looking at him "with measuring if not critical eyes. These men represented the best in their professions and businesses."[12] By this time Friday had returned to Canada, so Keltner was on his own. He made an impassioned pitch to participate for one year in an experiment that had the potential to revolutionize "youth work and family life." He had brought a piece of birch bark, and at the conclusion of his presentation he asked all those present to sign it. The first tribe of what came to be Y-Indian Guides was born.

THE FORMATION OF THE PROGRAM

As Keltner freely admitted in 1955, "When [Joe Friday] returned to his native land, I put together the elements of the Woodcraft League best suited to our purpose, the Friendly Indian ritual, and added the original Indian Guide aims, which we had made from Indian standards." (In other words, Friday spoke and Keltner listened.) As he wrote elsewhere, "Too much cannot be said in appreciation of the work done by Mr. Joe Friday, our Ojibway Indian Guide. Many the night he has sat up with me until the early hours of the morning talking over his experiences as a boy in the wigwam of his father. The Eight Aims of the Indian Guides really came out of these midnight discussions."[13] Those aims were: (1) to be clean; (2) "to complain never"; (3) to put the other fellow first; (4) to be silent while elders speak; (5) to love the sacred circle of the family; (6) to love honor and truth; (7) to be reverent; and (8) to see the beauty of the Great Spirit's work.[14] These aims would be consolidated in the ensuing years and adopt the overtly Christian aim, "to love my neighbor as myself."[15]

The minutes of the very first Indian Guides tribe, the Osage, along with a number of other records and artifacts, were kept by Keltner's youngest daughter, Gene Keltner Cannon, until her death in 2015.[16] As they reveal, on the evening of November 17, 1926, "a group of Friendly Indians as yet unidentified met at Brave Arthur A. Hapke's wigwam in the hunting grounds of the Osage's for the purpose of organizing a Big-Brave-Little Brave council. The skies were dark and full of moisture but the braves were all there." The adult men present were "Big Chief" Keltner (who adopted the name "Chief Lone Wolf" because he had no sons); YMCA's visiting chiefs Lansing Smith, Buren Holmes ("a wonderful old gentleman who understood rocks, trees, birds, and boys"), and J. A. Wolf; and Big Braves Hapke ("of the Federal Courts"), Dr. F. W. Fender (a dentist whose boy was anxious to become a scout), H. L. Parsons, D. D. Holmes (Buren's brother, "a lawyer and enthusiastic trout fisherman"), Henry Cleino ("another lawyer—the humorist of the group, and story-teller par excellence"), Fred O. Lutz, Augthins, and William Hefelfinger ("a bricklayer and contractor who proved to be the most talented of the group in his use of Indian language, forms of speech, handicraft and understanding of the same"); and "Medicine man" Howard B. Phillips ("a kindly social type of man"). The Little Braves were Jack Martin, Robert Lutz, and the sons of Augthins, Cleino, Fender, Hapke, Hefelfinger, and Parsons.[17]

Figure 7. Members of the original Indian Guides "tribe," the Osage. Harold Keltner is standing second from right; William Hefelfinger, third from left. Gateway Region Young Men's Christian Association (S0473).

There were "several surprises," noted Keltner years later, at the first meetings of the Osage "tribe," including the success of the story-telling period. One father after another told stories about going hunting. Mr. Cleino confessed that in trying to shoot a hawk he had neglected to remove the ramrod from his gun before pulling the trigger. "Mr. Wolf and I will never forget the look of wonder in the eyes of the boys," wrote Keltner, "not only at the stories of the other men, but from experiences of their own dads, many of which had never been related to them before. . . . The score stood 10-0 against "It can't be done."[18]

One of the secrets to Indian Guides' success, then, was in creating a space that easily and naturally developed camaraderie between fathers and allowed sons to observe and benefit from it. These light-hearted adult interactions humanized fathers in the eyes of their sons and the other boys, which in turn created a context in which fathers were better prepared to engage in playful activities with their sons. The great enjoyment fathers derived from these experiences was another great surprise. It should be noted, however, that this program and these benefits were largely reserved for middle- and upper-middle-class families who owned homes large enough to host such events, whose mothers stayed home and could provide refreshments at the end of meetings, and whose fathers had the disposable time and income to facilitate meetings and events central to the program.

At some point during the early days of Indian Guides (Keltner remembered it as the winter of 1925–26, but since Indian Guides did not exist until the following year, he was likely a year or two early), Keltner decided to create an event with "Indian atmosphere." Friday's brother William brought a "quarter of moose meat" from Temagami, and the Keltner family hosted an Indian-style meal for "several prominent men," including Boys' Work Commission member and baseball pioneer Branch Rickey.[19]

The Osage minutes, as well as mimeographed copies of the group's very first newsletters, show a program still very much in the process of formation. This initial collection of fathers and sons referred to themselves as Friendly Indians. In fact, as Keltner wrote at the bottom of the first page of minutes, they "used Friendly Indians headbands." The minutes for April 12, 1927, described a meeting of the "Forest Rovers." It was not until December 2 that it was "emphatically stated by Chief Red Feather [William Hefelfinger][20] that the name no longer was 'Indian Rovers' but 'Indian Guides.'" The group had found its name and its purpose. Fathers would, perhaps paradoxically to some, play with their boys in order to lead them into manhood.

In Keltner's view, Indian Guides was unique because "it was home-centered; membership was a father and son unit; program responsibility rested on the fathers. The age group was 9 to 12. . . . One hundred per cent attendance was a definite requisite."[21] The feature that created some tension at the beginning was that fathers and sons had to attend together. The first test arose when a boy arrived one evening without his father and was sent home sobbing. "It was hard," remembered Keltner, "but the rule said, 'No father without a son, no son without a father.'" (As founder, Keltner, who had no sons, was the exception to the rule.) "If infractions were permitted, the program would collapse. Within 20 minutes the boy was back, with his hand in his father's hand."[22]

Participants in Y Indian Guides found in their imaginative play a palliative to the ills of modern, industrialized, corporate America. Participants could revere Indians and promote American exceptionalism at the same time, as Hefelfinger, who became national Indian Guides president in 1945 and adopted the name Negaunee, made clear: "I believe by any standard you choose to take, the Indian was the highest type of primitive people in the world."[23] Of course, even while extolling Indian culture, the Y never lost sight of its own Christian identity. Any reference in any Indian Guides publication to the nobility of Native culture concluded with its inherent, intuitive respect for and acknowledgment of the Great Spirit, which in the eyes of the YMCA meant the Christian Triune God. This understanding was both implicit based on historic identity and mission of the Young Men's Christian Association, but also made explicit in publications and events. In 1942, for example, Dr. Milton Towner summed up his presentation at the fifth annual National Longhouse meeting by saying that Indian Guides helped fathers show their sons that American society, understood to be a Christian society, "takes its meaning from and finds its worth in a great faith in God and in loyalty to the leadership of Jesus Christ."[24] While Joe Friday had inspired this experiment, he was not present at the first several meetings. His return from Temagami, however, was heralded in the 1927 Valentine's Day minutes of the Osage tribe:

> Great was my astonishment when I saw a real specimen of the red man, —a man deep of chest and lithe of limb with muscles of whip cord. One that would be tireless on the trail and who could handle a canoe like a viking moored a ship. A man who had the poise of

an athlete and the bearing of a statesman, and from the serenity of
his countenance you knew he was at peace with the Great Spirit.
Chief, my hand is out and my home is open to this fellow-man,
Joe Friday, which I am sure is the sentiment of the fellow members
of this tribe.

Later in the meeting Friday "showed us some very interesting pictures
of the North country and gave a very interesting talk on the same, and
also an account of his early life which was very much enjoyed by all."[25] It
is clear from these comments that Friday was the object of tremendous
affection, even a kind of reverence. But this is not the same as being
understood or respected. Despite all the good intentions of his rapt
white audience, one can nonetheless assert that Joe Friday was what
they wanted him to be: what Robert Berkhofer has called "the white
man's Indian."[26]

But who was Joe Friday? Apart from the texts found in the records of
the Indian Guides, what can be known about this enigmatic man whose
way of life became the model for a program both beloved for its great
success at creating warm bonds between fathers and sons and reviled for
its appropriation, reinvention, and misuse of native culture?[27]

Joe Friday was born on November 10, 1887, in the northern Canadian
forest of Matagami, minutes before his twin sister Charlotte. He also
had four brothers—William, Thomas, James, and George—and two
other sisters, Ellen and Flora-Harriet.[28] He was given the name Ahtik,
Ojibwe for "caribou," because his father John saw caribou tracks outside
their birchbark wigwam shortly after Joe was born. After John's death,
which occurred when Joe was still a young boy, the family moved to
Bear Island on Lake Temagami, near Hudson Bay in Ontario, Canada.
There Ahtik was christened and given the name Joseph by his uncle
White Bear, who was the chief of the tribe and who also took on the
responsibility of raising Ahtik/Joe.[29] Friday left his native land to fight
in World War I, serving in Canada's 228th Battalion. It was during the
war that he met Eva Vanderlip, whom he married in 1918.

Indian Guides literature described Joe as a "real Indian, born in a wigwam." He was "a hunter, a trapper, a guide and a philosopher." While
readers may have assumed that these qualities were products of his isolated Native environment, Keltner stated that "the ambition of every little

Indian boy was to grow up to be a famous guide for fishing and hunting now that the white man had taken over his country." Friday, too, made it clear that part of his passage into adulthood included his uncle's decision to let him guide white fishermen on his own. As Canadian sports historian Andrew Holman relates,

> The Friday family was no stranger to commerce and no stranger to strangers. A prominent and widely-known group of hunter/guides, the Fridays of Bear Island, Temagami, were at the forefront among Native families who took advantage of a changing economy. A growing tourist trade . . . in the early twentieth century provided great opportunity for Natives to break their reliance on trapping furs for sale to the Hudson's Bay Company. By World War I some families did well enough as guides in the summer months that winter trapping (and sporadic attempts at farming) became a decidedly secondary source of income.[30]

So if one wonders how Joe Friday had the ability to visit St. Louis for long periods of time, or later to travel throughout the United States promoting the growth of the Indian Guides program, it is because he was part of a very successful family business that afforded him the time to pursue other interests during the off-season. Indeed, wealthy tourists, further mobilized by the increasingly popular automobile, came to northeastern Ontario to have a "real" northern Canadian experience, complete with a real Native guide. According to Patricia Jasen, "Travel books, guidebooks and other promotional materials provided lists of reliable guides by name . . . such as the Friday family at Temagami." One finds the following comment in a 1906 edition of sportsman's magazine *Rod & Gun in Canada*: "An integral part of Lake Temagami—Canada's newest and loveliest holiday island—is the Friday family, a worthy family of Indian blood. . . . [The wise adventurer] will close a contract with one of the Friday boys to be his guide, philosopher, friend, fisherman, canoeist, cook, and tentmate."[31] Joe and his brother Will were also regular winter fixtures in church and YMCA events, where they lectured on Indian life and closed most events with an invitation to meet them up north for some fishing. One can safely assert, therefore, that the Joe Friday who came to St. Louis in 1926 was not a naive fish out of water but rather a sophisticated businessman who knew how to play the role white tourists expected of him and in turn make a good living.

Friday's business interests were not limited to outfitting and guiding. Between December 1927 and February 1928—not much more than a year after visiting St. Louis and inspiring the creation of Indian Guides—Joe and Will organized a twenty-two-city tour with two Native hockey teams, the Cree and the Ojibwe, who barnstormed Canada and the United States, playing either against each other or against a local team. They played in large American cities like Boston, Philadelphia, and Cleveland, as well as small Ontario villages. At every stop the teams "wore buckskin jerseys with fringe and (in pre-game warm-up) ceremonial headdresses made of feathers." The Friday brothers were "shrewd promoters," writes Holman. "They had to be to run a tour that required a great deal of planning, a knowledge of the market for this 'product,' and an extensive network of contacts." The brothers would have had to manage a significant number of costly expenses: "a Gray Line charter bus (and driver) for two months' travel; accommodations in 22 locations for 19 men; and money for meals. The Fridays would have had to strike deals with a long list of arena owners and managers for ice use (and perhaps gate receipts) in an era when the bottom line . . . trumped all other considerations for ice arena owners." Holman tells us that "wherever they could arrange it, the teams quartered at YMCA facilities." Joe and Will already had a history with the Y, and it was likely the cheapest place to stay. One also wonders if some hotels refused to house First Nations people.[32]

When the teams weren't playing hockey, they conducted "specially orchestrated 'powwows'—demonstrations of canoe paddling, bow-and-arrow whittling and shooting, birch-bark canoe construction, moose calling, and snowshoe making." They harnessed the one dog they brought with them to demonstrate dog-sleigh techniques and "displayed 'authentic' artifacts, too: a tepee, axes, tomahawks, arrowheads, animal skins, and stuffed fish." Films featuring northern wildlife rounded out the affair.[33]

How white audiences viewed the "Cree and Ojibway"[34] Indians playing the original, "indigenous" form of hockey against modern white players may not have been significantly different from how Keltner, Hefelfinger, and other white Indian Guides members saw Joe Friday and Indians in general. In the hockey tour, audiences were allowed to witness hockey "played in its pristine form." In Indian Guides, fathers sought to recapture what was depicted to them as a pristine version of fatherhood.[35] Yet in the first case, popular narrative saw modern white hockey as superior; Indian Guides celebrated, though in ideal form, the superior parenting skills of the Indian father. "Archaic" and "quaint" Indian hockey was seen as no match for the more "progressive" and "modern" white hockey, though Natives' role in originating the sport had to be acknowledged. Yet the Indian father provided a model that had the potential, in the minds of Indian Guides devotees, to save American families besieged by the ills of modern industrialized society.

A story about Joe's brother Will, perhaps apocryphal and before the days of the Y-Indian Guides, features white assumptions about "Indian naivete" mirroring those we will soon see in Harold Keltner's stories about Joe. Harry Charlton, publicity agent for Grand Trunk Railroad, wanted to make his 1909 Sportsman's Show in New York a real success by featuring a "real Indian." He invited Will Friday to make the long voyage to the city. Charlton arrived at the station and couldn't find Friday: "The poor, primitive, inexperienced boy was nowhere in sight." Charlton later learned that Friday had arrived early, found his way to Charlton's hotel, and secured his key. "Willie was sitting in Charlton's easy chair 'contentedly smoking' when he returned." The charge for Friday's cab fare from the Jersey station, Charlton later discovered, had been put on his bill and signed in his name.[36] Joe too would often (though certainly not exclusively) be depicted as a naive fish out of water, yet there was clearly far more to him than the stories shared by white men in St. Louis.

In both the hockey game and in Friday's role in Indian Guides, the opportunity to capitalize on white stereotypes of Natives could be seized by both sides. Yes, sportswriters previewed and reviewed the games in crassly caricatured language, employing overwrought tropes they had already employed to describe franchises with Indian mascots (e.g., "Indians scalp Yankees"). Audiences were free to interpret the contest and contestants they witnessed in any form they pleased. Despite white spectators' racist stereotyping, the Fridays and their players capitalized on their time on the road by promoting their fishing lodges up north. In fact, Joe often concluded his Indian Guides talks across the United States by inviting people to come up to Canada and go fishing with him.

And in the case of the hockey tour, Holman suggests that the Native players saw themselves participating in "a subversive self-parody, a drama of racial mockery and power inversion. In dressing up and acting as 'imaginary Indians,' these *real* Natives were having a laugh at their paying customers' expense." Was Joe Friday having a laugh at the expense of Harold Keltner and the Indian Guides? This seems unlikely, given the amount of time and energy he put into the program, though far from impossible. But Friday was aware, in some cases painfully, of how he and other Natives were perceived by most whites, and he may well have created a message that he felt would best fit the preconceived notions of his white audience.

Another source of information about Joe Friday comes from Jocelyn Thorpe's *Temagami's Tangled Wild: Race, Gender, and the Making of Canadian Nature.* Thorpe recounts how some of the white visitors to the Temagami region began building cottages there. Indeed, in a 1928 *Toronto Globe* article the region was described as having almost magical powers. This "Land of Virgin Beauty" could "reconstruct a broken-down physical constitution and give a tired, worn-out man a new lease of life sending him back to his work with such a store of energy that he finds the following months of toil a thing to be enjoyed rather than feared."[37]

Joe Friday told Harold Keltner that he was a "treaty Indian, which meant that he had no rights as a [Canadian] citizen but could . . . hunt and fish as he liked. . . . This treaty, he told me, was made with Queen Victoria and the Ojibways years before which entitled them to hunt and fish 'as long as the rivers flowed and the grass was green.'" The spirit of that treaty as Friday understood it came under attack when the province of Ontario began issuing leases to non-natives, allowing them to erect cabins in the region. By 1933 there had been 223 such structures built in the area. Logging interests also began encroaching, and while the government allowed "conservation-based" logging (more a euphemism than a policy) in the area, natives like Joe Friday's brother George were discouraged from cutting down trees to build their own homes.[38] The Ontario government began to see the native people of the region as mere occupants rather than owners of the land and waters. "With the increased popularity of tourism," writes Thorpe, "came the consolidation of Temagami as a (now officially) Canadian destination, with the result that [the various Native People of the area] existed in even more isolation from one another." Cottage owners began to see themselves as "settlers," while Indigenous control of the many islands in Lake Temagami was recognized less and less. In a few years, only Bear Island was recognized as belonging to the "Teme-Augama Anishanabai." This left many other islands, including the one Joe Friday's uncle White Bear had left him, open to white settlement. Increasingly, whites were recognized as the owners of Lake Temagami islands, while Natives were mere squatters. On July 29, 1940, Friday wrote a letter to the Canadian Department of Indian Affairs. He described a meeting between himself and two American men who came to visit the island where he had lived "since I was a kid," and where he had built cabins and was operating a lodge. He was informed that the island was up for lease, and that if they proceeded he would be forced to leave. As a Canadian Indian agent explained to Friday, he had not paid rent on the island, and therefore was considered a squatter and could be removed by provincial authorities. "Neither the American men's ability to lease this island and to build a cottage on it," observes Thorpe, "nor Friday's removal from it were natural. Both were the result of the provincial decision to lease islands in Lake Temagami to cottagers."[39]

As the next several years passed, the Teme-Augama Anishanabai flatly refused to pay rents to the government for lands they considered theirs. "The Ontario government envisioned them," says Thorpe, "as too civilized to deserve special treatment and too uncivilized to require access to lumber." Ultimately, Ontario even sold Bear Island to the federal government, which raised white fears that it would be designated as a reserve.

As these events unfolded, the Teme-Augama Anishanabai made various proposals. One submitted in 1942 is re-created in full in Thorpe's book. It suggested, among other things, that the Indian chief of the Timagami Forest Reserve, in consultation with the chief forest ranger and the chief game warden, "shall direct his people to what they may or may not do"; that the Indian chief keep a tally of all lumber and game taken with his permission; that once a chief was no longer able to perform his duties, a new one would be elected; and that a chief be paid adequately for his services so that he need not spend valuable time hunting and fishing. "We present these proposals," concluded the letter, "in the belief that by having a voice in the game and timber regulations, we Indians will be able to achieve full and whole-hearted co-operation with the conservation program such as is impossible when our own legitimate needs are not taken into consideration." This proposal was submitted under the signature of Joe Friday.[40]

Ontario sold Bear Island to the federal government in 1943 and claimed the remaining Temagami region as crown land. As part of the sale, Ontario placed restrictions on logging and the construction of settlements designed to favor the experience of tourists at the expense of the Temagami First Peoples. The transfer did have a symbolic effect of transforming Bear Island "from part of the Temagami wilderness (for tourists to visit) to an Indian space (for Indians!)."[41]

The October 1944 edition of *Long House News* confirmed Joe Friday's central role in continued negotiations with the Canadian government. Taking the occasion to point out that Native Americans were playing a disproportionately large role in fighting for their country during World War II, while at the same time they were not allowed to vote in some states, the newsletter reported that "Joe Friday, our faithful guide of the north . . . has long championed the cause of his people and their hunting and trapping rights. This Spring he was chosen to attend an all-chief representation council on Ottawa, Canada. . . . Apparently the tribes are satisfied that justice in their hunting grounds is to be established along with other minority world groups when peace is achieved." Despite his role in these important discussions, Friday planned to spend January 1 to April 1 of 1945 traveling through "Indiana, Illinois, Michigan, Kentucky, Missouri, and the West central area" promoting the Indian Guides program.[42]

Over the next twenty-five years the Teme-Augama Anishanabai lobbied the Department of Indian Affairs for the creation of a reserve encompassing a larger area based on an 1884 survey. In 1971 Ontario finally canceled the condition it had placed on Bear Island for its transfer to the federal government and declared it a reserve. This allowed the Teme-Augama Anishanabai to become eligible for a variety of administrative programs, though the fight for land extending beyond Bear Island continues.[43]

The story of Joe Friday found in the historical record stands in stark contrast to the man described in Harold Keltner's writings. In the latter one can certainly identify ways in which white stereotypes about Indians manifest themselves. Accounts about Friday can mostly be classified as

Figure 8. As so often in stories about the creation of Y-Indian Guides, Joe Friday stands in the background behind Harold Keltner in this 1970 commissioned portrait. Courtesy Gene Keltner Cannon.

lore. Which detail is myth, which is embellishment, and which is truth is difficult to tell. In many accounts, even in a commemorative portrait commissioned in 1970, Joe comes off as a background player, more inspirational than influential.[44] In Keltner's manuscript, his descriptions of his Ojibwe friend cannot help but be as much if not more about Keltner's own perceptions than about Friday's true self. On several occasions Keltner describes Friday as semiliterate: "With difficulty he could read, learning it mostly by Bible reading." This was clearly false. Yet one must remember while reading the following paragraphs that Keltner wrote most of what he remembered about Joe Friday many years after the fact (though one would think he could remember that Joe could read). He wrote his recollections based on his own expectations, on those he assumed his audience had, and on the "kind of Indian" Joe Friday chose to be while living with the Keltner family and the citizens of St. Louis.

By no means should Keltner be viewed as anti-Native. His lifelong fascination with and affection for Indians is well documented. As his daughter Gene recalled, her father "adored" Joe Friday, who "always had stories to tell about animals and things—funny stories and he'd laugh and laugh. Mother always made him Sassafras tea—that's what he loved—and she'd always be sure she had some Sassafras roots for him." If Keltner had discovered "he had a drop of Indian blood in him," his daughter opined, "he would have died happy." If anything, she observed, her father was "kind of naïve in a way. He just thought any Indian was okay. And he also brought home other people—a house with three little girls and he [brought strangers to stay with us]." These strangers included a (non-Indian) man convicted of highway robbery who, along with his wife, stayed with the Keltner family. Keltner told his daughters about the man's criminal record but said, "He's all right now." "I don't know how long they stayed with us," said Gene, "but he threw my doll out in the snow and laughed. Dad didn't really know that, I guess." This same man went hunting with Keltner and "an Indian friend." While the trip was supposed to last for two days, the men returned that same night. Before Keltner came through the door, he announced, " I'm okay," but then said "I got a little shot in my eye." While the former convict claimed to have fired a shot that ricocheted toward Keltner, his "Indian friend" exclaimed, "No way it was a ricochet; that was intended."[45]

Keltner's recollections of Joe Friday are a mélange of narratives, from the tender and insightful to outright caricature. He took great pains, as seen earlier, to depict Joe as an able and amiable wilderness companion. On one of his first visits to St. Louis after the founding of Indian Guides, Keltner wrote that Joe's wife Eva had "left him and returned to the states, her former home." After the camping season, Joe lived with the Keltners. Curiously, the next sentence in Keltner's account is crossed out: "He [Joe] was much in love with his wife Eva, so we arranged to have her rejoin Joe in our home where they lived until they rented a house of their own that winter." It seems odd that, having already shared a highly personal detail from Friday's life, Keltner would excise this passage. In any event, Friday stayed in St. Louis over that winter without a job in hand. Keltner found him work "firing furnaces at night," but hoped that he could persuade the YMCA to hire him as a boys' work secretary. Keltner went to visit Friday "at about 1 a.m. in the basement of an apartment building," where he found him stripped to the waist and bathed in sweat, loading the furnaces with coal. This was clearly not the job either man had envisioned for Friday. As Keltner recalled, when he entered the room, Joe "straightened up . . . grinned and leaned on the handle of the coal shovel. 'Do you know what an Indian hates most of all?' he asked. 'No, what?' 'A shovel,' he answered, and then laughed out loud to show me that he understood this was the best we could do."

The relationship between Keltner and Friday is not an easy one to define. While we only have Keltner's version of this and other stories, there was clearly a warm bond between these two men that in part transcended the different backgrounds they had and even their different perspectives on Native history and life. Keltner writes of visits that he and his family took to Temagami to visit Joe and spend time canoeing, camping, and hunting. As a Y secretary, Keltner had nowhere near the salary necessary to pay Joe what his time and expertise were worth during their visits north. And Friday's salary, either as a camp guide for the St. Louis Y or as an emissary for the Indian Guides program, was meager. This story of Joe and Harold in the basement further humanizes our understanding of the relationship between these two men, but also shows that neither Keltner nor Friday had the kind of clout or status, even at the local level, that people later assumed. Seeing Friday soaked in perspiration, likely in the midst of his own dark night of the soul, led Keltner to take a bold step: "This was too much for me, and I hired him at once without, I am afraid, asking board or general secretary." Joe began making the rounds "with the public, boys, and our Y membership," and general secretary Lester Haworth "always forgave an executive if he produced with a wild scheme." Nonetheless, wrote Keltner, boys' work chairman Lansing Smith admonished him, "Don't hire any more Indians without proper clearance."

Keltner's manuscript is filled with other warm remembrances of Friday, though several do more to fulfill white stereotypes about Indians than to illuminate Joe Friday the man. Given Holman's observations about the Canadian Indian hockey tour, however, one might ask if Joe was a participant in the creation of these images. Was Joe Friday depicting to his white companions the kind of Indian they expected? Was Keltner projecting his expectations onto Friday? Are we, decades after the fact, able to properly understand their relationship?

Gene Keltner Cannon remembered her father as hopelessly naive about Indians, assuming that they were uniformly good people. According to Keltner, Friday had the same feeling about Christians. He related a story Joe told him about a wilderness trip Joe and his brother Will took together. Finding a spot to camp, they noticed a dirt path leading to a riverbank. "They were apprehensive at once since in such country did outlaws and criminals hide from the law and mounted police." They encountered a Native man living in a wigwam who invited them to stay with him. All concerns about the man's character disappeared when, upon entering his home, Joe spied a Bible. "'No one can go wrong,' said Joe, 'if he accepts the hospitality of a man who believes in the Bible; it's a sure sign of safety.'"

Keltner's reminiscences of Joe in the wilderness show him as adept, indulgent, and inventive. But once the stories turn to his exploits in the St. Louis area, Keltner's stories adopt a different tone. While Joe made Camp Niangua "a famous place for boys with canoeing, stories, and camp craft," letters from mothers informed Keltner "in no uncertain terms that they objected to their boys eating muskrats." It seemed Joe had taught his young charges to trap muskrats just as he had in his youth. "We got this settled," wrote Keltner. Joe had told so many stories about moose that he thought it would be fun to strap a pair of moose horns on a mule and let him loose in the woods. This too was discouraged. On another occasion Friday staged a "mystery murder" featuring a "fake scalping." Joe staged an argument with another camp leader and then proclaimed loudly that he would have the last word. After the two spent days exchanging hostile stares, a loud shriek in the night brought campers out from their tents. They found the man Joe had threatened with (ox) blood on his head, and Joe was nowhere to be found. There was blood found on a paddle, and a canoe was missing. This prank led to a sleepless night for the campers. The camp director intervened, insisting that the two men bring their ruse to a swift conclusion. The next morning Joe and his alleged victim walked into the dining hall arm in arm. But the days of pranks at camp were over.

Joe's dog Brave, a large white husky, features prominently in many of Keltner's tales. When Joe first arrived in St. Louis, Keltner met him at the train station. They walked to the baggage car, where an agitated baggage man "was scared to death by the huge animal chained inside." Brave jumped up, placing his paws on Joe's chest, and greeted Keltner in the same fashion. "This gentle animal could bring down a deer by itself but was as gentle as a lamb with our children who played horse with him on Joe's island." On the way from the train station to Keltner's, Brave leaped against the window, causing Keltner to crash, because, said Joe, "He saw a mule on that old wagon and thought it was a moose."[46]

In 1927 Joe and his wife Eva worked weekends at the St. Louis YMCA's Camp Taconic. At that time Keltner's office was in the Railway Exchange Building, and one day Friday rushed into Keltner's office out of sorts, exclaiming "Oh my, Oh my. . . . It's awful." Once Friday calmed down, he explained that while he was out walking with Brave, a homeowner's door opened, and "a lady with her little dog came out. The little dog saw Brave and made a rush at him, nipping his heels." Brave proceeded to pick the dog up, and "with one swipe he broke his back." The owner of the small dog fainted on her porch. When Keltner asked Joe what happened next, he answered, "Why, I ran away as fast as I could." Keltner ends the story by simply saying he laughed until tears ran down his face.[47]

Comfortable and adept on his native soil, Friday (as depicted by Keltner) becomes the archetypal fish out of water. His dog Brave becomes an extension of the wilderness life he has left behind, refusing to play by the rules of civilized society, slaying both domestic pets and wild animals. (In one tale Brave hides in the snow and single-handedly kills a deer, which Joe butchers.) At camp he seems better suited to childish pranks than adult supervision, standing in stark contrast to the Indian father promoted in Indian Guides, yet displaying the playfulness that characterized the program. In other cases he simply conveys his own skills and values to boys but discovers that white adults don't approve. It is in the tale of Friday fleeing the scene of Brave's violence that he is depicted most unflatteringly. Here he comes off as childish, abandoning all the courage, honesty, charity, and nobility supposedly residing in the heart of every true Indian. (Of course, here we must avoid employing one stereotype to criticize another. Joe Friday, after all, was a human being, not an automaton.) He could inspire the men of the white world to be better fathers, but in Keltner's tales he struggled in St. Louis to navigate that world, relying on Keltner and others to make his way.

Keltner's depictions of Friday are sometimes more than just unflattering. On two occasions above, for example, Keltner describes Friday or Indians in general—or, more accurately, he depicts Friday describing himself or Indians in general—as "savage." And his tales of Friday at camp and around the environs of St. Louis serve to undermine the very image of Joe Friday—and Ojibwe people in general—that Indian Guides sought to propagate. And as we shall see in chapter 4, Keltner was not above disparaging Friday to YMCA staff even as he was sending him their way to promote Indian Guides.

Despite the warm rhetoric used to describe him in numerous Indian Guides publications, Joe Friday largely remained an outsider in the white world, relying on agents of the YMCA to mediate his involvement. The contrasting depictions of Friday—as the background character presented in many remembrances, and as the man who played a clearly active role in the program, as evidenced in the records for many years—in many ways mirror the diverging narratives of American Indians in popular culture. Invoked for their symbolic power, they are nevertheless frequently denied a voice of their own in the "official" record. Some may wish to criticize Friday's role in promoting Y-Indian Guides or the hockey tours as giving space for the appropriation of his culture, perhaps even being complicit in it. However, lacking his own words and reflections on his lived experience, that seems unfair. Furthermore, as discussed in the introduction, given the weight of colonization and the attempted eradication of Friday's people and culture, it is inappropriate to be overly critical of his chosen way of not only surviving but perhaps thriving in a hostile world.

CHAPTER THREE

The "Indian" in Indian Guides

FROM COLONISTS DRESSING up as Indians before tossing English tea into Boston Harbor to debates over the use of sports mascots like the Atlanta Braves, Cleveland Indians, Washington Redskins, or University of North Dakota Fighting Sioux, US history is riddled with examples of the misunderstanding and misappropriation of Indigenous peoples' symbols, rituals, and values, as well as crass caricatures of American Indians themselves. "Playing Indian" has been not only a time-honored tradition in playgrounds and backyards across America but also often ritualized in ways intended to bring "civilized" individuals closer to nature, maturity, or wish fulfillment. While these practices have often been motivated by economic, competitive, ideological, or artistic impulses, for some groups, like the Y-Indian Guides, they have a more complex origin and legacy.

The role of the American Indian (or more accurately a white-invented version of the American Indian) in defining American identity has been the subject of extensive scholarship. Philip J. Deloria's *Playing Indian*, for example, provided the first thorough examination of how the dominant Anglo culture co-opted Indian identities in its quest for both legitimacy as a new nation and escape from the monotony of modern life.[1] Jason Edward Black's explorations of the "mascotting" of Indigenous peoples show how this kind of appropriation commoditizes Native culture, granting outsiders the privilege of defining what constitutes Native culture.[2] According to Rayna Green, "playing Indian" has not only been the domain of white men but "draws women, even blacks, into the peculiar boundaries of its performance, offering them a unique opportunity—through playing Indian—of escaping the conventional and often highly restrictive boundaries of their fixed cultural identities based in gender or race."[3]

In a 2003 address at the University of Minnesota, Pulitzer Prize–winning author Michael Chabon ruminated on his childhood and its role in forming his sense of imagination and adventure. These were days, he reflected, when white remorse over the extermination of American Indians led to the creation of numerous mythological, sympathetic Indian characters in art, cinema, and television. These images, though inaccurate, inspired many to study the lives of historical Native Americans. Pontiac, Crazy Horse, Tecumseh, Sequoia, and other important figures became, to Chabon, subjects of keen interest and deep admiration. The problem, he observed, was that those reflecting wistfully and longingly on this vanishing culture were evoking "not an imaginary world of Indians, but a world of imaginary Indians." It was into this latter world that members of Y-Indian Guides would be invited.

Figure 9. An elaborate but entirely fanciful "Indian" ritual, St. Louis, date unknown. Gateway Region Young Men's Christian Association (S0473).

As Anne Braude has suggested, whites often perceived Indians as eternally childlike (for instance, their depiction in Peter Pan), and until the late 1960s or early 1970s, American Indians had little public voice, leaving whites to freely imagine, invent, and employ on their own terms the "Indian" of their choosing. This childlike depiction of Indigenous peoples in white society coincided with the playful tone set within Y-Indian Guides. While many members showed a genuine interest in the true history of Indigenous peoples, they also had or sought little historically accurate information, even from the very people they sought to honor and emulate.

Through the use of "primitive" symbols and rhetoric, Y-Indian Guides participants endeavored to bring themselves back to a "purer" self, revering family and nature, caring for the less fortunate, and respecting all people. Yet this very appropriation betrayed the privilege and power of the individuals engaging in these activities. Fathers and sons in Y-Indian Guides, largely from white middle- and upper-middle-class families, sought to revere American Indian cultures, but also exercised power over them and defined them subjectively. Herein lies the tragic irony of Y-Indian Guides: a program designed to develop youth found its success at the expense of American Indian youth. As research into appropriation shows, marginalized and oppressed communities are harmed by the contrived characters, stereotypes, and misuse of material culture by a dominant group.[4] Kevin Gover, then director of the National Museum of the American Indian, provided one such example when he spoke to members of the Saint Paul & Minnesota Foundation on October 30, 2018. Everything he read and heard as a boy taught him that Indians were "primitive and savages and all that. . . . Indians were somehow lesser, not as smart, maybe." Since he was one of the brightest children in his class, "I actually entertained the idea that it must be because my mother is a white woman. That would account for me being smart like the other kids. So, you can see the kinds of messages that kids pick up, not from any intentional degradation of them, but by continuing the pursuit of these narratives that are, in fact, ultimately demeaning and really advance what is essentially a lie."[5]

As Rebecca Tsosie discusses, appropriation harms tribal groups who depend on their cultural resources to stand and survive as "distinctive cultural and political groups."[6] One method of harm, and germane to Y-Indian Guides, is what Eric Lott, in his exploration of minstrelsy, calls the "haunted realm of racial fantasy" that "represses through ridicule."[7] This ridicule has a particular impact on the children of repressed groups by interfering with their ability to define and establish their own identity.[8] These practices led the American Psychological Association in 2005 to call for the "immediate retirement of all American Indian mascots, symbols, images and personalities," citing research showing that mascotting and other misrepresentations of native cultures have a negative effect on "not only American Indian students but all students."[9] This stance was affirmed in 2014 in a report by the Center for American Progress (CAP), which examined the research regarding the impact of mascotting on Native youth and found that it creates a hostile learning environment, directly resulting in lower self-esteem and negative impacts on mental health.[10]

Arguments against the APA's position, which tend to center on economics and "honoring" of native cultures, are recentered by the CAP report, aptly titled "Missing the Point." Enabled by their distance from Indigenous groups, whites engaging in mascotting "contribute to the development of cultural biases and prejudices" that undermine the vitality of Native cultures. A tragic outcome of this dynamic is found in the suicide rates for Indigenous youth ages fifteen to twenty-four, which are "2.5 times higher than the national average." Misconstrued narratives centered on Native lives form a body of misinformation against which American Indians must constantly contend. Complicating this process is the reality that much of the "Indian" presented in popular culture comes from the world of myth and fantasy and does not represent actual historical Native American lives and stories—a reality that most Indigenous youth understand and few non-native do.[11]

Ironically, Y-Indian Guides had the means to learn more about real Native Americans through the YMCA's work with these communities. The YMCA's work with American Indians began as a domestic missionary effort under its International Work department. The YMCA was "concerned" for individuals whose "plight was dramatized by the several military expeditions required to finally subdue them."[12] The YMCA organized student YMCAs at various governmental schools beginning in 1886 and expanded the work to include twenty-five Indian Associations. The largest and most enduring example of this work is with the Sioux in South Dakota. The Sioux YMCA (renamed the YMCA of the Seven Council Fires in 2022) was organized in 1879 by survivors of the Sioux Uprising of 1862. Thomas Wakeman, the son of Chief Little Crow, was a founding member. This group created what they called the "rules of Jesus" to guide their work and met regularly, unbeknownst to the larger YMCA movement. The YMCA would later comment that "these men knew nothing of our methods of work, but they were guided to its real spirit by a more earthly wisdom."

Once the Sioux YMCA was made known to the larger YMCA movement, efforts were quickly made to bring it into the fold. In 1891 a representative from the organization attended a state convention of

Minnesota and the Dakotas. There he reported twenty active American Indian YMCAs, though they differed markedly from the urban Anglo YMCAs. The Sioux YMCA had no buildings. Each association drew its membership from up to sixty miles away. Supported by the church, theirs was largely a prayer and social enterprise.

That would all change in 1894 when the International Committee hired Dr. Charles Eastman (Ohiyesa), a Sioux graduate of Dartmouth College and Boston University, to advance the YMCA's work in the Dakota territories. Eastman was recruited by Charles K. Ober of Minnesota, who spearheaded the effort to work among American Indians. Ober, who believed the Indian could only be civilized through Christianity, visited a gathering in South Dakota attended by over a thousand American Indians connected with the Congregational and Presbyterian churches and the Indian YMCA. In 1895, after one year, Eastman reported significant progress, having visited "all of the Associations on the Sioux Reservations in North and South Dakota."[13] Through his travels, Eastman formed the opinion that the people he worked with were "willing and enthusiastic . . . [and] anxious to take hold" of the work, but ultimately lacked competent leaders.[14]

In 1911 the YMCA highlighted its work with American Indians within the pages of its premier publication, *Association Men*. This work took place on a variety of fronts from reservations to government schools, all intended to make American Indians "more civilized," which essentially meant "more like the white man."[15] But as much as the YMCA wanted to "civilize" American Indians, it tried to make some accommodation for their uniqueness. According to Indian secretary Robert Hall, the Y's goal "should not be to make an Indian-white man, but an Indian citizen of a cosmopolitan republic."[16] Interestingly, the expectation of and strategy for American Indians becoming citizens mirrored child development theories articulated by G. Stanley Hall. Premised on the belief that as youth mature they re-create the race memory of our species, his recapitulation theory had a profound impact on the YMCA, as evidenced by progressive programs like Y-Friendly Indians, Pioneers, and Comrades.[17] With regards to American Indians, Hall counseled patience in measuring their progress, proclaiming that the white man spent centuries "imperfectly" refining his own culture.[18]

As one can imagine, the work of the American YMCA with American Indians has not been a straight line of progress, but one of gains and setbacks. However, in spite of the paternalistic and condescending language frequently employed, there have also been moments of radically progressive and honest soul-searching where white culture is castigated for its treatment of American Indians. One such example is found in the proceedings of the 1913 gathering of American YMCAs. There, a delegate from Washington, DC, lifts up the cause of the YMCA's work with "special classes." He calls American Indians the "first Americans," the original owners of this country, which was taken from them (though he remarks that his home state of Pennsylvania took the land "honestly"). He reports that, with at least 2,500 American Indian men and boys participating in the YMCA, "those Indians have the Association spirit, which is, 'Not to be ministered unto but to minister.'"

The YMCA's efforts to improve the condition of American Indians remained under the auspices of its International Department, and by the time Y-Indian Guides became a national program in 1935, the work with the Sioux was in decline. The program continued to rely on Joe Friday to provide any semblance of an American Indian perspective. Whether this role was inspirational and fanciful or consultative and authoritative, one might fairly ask: Who was the "Indian" in Y-Indian Guides? What set of behaviors, garb, and language allowed a set of predominantly white middle-class Americans to take on the mantles of Chief, Tom-Tom Beater, Tallykeeper, Indian Runner, Wampum Bearer, and Brave?

Indian Guides was a peculiar amalgam of the fantastical, contrived, and mundane. Where the Indian is invoked, he is often presented as a monolithic entity whose identity is drawn from many and represents nothing recognizable to actual Indigenous peoples. This pattern was maintained when young girls were eventually added to the program through the creation of the "Indian Princess," a role not ascribed to any federally recognized tribe. Y-Indian Guides would regularly make "totem poles, headdresses, tom-toms and other articles for use in ceremonials of a tribe."[19] These were elements taken from tribes of the Pacific Northwest and the Plains. In the case of the tom-tom, the word itself was projected onto Native Indian drums but has its roots in India. In addition to handicrafts, "tribes" would tell stories. The stories that would have been familiar to Y-Indian Guides tribes conflated Indian identities, contributing to confusion rather than familiarity. When invoked by non-Indian writers, American Indians were frequently portrayed generically and as a vehicle to teach Western Christian values.[20]

One such collection published by the YMCA and used by Y-Indian Guides tribes, *Treasury of American Indian Tales*, purports to bring twenty-seven American Indian tribes to life again in "vivid, authentic short stories written for boys and girls aged 6 to 12."[21] The author, Theodore Whitson Ressler, claimed to have "created" the stories which were based on "Indian lore and customs . . . related to him by his Indian friends, descendants of the braves who first recounted them many generations ago." The author clearly believed, much as the Y-Indian Guides founders, in the power of the "Indian" model. Parents and youth leaders were encouraged to observe "that stress is placed in several stories upon the close father-son and mother-daughter relationship—completely true in Indian culture, and as much coveted in the formative pre-teen years of our own children today."[22] However, the source of the stories is unclear. The book simultaneously holds up the authenticity of the narratives, which are truly fables, while describing some as original and others as traditional. The authority to present these stories comes from the author's "Indian friends." The tribal origins of the author's friends are unknown, though *Tales* lists Cherokee, Iroquois, Nez Perce, Wyandot, Apache, and twenty-two other tribal nations as sources for the various narratives, and in the process portrays Indians as factional groups within a monolithic ethnic identity. In fact, apart from a sprinkling of well-known regional words—*wigwam, tee-pee, moccasin, tomahawk*, and so on—these stories offer no insight into the lives of real tribes. They serve as literary tourism, showcasing Anglo-Protestant values under a thin veneer of Indian window dressing.

THE WHITE HERO IN THE FABRICATED INDIAN STORY

This fascination with a constructed Indian mystique was not limited to the United States. Karl May, for example, has been described as the most influential German author between Johann Wolfgang von Goethe and Thomas Mann.[23] Though he profoundly shaped the European view of the American West, his depictions were pure invention, and varied significantly from both the mythical and actual West held in American memory. Born to a poor weaver, May (pronounced "my") was blessed with a rich imagination. At sixteen he had already written and attempted to publish his first short Indian tale. Unfortunately, his creativity also led him down the path of crime. He was sentenced to five years in prison for insurance swindle, medicine fraud, and theft. Having feasted on the prison's wide collection of adventure fiction, May was released four years later with a head full of potential stories. Imprisoned again only six months later, this time for impersonating a civil servant, May spent another eight years behind bars. Managing to publish several short stories in "sensational tabloids" while still incarcerated, he emerged from prison at thirty-three an in-demand author and editor. He wrote some seventy volumes on the Middle East and the American West without having visited either.

The main hero in May's books on "the West" was "Old Shatterhand," a young man named Karl (of opportunistically physical similarity to the author) who travels to St. Louis to tutor the children of Mr. Henry, a German immigrant and weapons maker. Recognizing in Karl all of the strengths and virtues necessary to become an invincible "Westmann," Mr. Henry awards him two of his best weapons "and secures his young charge a position with a surveying crew of the westward-expanding railroad. While surveying, Karl becomes acquainted with the revolting crudity of the American, and must frequently exert his Teutonic wisdom and strength to teach a few Teutonic manners." Early in their journey, Karl and company are captured by a band of Kiowa, whereupon he is forced to do battle with the tribe's mightiest warrior. "Wielding a lightning-fast, dynamite-packed fist as his only weapon—Karl dislikes bloodshed—the German stretches his opponent on the ground with one blow." Awed and impressed by his abilities, the Kiowa rechristen Karl "Old Shatterhand."[24] Countless German readers assumed the author and the character were the same man, and May did nothing to disabuse them.

After a grueling test of endurance and strength that gains him admission into the Apache tribe as a chieftain, "Old Shatterhand" is embraced by Winnetou, who becomes his blood brother and a coprotagonist in May's tales. Winnetou patiently teaches Karl the many dialects of the Apache and the Navajo, making him "an invincible, infallible western hero." Of course, there is room for only one woman in all of May's Western adventures, and she is, predictably, the sister of Winnetou, who falls madly in love with "Old Shatterhand."[25]

While May did exhaustive research on Indigenous peoples, the story always came first. Like those of James Fennimore Cooper, his tales are filled with laments over the "destruction and degeneration" of Indian nations. But these elegiac observations ring somewhat hollow. For example, May repeatedly demonstrates Winnetou's innate nobility as a "savage," but what makes him noble is his willingness to blend his own culture with that of the white man. When on one occasion Winnetou comes to rescue Shatterhand, carrying a copy of the "Song of Hiawatha," the German thinks, "This Indian . . . possessed the mind and taste for culture. Longfellow's famous poem in the hand of an Apache Indian! I would never have allowed myself to dream such a thing." Winnetou speaks to Karl in High German and embraces at least the manners of a Christian. He does, however, retain the one word that, according to May's books, all Indians use: "Howgh." Any Indian hearing that word, he explained, would reply, "Uff uff," which meant a variety of things depending on context.

May had a gift for sustaining a thrilling and believable narrative that captured the hearts and minds of his white readers.[26] Fans included Albert Einstein and Albert Schweitzer. As Richard Cracroft related in 1962, a time when Y-Indian Guides was reaching its height in the United States, "few German readers have been able to resist May's image of the American West as the bona fide image."[27]

Harold Keltner himself took a turn at writing an Indian tale. "Eric among the Savages," a tale set broadly in the Age of Exploration (pre-colonial America), was his graduation thesis from the International Young Men's Christian Association College (now Springfield College) in 1915. This tale, which he dedicates to the founder of the YMCA Archives, J. T. Bowne, for introducing him to the "real American," sheds insight into Keltner's early fascination with Native Americans, as well as his belief that stories related to them have the ability to rouse the interest of youth. "Eric among the Savages" tells a tale of Scandinavian discovery in the New World and foreshadows the conquering of the Americas. When the Vikings discover Vineland, they immediately kill three sleeping natives (which they called "Skrellings"; that is, barbarians), and each encounter described between the Vikings and the Indigenous people ends in some sort of conflict. Keltner, however, also makes an attempt to depict both the Vikings and the Indians in a similar fashion. Eric, a descendent of the Vikings, is told by his father that his ancestors were true and steadfast to their friends and unfailingly honorable. Eric desires to become a sailor and travel the world like his ancestors. His first true voyage takes him to America. His shipmate Pierre tells him of the "Indians [who] are fierce and crafty men." Even so, Pierre admires "many of the fine qualities of the red men" and cannot blame them for their savagery, which he sees as a justified response to their harsh treatment by Europeans.[28] Like May's Old Shatterhand, Eric and other enlightened white observers frequently bemoan the poor treatment of Indigenous peoples meted out by their new invaders. They are imprisoned and enslaved, cheated in dealings and trade, and held in exceedingly low regard.

Eric first encounters the Indians after he is captured by Spanish pirates. His observation of pirate behavior and their treatment of the Indians convinces him that he would be better off to "flee to the savages" than to remain with the Spaniards. At his first opportunity Eric jumps overboard, escaping the pirates and joining the "savages." He is now ready to live out the tales Pierre related to him, tales encouraging him to "admire the Indian character" and "to live such a free life as the Indian boy, who learned his lessons through touch with the beautiful hills, trees, birds, and plants." Eric is immediately adopted by the Algonquin tribe and begins to learn their ways with the help of his new friend Nequassen.

These three examples underscore the pervasive image of the constructed, amalgamated Indian. *Tales* was used by YMCAs, churches, and parents to teach morality and most importantly the need to honor one's parents. May's depictions of the noble savage reinforced an increasingly distorted stereotype. And both May and Keltner (along with Michael Blake/Kevin Costner) romantically positioned both the Viking Eric and the German Karl (and John Dunbar in *Dances with Wolves*) as one of the tribe. These stories are examples of the ubiquitously false narratives of Native lives consumed by children and adults. In such a social and literary context, the likelihood that Y-Indian Guides could convey accurate depictions of Indigenous peoples seems very low—far less so as it blossomed from a local and then regional curiosity into a national phenomenon.

As we further explore this disconnection between the Indian in Y-Indian Guides and actual living Native Americans, we should pause to reflect on what one should expect as possible or realistic for a well-intentioned white male YMCA secretary of the 1930s, '40s, or '50s to believe or accomplish. One also should consider the still-widespread antipathy toward Indigenous peoples in many hearts and homes in the United States. In fact, William Hefelfinger's explanation for why the YMCA used the American Indian as a model for the Y-Indian Guides program is, as much as anything, a defense of the "worthiness" of Indigenous peoples to serve as a role model for white fathers and sons. While also acknowledging the "romantic appeal of the Indian" in both American and Europe, Hefelfinger also spoke of "real world" Indians: "The Indian is part of our history. Some of our streets are named after him and every state has rivers and cities with Indian names. Such great Indian athletes as Jim Thorpe, Chief Bender and Chief Meyers who wrote such brilliant pages in the history of football, baseball and track, have thrilled the peoples of many countries. The Indian has served this country well in the present world war as well as in World War I." As would have been the case for the vast majority of white men in his day, Hefelfinger gave no thought to any potential offense to Native American tribes of his day in appropriating versions of their identity and heritage for his own purposes. Instead, his editorial seems to discourage any idea in the minds of his white audience that Indians were unworthy role models and had nothing of value to teach them.[29]

While we wrestle in the early twenty-first century with the cultural inadequacies and insensitivities of the Y-Indian Guides program, we must acknowledge that even though the white man's conception of Indigenous peoples was naive, conflated, and inaccurate, it nonetheless encouraged in many a curiosity and sense of compassion toward (what they believed to be) real Indigenous peoples. This intense interest in all things native was present in other youth spaces as well, particularly in the burgeoning world of camping. In the YMCA's case, the idea of pitching a tent drifted from its initial goals of religious reflection and seeing the beauty of God's creation, which one might miss in an urban setting, toward the development of young boys into manhood.

CAMPS AS CRADLES OF "IMAGINARY INDIANS"

In 1885 a YMCA volunteer took a group of young men into the woods for swimming, canoeing, hiking, and spiritual reflection. In the process, Sumner Dudley became the originator of what would become a signature Y program: camping. Camping, in the context of the YMCA, was an extension of the growing area of youth work, which, as discussed in chapter 1, was initially centered on Sunday school and Bible instruction. As the YMCA's work with youth expanded beyond religious instruction, it came to be organized through a Boys' Work department, which brought to bear the rapidly evolving YMCA program of holistic development. At first, camping was less about a specific location and more about an excursion into the wilderness. This addressed many of the concerns the YMCA and its supporters had for urban youth, specifically the cultivation of a boy's masculinity and a nurturing of his personal faith.

The first decade or so of YMCA camping trips were conducted along these lines, and the legacy of Dudley's approach is still present in the many camps that conduct religious services, have outdoor chapels, or offer the YMCA Raggers program.[30] By the early 1910s, however, camps began responding to the same worries about the perceived threats of modernity: new immigrants from non-Anglo-Saxon lands and the closure of the West. Abigail Van Slyck framed this dynamic as camps addressing "modern anxieties about boys—particularly white, privileged ones—and their needs."[31] This response took the form of "mimic[king] the trappings of Native Americans and rural mountain folk."[32] This back-to-nature impulse was contemporaneous with the formation of Y-Indian Guides and, as discussed in chapter 2, informed Keltner's process of constructing the program. A particular influence on both camp and Y-Indian Guides was Ernest Thompson Seton, who, in addition to forming the League of Woodcraft Indians and influencing the Boy Scouts of America, traveled the nation during the early twentieth century consulting with camps and instructing camp leaders on how to instill the mystique of the Indian into camp life.[33] Seton's fascination with Indigenous peoples was born out of the same antimodernist sentiment captured in his description of the role of the campfire, which would become a central fixture of Y-Indian Guides: "manhood, not scholarship, is the first aim of education." In other words, the campfire, the woodcraft, the playful engagement in "Indian life" was a means to re-create a (perceived) lost masculinity. While there were many forces at play in Seton's recasting of Native Americans from primitive savage to noble proto-American, and his subsequent cherry-picking of contrived cultural elements, his work had a profound impact on the use of "the Indian" in youth development.

Many issues of the Y-Indian Guides' newsletter, *Long House News*, included historical information about or photographs illustrating the surviving evidence of individual indigenous tribes. New books, films, maps, and other resources about native peoples were frequently introduced. But Harold Keltner's editorial in the very first print version of *Long House News* suggested that from the start the "Indian" in Y-Indian Guides was more a means to an end than a real person:

> The Indian Guides remind me of a little river of clear friendship flowing silently through a dense forest of life's problems, but ever increasing in its depth and usefulness as it contacts new streams of human interest. *It is this friendship that counts most with us and our boys. Anything that adds to that relationship is welcome.* The "Long House" paper hopes, above all, to bring us more closely together in thought and purpose. Through all of your activities we seek one attainment—the permanent confidence and comradeship, one with the other, of our boys and their fathers.[34]

Even if Keltner, Heffelfinger, and other early leaders sought to make Y-Indian Guides a program that educated members about real Native Americans, at least two inevitable obstacles arose. First, as already noted, the educational resources offered were created by whites for the consumption of whites. However serious-minded they might have been, they were part of the same cycle of appropriation and fanciful reinvention. Second, as Y-Indian Guides moved from a local to a national phenomenon, Keltner, Friday, Hefelfinger, and others like them lost their ability to control the program and ensure uniformity and the kind of seriousness of purpose they intended.

LOOKING FOR "THE INDIAN" AT A Y-INDIAN GUIDES POW-WOW

In March 1938, the Sixth Annual—but first national—Y-Indian Guides Pow-Wow was held at Webster Groves Gymnasium. Not long before the event, the *St. Louis Globe-Democrat* ran a two-page story loaded with photographs in its Sunday edition. Oddly, its description of the founding of Y-Indian Guides makes no mention of Joe Friday whatsoever. Instead, the paper reported: "Twelve years ago, Harold S. Keltner . . . took a camping trip in the Canadian wilds. He met up with some Ojibway Indians, and after the unusual ceremonies, Keltner . . . began to talk shop. The Ojibways were blunt. Americans didn't know how to teach boys. . . . Fathers should pal with sons, set an example. Keltner listened carefully. . . . He returned to St. Louis to found Y-Indian Guides, an organization fostering companionship of father and son." A photo caption in the same article reads, "More than 20 tribes have been founded in the St. Louis area since Keltner came back from Canada with the idea."[35]

The absence of Joe Friday from this narrative is jarring, especially considering how much credit Keltner gives to Friday in other sources, including an article in the *Globe-Democrat* the previous December.[36] Whether Keltner himself chose to delete Friday from this account or the reporter and/or his editor made that decision, the process of erasing Joe Friday from the public narrative about Indian Guides had begun.

In any event, the 1938 Webster Groves powwow was the first national gathering of Y-Indian Guides tribes who came to display the fruits of their individual and collective endeavors from the previous year. The strong bonds formed between fathers and sons and between members of the tribes were illustrated especially poignantly by the story of young "Swift Eagle" (Edgar Kirtley) of the Pawnee Tribe of Kirkwood, Missouri, who was given a special award because "this Little Brave had lost his father in death something over a month ago, and yet he had carried on his Indian Guide work, and with the help of the chief and some of the other Big Braves of his tribe, completed his part in their tribal exhibit."

Ribbons were awarded for Best Tribal Project; Best Individual Project (Little Braves Only); Best Individual Father and Son Project; Best Display of Ritual Properties; Totem Pole Award; and Most Attractive Charter Frame. But to what extent did the contestants need to adhere or aspire to any specific, authentic cultural traits relating to any individual Native American tribe? What kinds of guidelines for evaluation did judges receive? And what, in the final analysis, was the purpose of the powwow?

Figure 10. Fathers and sons from the 1938 Webster Groves Pow-Wow, the first national Y-Indian Guides event. Gateway Region Young Men's Christian Association (S0473).

Y-Indian Guides as an organization, which communicated primarily through *Long House News*, gave tribes little information to use in preparing their exhibits. Certainly between 1935 and 1937 there were numerous articles with information about distinct Indigenous peoples (or at least illustrating that there were differences in practice between different tribes). Some seem to bear Joe Friday's fingerprints, such as February and March 1935 articles on "Life in an Ojibway Tepee." But many are syncretic or ambiguous, such as the dozens of "Indian symbols" on the back page of the February issue. Were these also provided by Friday, and if so, why were they not properly identified as Ojibwe symbols? Or were they perhaps more invented or fanciful in origin?

With little guidance from *Long House News* and little likelihood that fathers spent time steeping themselves in cultural and historic knowledge of any individual Indian tribe, it seems unlikely that Y-Indian Guides powwows were celebrations of Indian culture. In fact, the criteria issued to judges validates this assumption. All they received was a scorecard with all of the different "tribes" listed on a vertical column on the left side and a list of the awards given across a column on the top. Judges were simply encouraged to use their "independent judgment," but to keep two basic ideas in mind: "First, emphasis should be placed upon father and son joint activity, which is the primary purpose of the Y-Indian Guides. Second, in considering a tribal exhibit, first consideration should be given to the one showing the greatest cooperation between the members of the tribe, both little braves and big braves. This is to discourage tribal exhibits developed by only one or two members." No criteria concerning adherence to any particular tribal tradition, image, dress, or practice can be found in any of the literature provided to contestants or judges, nor was a need for such criteria mentioned in the final report issued after the event. All suggestions for improvement centered on logistical concerns or the need to offer more awards since the event had gone national.

Clearly, then, the purpose of the powwow was not to create near-authentic reproductions of unique tribal artifacts. The purpose, at least for the contest and the awards, was explained by William Hefelfinger in a letter preparing leaders for the following year's powwow. There seemed to be, he observed, too much emphasis on winning prizes. "They have become," he observed, "paramount instead of incidental." Awards were important, he acknowledged, but "we are extremely aware of the harm that can be done by the wrong use of that incentive. The main problem is to get our boys to realize that the big value is in the doing in the best way he knows how and that he is not a failure if he fails to be on top all of the time."

So if not primarily to win, why, according to Hefelfinger, should fathers and sons, as well as tribes as a whole, work on projects for competitions such as the powwow?

The object of the awards is primarily to stimulate the objectives of the Exhibition which are as follows:

It gives each tribe a definite program of its own choosing.

It provides an opportunity for each father and son to compare his skill, ingenuity, originality, sportsmanship and ability to carry through with that of others.

Each tribe is given a chance to see what others are doing—an exchange of ideas which may be the basis of future programs for younger tribes.

It is the big opportunity to show our friends what the Indian Guides are doing and the progress they are making and is also the main medium of getting new friends and tribes.

So, in short, the purpose of the powwow was twofold: to create projects that encouraged fathers and sons to work together, and to recruit new participants. And as both new recruits and seasoned veterans sought to keep their powwows engaging for their sons, they could turn

Figure 11. Cover image from the first printed issue of *Long House News*, January 10, 1935. (Earlier issues dating back to 1933 were typed and hand-illustrated.) All issues housed at the Kautz Family YMCA Archives, University of Minnesota Libraries.

to *Long House News*, which served primarily as a vehicle through which they could gain new knowledge, learn new skills, and plan new activities for their tribe, extending the usefulness and enjoyment of the Y-Indian Guides program for all participants. "With one tribe nine years old and still going strong," observed Harold Keltner in 1935, "it is probable that the average tribe's length of life will increase from four to several more at least."[37]

This enduring and ever-warmer relationship between father and son was the real object of the program, and the key to its success was the real "Indian" in Y-Indian Guides: not any particular nation or individual, but the Indian father as described by Joe Friday, the role model for all non-Indian fathers to emulate. Arthur Martin's 1939 essay "What the Indian Guides Mean to Me" made these sentiments clear:

> The Indian father intrusted the training of his boy to no one except himself. He taught him to hunt and fish, to endure pain, to be brave, to learn and to practice the code of his tribe. He did not depend on others to do what was his duty to his boy. . . . Indian Guides has made me conscious as a dad that I can be a better companion of my boys, grow up with them, share their joys, their sorrows, and their disappointments. . . . Fathers, be boys again with your boys, play their games, sing their songs, do what the boys do, enjoy together the great outdoors and commune with the great spirit. Indian Guides has taught me that some of my time belongs to my son[s], to share my life with them . . . like the Big Brave—the kind and loving Indian Father.[38]

In 1950 another *Long House News* contributor echoed the same idea, though far less sentimentally: "Their arrows are broken; their springs are dried up; their tepees are in dust. Their council fires have long since gone out on the shore, and their war cry has faded to the untrodden West. As a race, they have withered from the land. But we remember them for the relationship between big and little braves."[39]

CHAPTER FOUR

A National Movement

ONE CANNOT KNOW if, in the midst of its creation, Harold Keltner and Joe Friday envisioned Y-Indian Guides being copied in cities and towns across the United States and beyond. It *is* clear, however, that Keltner's misgivings about its potential failure were not entirely imagined. Even as he described his first meeting with the original group of fathers at Rev. Howard B. Phillips's house in October 1926, Keltner wrote, "There was one fear in their minds that was very evident." They couldn't imagine that their boys actually wanted to spend time with them. "In fact it is my belief that some who signed the agreement thought it would get no further than the first or second meeting."[1] As a letter from the Y-Indian Guide National Longhouse stated in May 1967, "For nearly one quarter of a century, this program for fathers and sons was laughed at and scoffed at by professional staff and local association laymen."[2] Indeed, though Y-Indian Guides spread quickly throughout parts of Missouri, Kansas, and Illinois,[3] it was not initially taken seriously by the national YMCA. After all, it was a serious departure from the Y's traditional youth development programs focused on turning young boys into productive, devout citizens and mature adults. Y traditionalists likely viewed the program as a whimsical, insubstantial annoyance. How, then, did Y-Indian Guides survive not only an extended period of disrespect but also the Great Depression?

Part of the answer is the dedication of its adult membership and Y secretaries, often with young sons of their own, who supported, even fervently believed in, the program. As they established their own "tribes," they slowly began to see potential for not only boys but families. This had become apparent already in 1930, when the National Council of the YMCA sent representatives to St. Louis to study the program. "There was plenty of evidence among the fathers," said the report, "to

97

show they believed other fathers and sons ought to have the advantages which their tribes were bringing to them. Some of them wondered if it might become a national program."[4]

Figure 12. William Hefelfinger, second "chief" of the original Osage "tribe" in Richmond Heights, Missouri, strikes a pose intended to convey reverence for Native Americans during a camping trip. "Junior Gets a Break with Dad in St. Louis," *St. Louis Post-Dispatch*, c. 1934. Clipping found in collection of Gateway Region Young Men's Christian Association (S0473).

Young fathers displaced from rural into urban settings, from a life of study to one of work and responsibility, and often from the emotional and/or physical scars of the Great War to the demands of civilian life were ripe for recruitment into Y-Indian Guides. There they found opportunities to reconnect with nature, pastoral life, and working with their hands; to commiserate with other fathers who were often experiencing similar struggles in their personal and professional lives; and to find a form of intimate companionship with their sons that they might not have enjoyed with their own fathers, all through a fantasy world that Y-Indian Guides encouraged them to create. An important aspect of the program's early success was the lighthearted nature of Y-Indian Guides, which helped break down barriers between fathers and sons, but also between the fathers themselves.

The motto "Pals Forever" and the many programs initiated through Y-Indian Guides suggested that in order to be a better father, one had to remember what it was like to be a boy and what it meant to play. This message shines through from the earliest days of Y-Indian Guides meetings and newsletters. Given the stiff formality with which YMCA staff normally communicated with and about one another, it is especially telling how they were depicted within Y-Indian Guides. Keltner himself was sometimes the butt of jokes recorded in the minutes of the Osage "tribe." When he returned from a turkey hunt, the January 10, 1927, minutes reported, "space will not permit a full account, but there was a couk, couk, here and a gobble gobble there, but no turkey, only a crow." On March 14 a powwow was held at Keltner's home. At the end of the meeting, read the minutes, "The tribe all enjoyed the feast by Mrs. Keltner and now we all know why the Chief is getting so fat." In the second issue of the St. Louis-only, as yet unnamed *Long House News*, highly regarded boys' secretary Joe Causino, a legend in the city's Italian neighborhoods, is called "Brave Snow on the Schnozzle."[5] Though the program was ostensibly for their children, the fathers gained much from Y-Indian Guides.

The Great War, said Keltner, had been a proving ground for men. In his (retrospective) opinion, those "who withstood the destructive influences of wartime were those whose fathers and mothers came first in their lives. Only close companionship in work and play over the formative years developed such character bulwarks."[6] The physical and psychological scars inflicted on some of the first generation of Indian Guides fathers, and the economic ravages of the Great Depression— followed by more wartime trauma suffered by the second—encouraged a greater desire for escape, adventure-seeking, and fantasizing.[7] Indian Guides helped fathers and sons engage in various forms of wish fulfillment, including escapist desires and aspirations for personal growth and a more tight-knit family. The primary long-term gains were not,

however, a greater understanding of American Indians but rather the
warm bonds established between fathers and sons, and often the mutual
support shared between fathers as well. Keltner himself noticed this with
the very first tribe, the Osage, when the boys in the tribe turned twelve.
It was at that age, he noted, that the boys' interest in Indians began to
wane. "Never will I forget the evening when I called a social council,
and told them it was now time for them (the boys) to join the scouts,
no other program being in existence in the [St. Louis] Y. There was a
long silence before one of the boys arose and said, 'Oh chief, it is true
that we are tired of playing Indian but we want to stay with our dads.'"
This reply, remembered Keltner, "thrilled me to the very soul," and in
fact Osage "chief" William Hefelfinger spent the next six years finding
new interests for the fathers and sons to share until the latter went off
to college.[8] Thus even as the Indian in Indian Guides was cast aside, the
bond between fathers and sons remained. This bond, however, would
pose a challenge to the YMCA when it formally adopted Indian Guides
as a national program in 1935. Here, too, each tribe's primary loyalty
was not to the Y but to itself, to the warm and durable bonds created
between fathers and sons.

Figure 13. This float from a 1949 Community Chest parade in Kansas City
shows how the YMCA intended Indian Guides to fit into its broader pipeline
of youth development programs. Boys were expected to "graduate" out of
Indian Guides by age nine, move on to Gra-Y (grade-school Y), and then on
to Junior Hi-Y and Hi-Y. *Long House News* 14, no. 1 (October 1949).

THE SHAWNEE FATHER AND SON "Y" INDIAN GUIDE TRIBE

From left to right, the men are: Mr. R. Salveter, Mr. Nye, Oscar Zabner, W. H. Willockson, John Long-
mire, R. W. Chubb, and Fullerton Place. The boys in the second row are R. Fullerton Place, Jr., Rising
Sun; Donald Zabner, Brave Wolf; R. W. Chubb, Jr., Silver Heels; W. Harry Willockson, Jr., Little Bear.
In the front row, R. Earl Salveter, Jr., Whistling Water; William T. Nye, Little Eagle; David M. Longmire,
Sleeping Bear.

H. S. Keltner, Executive Secretary of the South Side St. Louis Y.M.C.A, writes of the Shawnee tribe,
"To us, who remember these big fellows as only youngsters nine years ago, it has real significance. This
tribe has been going eight or nine years, until all the boys went away to college this fall."

Figure 14. But as this photo illustrates, the strong bonds between fathers and sons created
by the program sometimes meant that "tribes" remained intact for much longer, and
Indian Guides failed to become the kind of feeder program the YMCA had envisioned.
Long House News 6, no. 6 (1942).

THE INDIAN GUIDES MEETING

As more and more tribes were established, they were encouraged to
adopt the name of American Indians that had or still resided in their
area, indicating an understanding that Indigenous peoples were not a
monolithic group.. As the program grew, however, this became impossible without some redundancy. Some turned to literature, movies, and
later television for inspiration. Keltner kept record of the progress of
the first thirteen "tribes" established in the St. Louis area. Three of them
failed, one because a key leader moved away, two because there were
not enough "high grade men" to keep the program going. The successful Mohican tribe, established in March 1929, was described as a "city
group" (not in the suburbs) of "Jews and Gentiles."[9]

Central to the success of any Indian Guides "tribe" were the twice-monthly meetings held in the homes of tribe members. Each tribe elected its own officers. The chief, a "big brave" who served as the tribe's senior representative, created programs for and presided over all meetings, and was "responsible for the success of the tribe." He usually held his position for a year before a new chief was elected, though serving for longer periods was common. Upon stepping down from office, the former chief became a sachem, an honor he held "until such time as the Great Spirit calls him to the Happy Hunting Grounds." Sachems were expected to help the chief find new activities and ensure the tribe's ongoing well-being. The tom-tom beater was a "little brave" who beat the drum calling the council meeting to order. He "must know his part in the ritual. He must be punctual and allow no one else to beat the tom-tom." The tally-keeper was a big brave who served as the tribe's recording secretary, keeping minutes from every meeting and handling all of the tribe's correspondence. Already in the earliest handbooks, it was suggested that if the tally-keeper "has a sense of humor and is willing to attempt to put the Indian atmosphere into his records, he can furnish an interesting part of the council program."[10] And so, for example, when "Bald Eagle" kept the minutes of the Chickasaw tribe in Kirkwood, Missouri (a tribe of which William Hefelfinger, known as Negaunee, was a member), his minutes read thusly: "Chief say we need representative to Long House and appointed Big Thunder. Big Thunder say 'No can Do,' as he is little brave now. Negaunee is chosen next but say he is too busy. Flying Cloud say he no good. Big Thunder save day, he say he be big brave for while and take job. How."[11] The Indian runner was a little brave in charge of wardrobe, collecting all of the "Indian" regalia, books, and other effects of the tribe, "returning with them sufficiently early at the next meeting to be ready for the calling of the council by the tom-tom beater." Finally, the wampum bearer, a big brave, served as tribal treasurer and ensured that all tribal and national dues were paid. The tribe also had the power to award anyone they deemed worthy the title of honorary chief. Many elected officials, mayors, governors, and other public figures accepted this title over the ensuing years. (While famed St. Louis and Brooklyn baseball legend Branch Rickey spoke at a 1935 National Longhouse event, it is unclear whether he was ever made an honorary chief.)[12]

It was not enough to simply schedule a meeting and expect members to put it on their calendars and show up. Fathers and sons were expected to put significant effort into creating invitations for the meeting they would host. Preserved in the Thomas Jefferson Library's Western Historical Manuscripts Collection at the University of Missouri–St. Louis are numerous invitations sent from fathers and sons to the other members of the "Chickasaw tribe": one can see paper made to resemble birch bark, construction paper cut in the shape of a Thunderbird or a tomahawk, ornamental feathers, a totem copied straight out of the Indian Guides Manual, pictographs, "Indian" landscapes, and many mixtures of the above. Some invitations were clearly created by young sons, some more of a cooperative effort, while others seem to have been crafted largely by the father. Even decades later, Pam Atkins of the Dallas YMCA stressed the importance of invitations. "Back in the day . . . everybody . . . [made] little teepees or the canoes . . . and you spent Sunday afternoon driving around [delivering] them. Computers came in and people . . . just would send an email. . . . I started having to tell

Figure 15. This invitation, sent out to members of the Chickasaw "tribe" of Kirkwood, Missouri, shows the lengths to which some members would go to encourage attendance and demonstrate both hospitality and creativity to other members. The personal inscription on this invitation suggests that Mr. Batts is inviting a potential new father and son to the "tribe." Gateway Region Young Men's Christian Association (S0473).

directors . . . 'What do they have to do to make that invitation?' 'Well, they . . . spend Saturday afternoon making the invitation.' 'Yeah. And then what do they do on Sunday?' 'Well, they spend all day in the car.' 'Are you getting it? We're forcing them to spend time together!'"[13]

What happened once a tribe assembled? If they followed the guidelines set forth by the Indian Guides manual, they gathered to the "solemn" beating of the tom-tom. All talking would cease as fathers and sons stood in a circle to simulate a campfire. Next, as a clear indication of both the YMCA's emphasis on Christian citizenship and Indian Guides' reinterpretation of Native American history, the tribe would sing "America." (Most likely "America the Beautiful" rather than "God Bless America.") After the tom-tom sounded twice, fathers—except for the chief—took their seats while their sons stood behind them. (In later years sons were instructed to sit on the floor "Indian style" in front of their fathers.) The chief would then give a speech "concerning the seasons of the year, traditions of the tribe, meaning of the gathering, or anything that will give the proper atmosphere." In an extended footnote, the manual explained that the "atmosphere" of the meetings would depend greatly on the season. In spring, one should note the return of geese and other birds, of "all growing things coming to life, the different songs that the birds sing, and the sweet odors of blossoming trees." The summer was a time to contemplate the sound of waves on the shore, "the little night sounds, splashing of fish, a little squirrel at night, the life of a loon, running streams and echoes." The fall invited the tribe to consider "falling leaves, whistling winds, dying flowers," animals hibernating, birds flying south, and "the calling of the moose," while during winter one could emphasize the falling snow, the howling of wolves, and the tracks animals left in the snow.[14]

When the chief's speech was concluded, the tom-tom was struck twelve "deliberate" blows before the tribe was called to one minute of silent prayer. During this time fathers would sit "Indian fashion" on the floor with their sons standing behind them. The tom-tom was struck twice more to announce the end of prayer time; fathers returned to their seats. The chief might next engage in a review of the duties of the officers and then have the tally-keeper call the roll using the members' "Indian" names. There would then be a time to discuss the business of the tribe, followed by a time for storytelling and handicrafts. The tribe would then sing together and play games before closing with the "Omaha Tribal Prayer," which came from Alice C. Fletcher's *Indian Story and Song*. With hands and faces raised upward, they would sing "Wakonda dhedhu, Wapadhin atonhe" (Father, a needy one stands before thee; I that sing am he). The manual explained that not every meeting had to be conducted in this way. Some tribes reserved it only for special occasions. "One of the features of the Indian Guide program is its flexibility. Starting with an Indian background, the chief of the tribe may use any material which he desires. In this way the tribe may benefit from the originality and ingenuity of every member."[15]

Over the decades some "tribes" deviated significantly from the manual, but at least some retained numerous elements. Jim Wotruba, who didn't join a St. Louis–area Indian Guides program until 1999, described a meeting that Harold Keltner or Joe Friday could have easily recognized: "We would have our Wampum drum and whoever is hosting the meeting with their kid would beat the drum whatever number of times to equal the number of children present for the meeting. And then that child would take the talking stick and he would stand up: 'Hi, my name is Jim, my Indian Guide name is Big Fish. . . . My dad's name is Jim, his Indian Guides name is whatever, then you would go through if you saw any wild animals since the last meeting, what they were, where were you saw them, then what the good deeds you did. . . . But the most amazing . . . would be like you to have . . . a Kindergartener standing there, and he's futzing with the stick and they are hiding half-behind their dad, and you could barely hear them. Some wouldn't even do it! Then you see them progress through the years . . . to where they're in fifth-grade, and it's like 'It's my turn to talk, give me that stick!'"[16]

An explanation for the enduring consistency of the basics of Y-Indian Guides—parent-child focus, gathering in small groups, and activity-based experiential learning—is found in the ways the program incorporated the YMCA's historical focus on "group work."[17] Though the first YMCA offerings were small and intimate as described in chapter 1, in the buildup to and during World War I, the YMCA increasingly engaged large groups, particularly in the areas of religious and physical work. Postwar, the YMCA began to give increased emphasis to engaging men and boys in groups. As it developed its Christian citizenship programs, it envisioned the group setting as a workshop of democracy. When Keltner and Friday created their vision for the program, the concept of group work was being actively promoted within the YMCA, both as a foundational approach for programming and as a method for training staff via Paul Super's "project method."[18]

But clearly, almost from the very beginning, one sees chiefs, tally-keepers, and others seizing creative license and whimsy with gusto. As previously mentioned, the Osage tribe reveled in teasing "Chief Lone Wolf" Harold Keltner, including singing "Old Man Keltner Had a Camp" during a field trip in 1928. Chief Roaming Wolf of the Chickasaw Tribe (only his last name, Knierim, is preserved in the records), began a story about the history of his own "tribe" by asking "How many of you little braves believe the Indians were ever Jews?" (Whether or not he asked this question because he and/or any of the members of his tribe were Jewish is difficult to determine.) It turned out that "Roaming Wolf" was referring to a white trader, James Adair, whose writings provided a rare outsider's view of the Chickasaw people. It was Adair who theorized, based on various observed words (*Halelu* and *Yahovah*) and cultural practices (burial rituals, division into tribes, sacrifices, etc.) that Chickasaws were descended from the lost tribes of Israel.[19]

"Roaming Wolf" concluded his single-spaced nine-and-a-half-page speech with an oft-repeated theme: "I want to leave with you the thought that we have adopted the name of a tribe often called savage, yet peaceable. There was never a nobler branch of the human race, purer, [or] cleaner [of] spirit." Less flattering was this conclusion from a January 1935 article in *Long House News*: "May I leave this concluding thought—that although Indians were very savage and crude in their beliefs, they seem to have had a very religious and tender heart."[20] No matter their attempts to admire or even emulate Indigenous peoples, white authors often failed to extricate themselves from colonial mindsets that centered their own sense of cultural, intellectual, racial, and spiritual superiority.

Clearly ritual was an important component of the first Y-Indian Guides tribes. As discussed in chapter 3, rites fostered the creation of a seemingly magical atmosphere where new identities were formed and

Figure 16. Creation of rituals was an important element for many Indian Guides participants. Here we see an induction of a "tribe" from Boulder, Colorado, by another from the South Denver YMCA, c. 1960, while proud moms look on. Kautz Family YMCA Archives, University of Minnesota Libraries.

where father and son could experiment with new, more intimate ways of speaking and interacting. That interaction and play was the glue holding the tribes and individual relationships together. As Keltner's initial tracking of the first tribes demonstrates, a high level of commitment and participation from all members was key to a tribe's success and longevity. When not in each other's homes, tribes engaged in a host of activities designed to keep fathers and sons in close communion with each other.

Many of the activities, unsurprisingly, centered on the natural world. Camping, a common excursion that had the additional benefit of placing father/son pairs together for an extended period, took the tribes into the wilds of the big and little braves they sought to emulate. In fact, National Boys' Work Committee member and longtime Indian Guides supporter Lansing Smith donated a "beautiful $15,000 camp on Lake-of-the-Ozarks near Ha-Ha-Tonka Park" to the St. Louis Y, which would have made an enticing destination for Missouri "tribes."[21]

In addition to camping, cataloging local flora and fauna (often from the back seat of a car) allowed the boys to identify and appreciate the countless variety of God's creation. Osage "tribe" minutes from June 2, 1927, for example, describe a contest in which boys from different cars, all on their way to Camp Taconic, competed to see how many different birds they could identify. On June 5, 1928, the minutes reported that one of the fathers introduced "Squaw Lee, his sister from California, who had started him, when a lad, [on] how to study nature. Chief Red Feather told of a workman in a brick plant encasing a toad in a pressed brick. When the brick was broken open the toad shrugged its shoulders and jumped away. The other scout reports were confined to toad stories, birds, birds' nests, flowers, and how the Indian got fire."

Beyond exploring the natural world, fathers and sons dabbled in arts and crafts. In addition to constructing the "Indian" artifacts needed for the tribe meetings (headbands, tom-toms, tomahawks, and totem poles), fathers and sons made slot cars, model airplanes, and dioramas to hone their craft abilities. Photography, painting and sculpture were encouraged and cultivated creative impulses in the boys. These projects were often showcased as exhibits at powwows where tribes would gather on a local, regional, and (ultimately) national basis to show off their handiwork and celebrate the growing movement.

But more important than any of the activities was the uninterrupted time and undivided attention that fathers gave their sons. As Stephen Hanpeter made clear, his and his twin brother's relationship with his father was "slim." But joining Indian Guides created the structure by which that relationship could be enhanced. "At home I would see him at his desk and there he's King, Emperor at the head of the table, getting dressed to go out to the job. . . . He's a professional, he's an engineer and he spent most of his hours, weekly, daily, yearly with business. He did set aside time and I think having Indian Guides was one way for him to do that. . . . We did these activities . . . and by doing [them], we got a positive sense that he did care and that he was there for us. . . . But the biggest sense I have is that we knew he was there." Greg Norman of Richfield, Minnesota, expressed a similar sentiment: "Well, just the fact that my Dad took time to bring me to Indian Guides and do stuff with me showed me that he cared. And that meant a lot."[22] Indeed, fathers not only took time, but "came down" to their sons' level to play. As Hanpeter observed, "There we are on the floor literally down . . . and free of his desk, free of his car, all these status things that . . . [put him] up on the pedestal, maybe a little bit less the father, the enforcer, the leader, whatever, but more of the partner. . . . That's the really important thing."[23]

The success of the program in the St. Louis area, and its expansion to neighboring states, set the stage for the national YMCA to voice its support for the program. It was at this point that Y-Indian Guides truly embarked on its journey to become the YMCA's signature youth development program. By 1930 Indian Guides was receiving some attention in *Christian Citizenship*, a newsletter of the YMCA's National Council. One unnamed father interviewed for the story made it clear that he had a "double interest" in joining Indian Guides: "It's a great joy to me to watch my son take part, and I enjoy the exchange of interests with the men." It was his belief and that of his fellow "tribe" members that "while the activities of the meeting were largely centered around what boys could do . . . there were enough by-products of interests for fathers around the meetings and in the general running of the tribes, the longhouse of the chiefs and the general Pow-wows to make their interests continuous and their growth assured." Often to their surprise, fathers and sons enjoyed spending time with each other in this setting, which seemed to "stimulate boys to make suggestions" to their father about what they would like to do. "The boys evidently enjoy the security which the presence of their fathers afford," reported the article, "but under that sense of security they are more likely to initiate suggestions and to participate whole-heartedly in the group programs." Fathers interviewed felt that they had derived great benefit from Indian Guides and believed other fathers would as well. "Some of them wondered if it might become a national program."[24]

THE STRUGGLE FOR NATIONAL RECOGNITION
A plan was hatched in the spring of 1935 to bring Indian Guides to the attention of the national YMCA. With support of his South Side branch, Keltner traveled east on a whirlwind tour of YMCA conferences and events to promote the program. In Montreal he attended a meeting

of the general secretaries of North America. He visited his alma mater, the International YMCA College (now Springfield College), and then moved on to YMCA national headquarters. In a meeting that included Lansing Smith, Abel Gregg, Harrison Elliot of Union Theological Seminary, and national YMCA general secretary John Manley, the assembly decided to draft and support a resolution to make Indian Guides a national program. The resolution would first be presented to the National Boys' Work Committee and then, if approved, move on to the National Council. The two bodies met only a few days apart in late October under the auspices of the national convention in Niagara Falls, New York. Once this decision was made, Keltner "went up to Croton-on-Hudson and spent a half-day with an old friend of his, Harold Gray, the creator of 'Little Orphan Annie.'"[25]

A pivotal moment in the promotion of Indian Guides as a national movement occurred on April 29, 1935, when the National Boys' Work Committee met in New York City. A story of this meeting was shared either by Charles Keltner Shanks, Harold Keltner's grandson, or one of William Hefelfinger's descendants, and repeated in National Longhouse, an organization that has sought to preserve the original Indian Guides program since the YMCA phased it out in 2003. In this account, St. Louis "chief" William Hefelfinger was so bent on making Indian Guides a national program that he asked Abel Gregg to put the proposal as the first order of business on the agenda. Gregg called the meeting to order with only the two of them in the room; they passed the proposal two votes to none, making Indian Guides an official national program of the YMCA.[26] But the authority to make this decision did not rest with this committee alone (it still had to pass the National Council), and in fact the records of the meeting make it clear that the matter was discussed by more than just Hefelfinger and Gregg. As a letter from Boys' Work Committee chairman Harrison "Sunny" Elliott reveals, "the question was discussed of a program for younger boys known as 'Indian Guides.' . . . It has been tried out experimentally for a number of years and seems to offer possibilities for one aspect of Boys' Work [the development of the father-son relationship] for which we do not have adequate program material at the present time." Former St. Louis Y Boys' Work Committee chairman Lansing Smith paid to have Elliott send a copy of the Indian Guides manual to every member of the committee for their consideration. At their next meeting, scheduled for October 20 and 21 at the National Laymen's Assembly at Niagara Falls, Elliott wrote, "We shall be glad to have your appraisal of the program and your judgment as to whether or not it would be wise for us to seek some way of sponsoring it on a national basis."[27] While the timing and details in the story shared by National Longhouse are not entirely correct, it is nonetheless true that William Hefelfinger and Abel Gregg (who had grown fond of the program through his association with Lansing Smith) played critical roles in the advancement of the program.[28] It was in October, then, not in April 1935, that both the National Boys' Work Committee and the National Council of the YMCA approved Indian Guides as a national Y program.

In June, Hefelfinger traveled to the International Y's Men Convention in Silver Bay on Lake George, New York, to garner their support, "paving the way for a favorable presentation which was to come later in October at the National Convention."[29] Hefelfinger and Mr. Fullerton Place, the delegate from eastern Missouri, represented St. Louis at Niagara Falls in October. It was Place who submitted the resolution on behalf of the Y's Laymen's Assembly, asking the National Council to endorse Indian Guides as "a part of the Y.M.C.A.'s work with boys" and as "a Father and Son program." This would be "an experimental program in determining what the Y.M.C.A. ought to do in the field of work with boys below the age of twelve." Since, during this time of Depression, there was no way the Y could provide staff or a budget for "the Indian Guide work in the area around St. Louis," it was decided that "the lay and professional groups now interested shall carry on, with the encouragement and help" of the Boys' Work Committee and any other interested neighboring state or local Y. Keltner's friend Harold Gray even sent a telegram urging those assembled "in the name of 'Little Orphan Annie' to move forward with such a remarkable Father and Son program."[30] Keltner recalled that from the very beginning, "Mr. Hefelfinger reported there was some opposition by YMCA Secretaries" and that "Mr. Gregg's mail brought forth protests from Boys Secretaries from many parts of the country. They expressed amazement at his lack of judgment, although they all conceded that they had not tried the program personally."[31]

Ignoring ardent critics, the St. Louis YMCA struck while the iron was hot. They had received the imprimatur of the national YMCA and now saw themselves as responsible for making St. Louis the capital city of the Indian Guides program. The best way to do this, they reasoned, was to aggressively recruit more fathers and sons into the movement. Advertising itself as "An All-American Program That Keeps Dads and Sons Together," the St. Louis campaign leaned heavily on guilt and sentiment, comparing white and (generic, idealized) Indian fathers in a way that left whites wanting: "The relationship between Father and Son among Indians was intensely personal. No Indian Brave ever allowed someone else to raise his boy. Early in life the Father took the Son on trips, taught him the wonders and language of the woodland and all the things he had learned out of long experience. Thus, the boy learned wisdom and how to care for himself and serve others. The Big Brave saw to it that the Little Brave got the best he could give him." Fathers busy making the grade at work often took little time to build meaningful relationships with their sons. "'Some day, Son, we'll do that together,' you have said a hundred times to that little fellow standing there looking up into your face. But of course, that day had not yet arrived. Dad," asked a promotional pamphlet, "is YOUR son the forgotten boy?"[32]

By January 1936, St. Louis leadership had developed what they called the Wampum Hunt. Fathers and sons would team up and canvass their neighborhoods, raising money from their friends, neighbors, professional associates, and playmates to fund the creation of new "tribes." As the training literature stated, boys and their fathers should tell prospective contributors that "Indian Guides originated in St. Louis and has now been made national in scope. We must therefore make St. Louis a strong official example for the entire country of how Tribes are started and how the program is carried out." Those who might be hesitant to support the cause should be told, "Crime or criminal tendencies simply cannot exist where there is real love between Father and Son, as is developed by Indian Guides. Crime costs everybody money. Tell the people you see that Indian Guides helps save them money." And to appeal to those who felt that the ills of modern life were destroying American society, one might say, "Indian Guides are bringing back good old fashioned home life which means so much to the family—but which we have gotten away from. Remind your friends that our programs are always held in homes."[33]

Fathers and sons were each expected to raise ten $1 donations. Generous patrons who pledged $5 or more were given a special card designating them as a member of the St. Louis Area "Reservation." All donors received a special thank-you card to which was tied a small piece of "wampum." The story of these pieces of "wampum" is itself a sign of how much times have changed since the inception of Indian Guides.

The wampum card was meant not only to thank donors but to educate them about Native American culture. The reverse side of the card, which bore the title "Some Facts about Wampum," told its readers about the different uses that different tribes of the East, Pacific Coast Indians, the Navajo and Pueblo, and tribes that, like the Osage, Shawnee, and Chickasaw, had once populated the St. Louis area had for wampum, and described their composition and construction. Yet on the front "Thank You" side of the card, the donor was told that the piece of replica "wampum" attached to their card was modeled after a genuine piece that Harold Keltner had found while roaming Monks Mound in nearby Madison County, Illinois. Of course, in the 1920s or '30s, few whites would have thought about returning a find like Keltner's to the native community from which it had come, even though the Antiquities Act of 1906 had made the acquisition of such items from federal lands illegal. (Monks Mound is part of a state historic site, which may have had its own prohibitions.) Keltner clearly prized this piece of wampum, which he felt linked him and his movement even more closely to authentic Native Americans. But his actions also highlight how easy and acceptable it was for whites to appropriate Indian culture without considering the potential implications of doing so.

While Y-Indian Guides preached unity, playfulness, and warm bonds of friendship, its founders in St. Louis also felt a strong sense of ownership over the program. They needed to demonstrate the power and value of Indian Guides to the rest of the country. An early success was the "First National Pow-Wow and Exhibit of Indian Guides of United States and the Western Hemisphere" (discussed in chapter 3), held over the course of two evenings in March 1938. This event marked the first gathering of a National Longhouse where fathers (Big Chiefs of area tribes) gathered to celebrate the program and plan its future.[34] But as it did so through the Wampum Hunt—increasing the number of "tribes . . . [with] full membership in each with virile programs by all"—and the National Pow-Wow, its main goal was to nationalize the program while providing "evidence that [Y-Indian Guides] National Headquarters should be maintained in St. Louis."

While understandable, this sentiment once again showed the potential for division that would accompany the national YMCA's adoption of Indian Guides. The St. Louis Y wanted national recognition for Indian Guides, but their own central locus of control. They wanted the national YMCA to bear responsibility for the program, but for the St. Louis Long House to maintain ultimate authority over it. And this civic-minded impulse came at the very time when, as even the St. Louis YMCA admitted, Keltner was able to spend less rather than more time focusing on the program. "Although the Big Chief's first love is Indian Guides," a Wampum Hunt bulletin announced, "more and more of his time was required on matters incident to the opening of the new South Side 'Y' building. . . . He must have help at Long House headquarters to take care of the many Indian Guide details."[35] Despite St. Louis' efforts, the national YMCA in New York City assumed authority over the Indian Guides program in the spring of 1940, also assuming responsibility for publishing *Long House News* and coordinating the various national and regional gatherings.

With the national office seemingly now in control of the program, what was foreshadowed a few years earlier would now become a persistent, existential debate between representatives of the YMCA and Indian Guides. To whom did Y-Indian Guides belong? Who controlled it? What was its purpose, and into whose plans did it fit? Increasingly, both parties came to learn that participants' primary loyalty was to their "tribe," and to a lesser extent the Indian Guides movement or the YMCA.

Two years after he had helped make Indian Guides a national program, Abel Gregg was clearly still getting an earful about it. In an attempt to help opponents better understand that to which they so vehemently objected, Gregg asked Harold Keltner to bring a father-son "tribe" to the 1937 Boys' Work Conference in Lake Geneva, Wisconsin.

Keltner was probably unaware that Abel Gregg was, by the summer of 1937, quite unpopular with his superiors and therefore not the best person to lead a high-profile campaign to make Indian Guides a national program. The tension seems to go back to at least 1934, when in the midst of the Great Depression, the YMCA was having difficulty raising money to pay salaries. Gregg had apparently been removed from the Boys' Work staff at one point but was reinstated by early 1934. A letter from YMCA National Council member Jay Urice claims that Gregg, having been told that the Boys' Work Committee would pay for his salary and travel, interpreted this to mean that "telephone, postage, stenographic service, retirement and every such cost will somehow be carried out of the general funds." At a time of national financial crisis, this comment, whether accurately conveyed or not, caused both consternation and resentment.[36] In addition, Gregg was part of a faction of Boys' Work secretaries who perceived the YMCA negatively as a top-down organization rather than the grassroots one they thought it should be. Boys' Work secretaries, who found themselves increasingly shouldering the burden of the YMCA's gradual though significant shift in programmatic focus from young men to boys, felt they lacked the influence, respect, autonomy, and representation they deserved on national committees.

Gregg and his peers reasoned that within the YMCA, "authority should proceed from committees [like theirs] upward rather than as delegated responsibilities." Boys' Work secretaries, claimed Urice, "resent[ed] the method of composition of the [National] Council [of Boys' Work secretaries] and National Board." In a memo to Urice, fellow National Council member John E. Manley described Gregg as "rather smug" and his arguments as illegitimate.[37] So as the Indian Guides tribe from St. Louis prepared their presentation, they likely had no idea that even if their demonstration was a smashing success, there were those who would have wished to see it fail simply because it was associated with Abel Gregg.

As Keltner recalled, "Some of us felt that we could not do justice to the program from such a demonstration. However, we finally agreed. Seventeen men and boys, paying all their own expenses, drove to Lake Geneva, eager for an opportunity to express their appreciation to the organization that had given them this father-son program. It never occurred to any of them . . . that the Boys Secretaries could appreciate their viewpoint as fathers. Fortunately, they never knew just what happened." It seems that after a long day of ponderous deliberations, many of the Boys' Work group began to crack jokes and make each other laugh in order to lighten their moods. It was in this spirit of levity that the secretaries arrived in the auditorium to see the Indian Guides demonstration. When the fathers began by placing feathered headbands on their heads, the laughter continued. "We did our best in the presentation," remembered Keltner. "To this day [1946], however there are Boys Secretaries who secured the wrong impression at Lake Geneva and made further trouble for Mr. Gregg. On the other hand, there were many men such as Arthur Crampton, General Secretary at Flint, Michigan, who were impressed."[38] Indeed, the Indian Guides program in Flint quickly became one of the largest in the country under Crampton's leadership. But a report written not long after the Geneva Conference shows that at least one secretary was deeply troubled by the inclusion of Indian Guides into the slate of well-ordered and high-minded YMCA youth programs.

After the Y's experiment with the Christian citizenship program described in chapter 1, it eventually settled into a threefold youth development program for boys in grade school, junior high, and high school. These programs had become well-established, stalwart programs in Boys' Work. White Plains, New York, Y secretary Tracy Redding asserted that Indian Guides was an attempt to plunge the Y into "another hodgepodge of different programs instead of the clear Gra-Y, Jr-Hi-Y, and Hi-Y stream." The national office, Redding claimed, had been all but blackmailed by Indian Guides leaders who threatened to go independent if the Y did not adopt their program. Many of Indian Guides' "unique" aspects, like its emphasis on active roles for fathers, its placement in homes, and its "dramatics, including Indian lore," he insisted, could be employed in any YMCA youth program.

They tell us boys fall for the spectacular features in "Indian" organizations. But boys will fall for almost anything that has color or novelty. They tell us of fathers who speak of "Indian Guides" with tears in their eyes. But grown men get emotional about a lot of things. . . . What share in the movement can we expect boys to carry who parade under false labels, American boys calling themselves some sort of Indians?

There are at least some in our ranks who would like to see us face up to the issues involved in this whole "Indian Guide" promotion. We feel that it has been foisted upon the Association, that the laymen's group was used as a tool.[39]

A counterpoint to Redding's scathing assessment came from Andrew Santanen, Boys' Work secretary at the Springfield, Illinois, Y. Santanen had been present for the Indian Guides demonstration at Lake Geneva and, like others, "saw little value in a program that placed so much emphasis on Indian ritual and headbands." With great reluctance he traveled with a group of fathers and sons from Springfield to visit St. Louis, where

Special Feature

Nationalizing the Indian Guide Movement

Mr. Keltner   Joe Friday   Mr. Zahner

A special feature of the Assembly will be the launching of the National Program for fathers and sons, known as the Indian Guides.

This movement to foster companionship between fathers and sons was started more than ten years ago by Harold S. Keltner a St. Louis "Y" secretary, and a full-blooded Ojibway Indian, Joe Friday. It has become so successful that the National Council of the Y. M. C. A. has officially adopted the program as part of its Boys' Work.

Harold Keltner is coming to Lake Geneva and bringing with him members of several of the St. Louis "tribes," Oscar Zahner, lay representative and Joe Friday. Together they will give an actual demonstration of the Indian Guide program and ways in which it joins fathers and sons in work and play.

Opportunity will be provided on the Assembly schedule for training sessions for local secretaries and laymen who wish to become organizers of tribes in their own communities. Use the special Indian Guide registration blank attached if you are interested in registering for these training sessions and in bringing the Indian Guides to your home town!

Figure 17. Flyer sent out to all attendees of the 1937 Boys' Work Conference in Lake Geneva, Wisconsin, where the question of making Y-Indian Guides a national program was put to a vote. Once again, the image of Joe Friday is smaller than that of Keltner. Gateway Region Young Men's Christian Association (S0473).

he had a change of heart. "I found an enthusiasm on the part of fathers and sons that I could not resist." The programs were well planned and allowed for "a variety of self-expression by the boys." Upon their return, the Springfielders began their own tribe. While he meant no disrespect to other Y youth programs, Indian Guides, he asserted, made it "possible to secure parent participation to a degree that is not easily attained in other groupings." Indian Guides was in no way a simple carry-over of the old Friendly Indians program, as the former had no role for fathers to play. In explaining the "four explicit functions of the movement," Santanen quoted a letter sent to Abel Gregg from A. S. Arnold, general secretary of the Cone Memorial YMCA of Greensboro, North Carolina, who employed a kind of proto-psychological defense: (a) being in close relationship allowed the father to observe emerging "individual personality difficulties" in his son and "clarif[y]" them before they became "suppressed or ill directed"; (b) "expansive, creative activities" shared by father and son in the presence of others produced "desirable maturation and integration of the boy"; (c) "wholesome group activities in which the boy may participate with his father make possible the growth of friendships and fellowships with other boys and fathers in a small favorable unit which serves as a sort of personality shock absorber in adjusting the boy to the larger social environment which often causes introversion and the welling up of emotional problems"; and (d) Indian Guides' "creative recreational and educational activities in sports, hobbies, crafts and the wide variety of project[s]" united "father and son and the entire group on the bases of common, interesting ideas and religious standards."[40]

Despite any criticism he may have been hearing, Gregg reported in January 1938 that an additional step toward "Indian Guide nationalization" had been taken through Lansing Smith's trip to St. Louis, where he met with "the chiefs of all the tribes" to discuss "the problems of promotion and programming of this newest development in the Boys' Work section." These discussions would be carried forward at the National Longhouse in March, also held in St. Louis.[41]

At the January gathering, unsurprisingly, Harold Keltner was elected chair, but he said he had no desire for the St. Louis Y to dominate the proceedings. Since, as we shall see, members of Indian Guides would have a tremendous amount of autonomy, it is ironic to see Keltner spend so much time in his 1938 remarks sharing concerns about new tribes needing to conform closely to older ones. Perhaps he understood the kind of trouble that might come from too much creative license. Everyone should have the same pin, the same headband, the same handbook. In fact, perhaps each tribe really needed to formally apply for membership to the Boys' Work secretary at their local Y, where their petition would be sent up the YMCA hierarchy and receive final approval from the local Y's board president and general secretary. Publication—in St. Louis, he hoped—of *Long House News* would further encourage congruence from tribe to tribe; it could be supported by dues (it cost $20 to print and mail out an issue in 1938) and distributed out of New York City.[42] Yet despite Keltner's dream of both a uniform standard in Indian Guides and a close relationship between tribes and their local YMCAs, neither of these goals were ever significantly achieved.

Despite the opposition, even scorn, of some Y secretaries, a March 1938 report indicated that the number of Indian Guides "tribes" had grown by "33 per cent in the last two years."[43] A year later the program had three times the budget surplus it had projected—during the Great Depression—and boasted tribes "scattered in cities from California to New York, and from Maine and Idaho to Florida. Until 1938, most activity around this project centered within a small radius of the city of its origin, St. Louis. It is now expanding in response to the growing interest in work with parents, and because of the awareness of the importance of the contribution of the family in child development." Plans were under way to set up "demonstration centers" in Greensboro, North Carolina, Birmingham, Alabama, and perhaps Springfield, Ohio, to further spread the "gospel" of Indian Guides.[44] By November 1939, Abel Gregg's passion for the program seemed unabated. The goal for 1940, he wrote, was to pursue further growth "relentlessly, with increasing force." He wanted a bigger budget, better stenographic and clerical services, and preparation of "literature more adequate to the opportunities in this field." He envisioned "tremendous possibilities" for the further development of the "father and son and home relationship" that Indian Guides helped develop.[45] What Gregg released for public institutional consumption, however, did not match what he wrote privately to the man who in many ways embodied the Indian Guides program, Joe Friday.

In the winter of 1939–40, Friday was traveling from city to city in the Northeast, doing his best to establish new "tribes" wherever he went. He had been conducting such campaigns for several years, as editions of *Long House News* attest. (In December 1937, for example, an article announced that Friday was available to travel across the country to promote the program and instructed readers to contact "Abe Gregg" if they were interested.)

Keltner had produced a flyer to attract interest in Friday, describing his friend as "an Indian Guide of the Great North Woods," a "Woodsman, a keen Hunter, expert Canoeist, Fisherman, Philosopher, Guide (much sought), Lecturer," and "one of the last of the real Americans," who "was 15 years old before he saw his first white man. Until they came, disease was rare, and the forests were full of game." Friday's specialties, read the flyer, were public schools, churches, service clubs, and father-son groups, and potential topics were listed for each. Keltner provided a personal testimonial, as well as comments from some of those who had recruited Friday for their events. In Keltner's own words, Friday was "an intelligent man, good judge of character, and has a discerning mind. . . . He is widely traveled, a sharpshooter in World War I, guide of European Royalty in Hudson's Bay and the North. . . . He has conversed with many of America's best minds around Canadian Camp Fires and has their respect for his philosophy of life, decidedly Christian." Sadly, Keltner felt compelled to add, "Of course, he is Indian. He is not an organizer, but can open many doors. Newspapers will see value in his presence in your city." Despite his longtime friendship with Friday, despite his proclamation of being "nuts about Indians," despite his desire to see white fathers and sons admire, emulate, and benefit from the values and cultural richness of Indigenous peoples, Keltner was not inoculated from a colonizing mindset.[46] In addition, as we saw in chapter 2, Friday and his brother had sufficient organizational skill to shepherd two hockey teams across the eastern halves of Canada and the United States. One is left to wonder just how well Harold Keltner really knew Joe Friday.

On January 31, 1940, Joe Friday wrote Gregg asking for assistance. (This is one of only two occasions in which we hear from Joe Friday in his own words.) He'd enjoyed a fine visit with a "Mr. Duran" of Pleasantville, New Jersey and nine boys, which had gone so well that the

Durans invited him to stay with them. "It is my duty to get the fathers and sons together and give them the spirit of the out of doors," he wrote, "but now it is up to Mr. Duran." Friday hoped that Gregg could follow up with Duran to encourage his participation in Indian Guides. He had tried to interest the local YMCA, but "there is no cooperation whatever with the Secretary. I had to work through the schools and churches and then hand it over to the Secretary." Friday's determination to promote the program, at least in this letter to Gregg, is clear: "In spite of all this difficulty with the Secretary, this has to go on—even if I have to work through school principals. They see the value of the Indian Guides. Also the fathers see it when it is presented to them." Friday was counting on Gregg, or someone in his office, to help book engagements and answer two letters of inquiry he had received. He was also hoping that, rather than simply being reimbursed for his expenses, the association might consider paying him a salary of $200 per month "so I can give my entire time to promoting Indian Guides for the month of March—and you do the booking. Also for April (not going home until May 10th)."[47] While these requests may seem presumptuous to the casual reader, it was clear that Friday was traveling with less than a full confidence in where he would be going next, whether he would have the money to get there, and how, or even if, he would be received once he arrived.

Gregg's reply to Friday seems rather brusque, considering the time and effort Friday was expending. No, he was not going to book events, and he was sending the two letters back. (He did provide one lead.) YMCAs of the eastern states, he averred, "have been and will be a conservative group. Their objections are of the sort which you cannot meet and which only time and demonstration of father and son tribes will slowly break down." Gregg further adjured Friday to avoid making any contacts apart from local YMCAs, as Indian Guides had no authority to go over their heads in starting "tribes." Gregg further expressed the view that it might never be possible for the national Indian Guides program to "assume responsibility for financing your winter time." If one were to read this letter in isolation, or if a critical reader were to select only the most negative comments found therein, it would cast Abel Gregg in a very unflattering light. While he must not be easily or entirely forgiven for heaping so many of Friday's concerns back on his shoulders, Gregg's

Figure 18. Joe Friday stands ready to participate in an induction ritual, date and place unknown. Kautz Family YMCA Archives, University of Minnesota Libraries.

long history of struggle within the Boys' Work Committee certainly puts his comments in a more appropriate context. Gregg's ruefulness, but also a bit of apology, comes through in this missive: "I would be foolish if I buried my head in the sand and did not recognize these facts which have been borne in on me as I have attempted to try and make your sojourn down here this time easier. Out of the two different sets of letters which I wrote offering to go with you to promote Indian Guide groups, we had only one offer. . . . Other ways have to be found of opening up the minds and readiness of these men for this effort." (An article in the October 1944 issue of *Long House News* shows that Joe Friday's fortunes on the recruitment trail improved significantly in the next few years: "We are glad to announce that Joe's schedule is completely filled from January 1st to April 1st, 1945, in the states of Indiana, Illinois, Michigan, Kentucky, Missouri, and the West central area."[48])

Despite the resistance of numerous Y secretaries, the obstacles set before Joe Friday, Abel Gregg, and others, and a decided lack of enthusiasm within the National Boys' Work Committee, Indian Guides was growing, a testament as much to the lay leadership of individual "tribes" as it was to anything done by high-ranking YMCA officials. Apart from Harold Keltner, who had no sons but who helped create the program, most supportive Y secretaries were also fathers with boys of a certain age, or were brought along, reluctantly at first, by avid fathers like William Hefelfinger, who insisted that a program be established. But even as Indian Guides began growing by leaps and bounds in the late 1930s and early '40s, the seemingly irresistible force of optimism generated by its aficionados met an immovable object: World War II. While the United States would not involve itself in the conflict until December 1941, the specter of impending conflict "stirred and threatened" boys in a way, wrote Harrison Elliott, that no previous war had. Looming conflict necessitated a more serious and patriotic approach to the father-son relationship and life in the home. Christian citizenship, as forged in and articulated by the Gra-Y, Junior-Hi-Y, and Hi-Y programs, came to the fore as the most important influence the YMCA could provide boys and families during a time of war. Mentions of Indians in general, to say nothing of the kinds of aggressive, optimistic language used only months before, began to subside. There must have been at least a few Y secretaries in 1942 who thought that the war had finally set things right in the Boys' Work Department.

CHAPTER FIVE

The Promise of the Program

In Indian Life, my name is Red Feather, and my dad's name is Little Big Man. I get many helpful things out of the Indian Guides movement. It has taught me a lot about trees, animals and birds and life in the open.

We studied about the Indian and his way of living—how he had to suffer many hardships.

A real Indian Chief visited our pow-wow and I liked the thrilling stories about their tribe. Another Indian danced for us to the beat of the tom-tom.

On summer nights we have our councils out of doors, around the campfire, and do our stunts and sing our songs together.

Sometimes we all go together to bakeries, dairies and airports: the dad and son have to write a theme about our trip. It is fun figuring out ideas for invitations. We like to make something typical of the Indian, such as miniature canoes, bows and arrows, or tepees, and write the invitation on them in Indian sign language. I think the Indian Guide Movement is swell because it means doing things and going places with Dad.

—Louis Yonley, Cheyenne Tribe.[1]

THIS CHILD'S TESTIMONIAL from March 1939 offers a glimpse into the childhood that families, in partnership with the YMCA and Y-Indian Guides, strove to construct for youth. Nurturing, wholesome, and filled with opportunity, the typical Indian Guide program during the period of and following World War II increasingly included civically oriented activities designed to teach youth about not only nature but also their communities. For most participants, however, as demonstrated by Arthur Martin's fatherly perspective, printed alongside Louis Yonley's, forging the father-son bond remained the central theme: "Indian Guides has made me conscious . . . that I can be a better companion of my boys, grow up with them, share their joys, their sorrows, and their disappointments. Many fathers do not know how to live with their boys but they know the finest experience in the world is to be a boy. . . . Indian Guides has taught me that some of my time belongs to my son[s], to share my life with them and be a boy again."[2]

Between 1945 and 1970, Y-Indian Guides experienced tremendous growth. Throughout this period, however, the program found itself in the midst of profound reevaluation, questioning its purpose, audience, and efficacy. The threat of war looming over the nation in the late 1930s

Figure 19. Abel Gregg, right, presents an Indian Guides charter to "Chief" David B. Treat, with his arm around Stanley King, as father A. A. Miller and son Bob Miller look on. Flint, Michigan, became one of the first cities outside of Missouri, Kansas, and Illinois to fervently embrace Indian Guides. *Long House News* 4, no. 4 (March 1939).

only heightened the sense of urgency within the YMCA to safeguard the childhood of young boys. The perceived idealism of post–World War II America, which ushered in the anxious years of the Cold War, placed greater pressure on Indian Guides to evolve while maintaining its core emphasis on shaping youth through parental influence.

Finally, the archetypal father-son relationship and the masculine ideal promoted by the YMCA were forced to change and broaden. World War II had brought millions of women into the workforce, enticed a million and a half African Americans to move north, dislocated individuals and entire families, and increased divorce rates and juvenile delinquency. Y-Indian Guides needed to address and accommodate these and other changes that affected the American family, while attracting new participants.

EXPANSION, FOR BETTER AND FOR WORSE

As Y-Indian Guides expanded, members of the National Longhouse, the program's national coordinating body, regularly expressed concerns that it was losing its focus on nurturing the father-son relationship. Fearing "a host of little things" that could impede the comradeship between father and sons, the Illinois Longhouse suggested a device to "bring out into the open a lot of these little things." The *Christian Herald* later described how this strategy was developed by sharing inspiring (if not verifiable) father-son stories.

Jimmie was a problem child until a neighbor intervened, asking Jimmie's father if he had ever tried to understand his son. He invited them to an Indian Guides powwow. "Six months later the transformation in Jimmie was striking. . . . Jimmie had found a real pal, the best pal in the world—his dad." Jimmie and his father forged their friendship through the power of honest facilitated sharing. As the *Herald* wrote:

> At some meetings the boys write on slips of paper what they like and dislike about pop. The latter does the same, then they swap. These bits of information can be plenty disconcerting to the old-sters. "The boys really light into us," one said. A plant foreman got this from his boy: "I don't like the way you come home with a grouch and snap at me as you did the other night when mom had

left the dishes and you ordered me to wash them. I was tired, too, and trying to get my homework done."

This was handing it pretty straight to the old man, and he faced it honestly. Yes, he often did come at home at night tired and irritated and took it out on the family. He'd try to be more considerate.

Next time he found a stack of unwashed dishes mom had left to attend a meeting, he put his hand on the boy's shoulder and said, "Son, let's you and I do the dishes. I'll wash if you wipe."

"Sure thing, dad," said the boy.

Another boy told his alcoholic dad that he didn't like it when he drank. "'Son, I've been doing a lot of thinking since our last meeting. I've decided that when a fellow can't feel proud of his pop, there's something wrong with pop. You told me what it is, son. . . . I'll never touch the stuff again.' The boy's face lit up as he exclaimed, 'Gee, that's great! Let's shake.' They did—'Pals forever.'" Sons in this article were not spared at least an occasional unstinting critique from their fathers as well. Their desire for "freedom" was often described as mere "license," though this impulse required understanding and proper guidance from Dad.

Another benefit of the program as described by the *Herald* was the fellowship between fathers. "A banker, lawyer and doctor will often rub shoulders with a janitor."[3] This egalitarian, democratic scenario would be regularly upheld as the promise of the program. Though there were communities where this mingling took place, later studies revealed that Indian Guides, like the YMCA as a whole, was (and remained for decades) a predominantly white, middle- and upper-middle-class institution.

The US entry into World War II re-created conditions that, in part, inspired the creation of Indian Guides. Once again a generation of fathers, dislocated, often traumatized by war, returned home, often unsure of how to interact with their families. But given the United States's longer and more transformative role in World War II, a new fatherly model developed within Indian Guides. General Douglas MacArthur, awarded the title of "outstanding American Father" by the National Fathers' Day Committee, foreshadowed this new ideal in a *Long House News* article: "A soldier destroys in order to build; the father only builds, never destroys. The one has the potentialities of death; the other embodies creation and life. And while the hordes of death are mighty, the battalions of life are mightier still. It is my hope that my son, when I am gone, will remember me not from the battle but in the home repeating with him our simple daily prayer, 'Our Father, Who art in heaven.'"[4]

The articulated (if not entirely genuine) desire to be seen and remembered as a father, and not a warrior, paralleled YMCA and Indian Guides concerns that youth have strong, loving male role models. Men placed in horrendous wartime situations would return with a desire to shield their children from the harsher elements of the world. While they often accomplished this materially, whether by moving to suburbia or providing their children food, clothing, shelter, and education, they often lacked the personal wherewithal to actually develop warm relationships with their progeny. For many fathers, Indian Guides became the means by which they overcame this deficit. Norris Lineweaver's father was a YMCA boys' work secretary in Meridian, Texas, in the 1950s. As he recalls,

My dad came home from World War II with a lot of scars, emotional scars. . . . [He] would never talk about the war. Never. What I learned about his engagements I had to find out in the history books. . . . But other fathers . . . weaved an interpretation of their experience in a way to help us and their sons understand that war is the last thing you want to be involved with, but we did it to protect our country, etc. . . . We knew our Dad had seen some horrible stuff, but it was comforting to my brothers and me to hear the other fathers speak at least a little bit to give us the feeling that we weren't wrong in asking the question. . . . That's just one example where that bonding and the sharing with other fathers was very important to us in so many other ways.

Dad always [believed] . . . we should give our lives in service to others, and it was so others-oriented that . . . his idea of a vacation was to go to Lake Park, and . . . spend the entire time picking up litter. . . . We never had any fun. And the only time we had fun was when we went to Y-Indian Guides. It's almost like Y-Indian Guides gave him the permission all of a sudden to have fun.

Upon discovering the opportunities Y-Indian Guides provided them, fathers often developed a kind of missionary zeal to attract others into its orbit. As "Chief Thunder Cloud," aka A. A. Miller, wrote in October 1944, "There is no need of us keeping to ourselves the companionship that we have developed. This companionship should actuate the desire to reach many others through churches, schools, and communities and enlist them to help us carry on the understanding of each other and make our organization the only and the greatest father-and-son movement in the world."[5]

The specter of war also pushed the YMCA and Indian Guides to emphasize the need to protect American youth in general. Dr. Milton Towner's address at the fifth annual National Longhouse meeting in Chicago in May 1942, "Stay Close to That Boy," makes this clear. What did a boy need? To be courteous and kind, to gain the love of a good woman, and to exhibit Christian virtue—all consistent with the YMCA's youth development goals.[6]

Boys who had grown up and gone to war also continued to connect with their former tribes through Indian Guides. The Shawnee Tribe of Glendale, Missouri, for example, was celebrating its twelfth year in late 1944, and held meetings "when a boy comes back in uniform. Last Christmas [1943] Silver Star (Elliott Chubb), Chief of the Shawnee, sent messages to absent members, so that they were all united in Christmas spirit, even in the midst of war."[7]

Though Indian Guides continued to grow nationally during the war years, it was still not fully integrated into the National Boys' Work Committee. The national YMCA believed Gra-Y and Hi-Y were better suited to shepherd youth through the shocks and stresses of war and help parents keep their children free of foreign influence by properly interpreting the "high powered propaganda of every resourceful nation."[8]

Though it had yet to become the YMCA's premier youth program, the Indian Guides' twenty-fifth anniversary in 1951 offered an opportunity to celebrate its achievements and remarkable growth from one "tribe" in St. Louis into a national program with 943 "tribes" and a total enrollment of 19,800 fathers and sons. It was an auspicious year; its leadership expected Indian Guides to take its place alongside other historic YMCA programs also celebrating milestones, including basketball (sixtieth) and the North American movement (hundredth). They believed these anniversaries were "news 'naturals.'"[9]

One suggested editorial, from a twenty-fifth anniversary media play-book titled "Lo, The Vanquishing Indian," credited Y-Indian Guides for increasing "the red man's stock" among boys. All the suggested editorials claimed that Indian Guides was a cure for juvenile delinquency. There were several suggestions to combat "the Hopalong cowboy epidemic" by staging media events where youth turned in their six-guns for Indian headdresses.[10] This campaign was part of an ongoing effort to accelerate program growth. The ensuing expansion, however, elicited renewed scrutiny from the National Council, and sparked another cycle of debates concerning the role and prominence Indian Guides should play in the YMCA's youth development strategy.

Preparations for the anniversary also gave the St. Louis Y opportunity to highlight its role in creating Indian Guides. Plans were already under-way in early 1950 to create a "National Y-Indian Guides Reservation" from a portion of the Conference Camp on Sunnen Lake near Potosi, Missouri. In honor of his many years of service, the National Pow-Wow in Chicago passed a resolution in February 1950 to name the camp after William Hefelfinger, or rather his "Indian" name, Negaunee. Hefelfinger hoped the camp could provide "wonderful opportunit[ies] for . . . planned workshop[s] stressing conservation."[11] By October, as plans were taking shape, "Negaunee" further observed that boys should be taught how to live in the outdoors, how to find food and cook it. "We want him to learn about the flowers, the trees, and the birds. We want him to know about the stars, something about the weather and geology, something of conservation and above all how these things all fit in the master plan of the Supreme Being."[12] In conjunction with the twenty-fifth anniversary celebration, *Long House News* editor John Ledlie asked that the National Board award an "illuminated certificate" to observe the establishment of Camp Negaunee. "Such designation," said Ledlie, "would seem to me to have some excellent public relations value."[13] Public support for the National Y-Indian Guide Reservation was so strong that the National Board issued a charter for Camp Negaunee, which positioned it as an independent association similar to historic YMCA retreat centers in Lake Geneva, Wisconsin; Silver Bay, New York; and Estes Park, Colorado.[14] "Big Chief" Walter Brockman and "Assistant Big Chief" J. Edwards Dodds drew rudimentary plans intended to mold the eighty-acre plot of land adjacent to the YMCA camp property into a conference ground and demonstration center. It is unclear why the plans never came to fruition, except as a site used by local "tribes," but Hefelfinger and the St. Louis YMCA certainly placed too much faith in the campground's power to draw people from hundreds of miles away who had perfectly good campgrounds close to home. Like the volunteers whose enthusiastic presentation overcame significant obstacles to make Y-Indian Guides a national program, Camp Negaunee highlights a growing dynamic within and between Y-Indian Guides and the YMCA; the conviction of die-hard supporters regarding the "obvious" merits of the program and the ability of those supporters, frequently men of means and influence, to get YMCAs to either endorse their efforts or simply get out of their way.

One byproduct of this effort was the construction of the "Y-Indian Guide Museum," a forty-foot teepee-shaped structure built in 1962 to house "historical materials and documents" related to the founding of the program and to recognize the essential roles played by Joe Friday, Harold Keltner, and William Heffelfinger (and, of course, the city of St. Louis) in its creation.[15] While the museum was no doubt a stopping point for Indian Guides "tribes" using the camp, it slowly fell into disuse. Sometime in the 1990s, the building was vandalized and items were stolen. Though the structure remains, only its shape suggests any association with Y-Indian Guides.

As Indian Guides continued to grow—in fact, explode in the postwar period—the YMCA would regularly struggle with how to understand it, define it and its overall benefit, and turn it into a feeder program funneling thousands of young boys into the Y's youth development scheme. The potential of this dream becoming a reality kept Y officials tied to Indian Guides for decades but also led to repeated confusion, concern, and consternation.

TENSIONS BETWEEN THE NATIONAL COUNCIL
AND THE NATIONAL LONGHOUSE

For more than three decades, the YMCA and Indian Guides endured a sometimes promising, often troubled relationship that never truly resolved. One significant point of tension was the Y's expectation that Indian Guides be a fully integrated YMCA program. They expected all "tribes" to employ YMCA-produced curricula, program books, and other

resources to create a well-organized, uniform program. Most importantly, they hoped fathers, many of them well-connected men of means,
would "graduate" their sons out of Y-Indian Guides at age nine and
send them on through Gra-Y, Junior Hi-Y, and Hi-Y. Upon completion
of this cycle, the Y believed, millions of Americans (and ultimately the
nation) would be influenced for the better by the Christian young men
produced by the YMCA. What the Y repeatedly discovered, however,
despite their best efforts, was that young "Indians" rarely wanted to become "Y men." They also hoped that, out of gratitude for the Y's role in
their more intimate relationships with their sons, fathers would join the
boards of their local Ys and become loyal, reliable, financially supportive
members. While the Y often suggested otherwise, these expectations were
realized in some areas but certainly not all. Many "tribes" saw themselves
as connected to but also largely independent from the YMCA, leaving Y
national boards scratching their heads, wondering exactly why they were
tethered to a program they did not control and whose concrete benefits
to members and to the Y often remained difficult to quantify. Others
adopted a laissez-faire philosophy, allowing Indian Guides leaders to do
whatever they wished.

One attempt at standardization was the first national program manual
for Indian Guides, published in 1942 not by the St. Louis Y, which lost
its bid to maintain control over Indian Guides, but by the Y's National
Council. Now under the purview of the Boys' Work Committee, the
manual emphasized "explicit as well as implicit" character and citizenship training, a longtime focus of the YMCA.[16] Seeking to avoid the
social breakdown that characterized the American home front in World
War I, Y leaders included projects designed to mitigate against intoler-
ance. Democratic participation and community service were encouraged
through the tribes' organization and suggested activities. Emphasis was
placed on the boys planning and carrying out tasks themselves. Prayers
and references to the Great Spirit, whose blessing on tribal activities
and father-son relationships was always sought, reinforced the Y's desire
to promote Christian living. Indeed, the YMCA's National Council reworked the Eight Aims of the Indian Guides, making the fifth aim the
Gospel's Golden Rule: "To love my neighbor as myself."[17]

Harold Keltner's vision of a national Y-Indian Guide movement became a reality after the war through the unceasing efforts of the National

Longhouse, the sometimes grudging support of the YMCA national office, and the dedication of thousands of volunteers. By 1948, there were 231 "tribes" in twenty states, an increase of 34 from the previous year. One of those 34 was the Blackfeet tribe of Gary, Indiana. Dave Lehleitner, now a St. Louis resident, was seven years old when his father Glen was president of the Gary YMCA. Joe Friday was touring the Chicago area, and according to Lehleitner, Gary was his first stop. Lehleitner's father was so impressed with what he saw that "he said, 'Yes, we will form a tribe,' and Dad got all of these individuals, bankers, US Steel workers." Lehleitner continued,

> The Indian Guides have had a big impact on my life. . . . I was Swift Cloud, my [older] brother was Red Bear and my dad was Big Swift Cloud. . . . I think Joe Friday came back a couple of times. . . . The Ojibwe Indians believed in a father and son relationship and of course . . . that's what [Joe Friday] represented, was this ideal of a Father and Son Indian way. . . . You would learn as a son the obedience to your father and the father teaches leadership to the son. . . . My dad passed away a while back but do you know how we signed off [in our letters] until the day he died? "Pals Forever."[18]

The continued growth of the program only exacerbated the Boys' Work Committee's concerns that tribes lacked proper supervision and exhibited little to no allegiance to the YMCA. Establishing a pattern for the future, the national committee, after extensive discussion, decided this concern could be allayed with adequate supervision, though it set no standards for what that meant.[19] Though a 1949 Boys' Work Committee review determined that Indian Guides met the fundamental requirements of a program for boys ages six to nine, proper supervision remained a concern for critics.[20] The national committee, however, declared it "unrealistic" for Indian Guides to meet anywhere other than in their own homes.[21]

Lehleitner, who experienced the program as a son, father, and godfather, expressed an opinion not unlike that of his father's: "I always believed Indian Guides needed strong lay leadership. It is not a program that you can just depend upon the professionals at the Y. . . . It needs a real ramrod job from lay people." This competing sense of who was better suited to control Indian Guides never abated. During the twenty-fifth anniversary celebration, St. Louis area Indian Guide "chiefs" used the occasion to champion the role and authority of individual tribes over those of the YMCA. An unattributed 1950 document from the Webster Groves branch of St. Louis and St. Louis County, known collectively as "the Mississippi Nation," noted that "for several years the Indian Guides were considered solely a St. Louis Movement, and were not accorded national recognition." In the author's opinion, "the greatest growth of the Movement in the St. Louis area occurred in those sections where there were no preconceived patterns of boys' work." The Mississippi Nation operated under two principles: "1. The growth of the Movement in Webster Groves is the responsibility of the laymen. . . . 2. The role of [Y staff] . . . is [as] an advisor and counselor. This is not stated directly, but is implied." The success or failure of any tribe always rested "with the men who help make it up." Since the Mississippi Nation had sixteen tribes in 1950, the author noted, no Y secretary could possibly "act in an advisory capacity" to them all. To the author's knowledge, "every tribe . . . in the Mississippi Nation was organized by a member of another tribe. No 'Y' Secretary has had any significant role" in establishing any of them. Despite statements less than subtly inferring that the YMCA should leave the running of Indian Guides to its lay leadership, the article concluded with a familiar prediction best explaining why the Y continued its tenuous relationship with Indian Guides for so long:

> Following this program of placing responsibility on the shoulders of the men, who by the very nature of the organization have to run their own show, this Movement has been a rich source of good adult leadership, and [emphasis ours] *potentially it can produce more leaders for the YMCA than any other single program we are now operating.* It is at this point we should act with wisdom in keeping laymen active, and in strengthening their hand by furnishing them with resource material which will make their experience one of satisfaction.[22]

DEATH OF AN ICON

The April 1954 edition of *Long House News* detailed the story of "Little Running Bear." The previous winter, Joe Friday had visited his

Cherokee Indian Guides "tribe" in South Bend, Indiana, and invited them to come visit him in Canada. "Little Running Bear," his brother "Snapping Turtle," and their father "Big Running Bear" made the long trek, concluding with a four-and-a-half-hour boat ride from the village of Temagami to Joe Friday's island. They caught fish, which Joe fried for them. They took a boat to the mainland for firewood and watched Joe fell a tall, dead red pine tree "about 11 inches in diameter" located half-way up a rocky hill. As the boys climbed to watch, Joe "felled the tree up the hill. He then pulled the tree back across the stump and sawed it into eight foot lengths." Revealing a common white stereotype, "Little Running Bear" observed that "if all Indians worked as hard as Joe, they shouldn't ever be called lazy." Friday responded to this comment by pointing out "all the things there are to see in the great forest when you take the time to be 'lazy.'" He noted the reflection of the water on the leaves of the trees and shared a legend about the loons as they watched them swim in the waters below. After rolling the logs Joe had cut down the hill, the boys peppered him with questions about his life as a young boy and learned many Ojibwe words, which they shared with their readers. Friday also took his visitors to an old, abandoned gold mine on another island, where the boys collected rock samples. As "Little Running Bear" shared with his readers, "it was the best vacation a boy could ever have, especially with Joe Friday for a guide."[23]

On February 10, 1955, Joe Friday died. He had been ill for a year and had been diagnosed with bone cancer less than a month before his death.[24] When the National Longhouse executive committee met in South Bend eight days later, the committee noted that Friday's remains would not be buried on Bear Island until the spring, when he could be laid to rest next to his wife. They decided that an official committee of Y-Indian Guides would attend the interment service. Members considered the most appropriate type of memorial for Mr. Friday, including monuments at various Y camps, including Camp Negaunee outside St. Louis; plaques designed by Harold Keltner (who had retired from the St. Louis YMCA the previous September[25]) displayed in Y buildings; a flag bearing Friday's image; and a memorial page in a new edition of the Y-Indian Guides handbook. It was ultimately decided that Keltner and William Carmichael of South Bend make a decision and report back

Figure 20. A portrait of Joe Friday wearing his famous buckskin jacket. This image was used in many editions of the Y-Indian Guides manual. *Long House News* 19, no. 2 (December 1955).

to the committee. Before the evening session adjourned, they passed a resolution stating:

> In the passing of Joe Friday our Movement lost a man who was able to bridge the gap between two civilizations and gave to our Movement the inspiration and Christian leadership which served as a stimulus to all big and little braves who knew him as they worked in the Y-Indian Guide movement.
>
> Therefore, be it resolved THAT this body go on record:
>
> 1. To extend sympathies and best wishes of this Long House to his family

2. That we memorialize his services by a rededication of our lives to the principles of Christian service and Christian fellowship by increasing the Y-Indian Guides movement through closer relationship of father and son.

The board's resolution was sent to Friday's nephew, Donald Potts, as well as the chief of the Canadian Ojibwe tribe.[26] The May edition of *Long House News* made note of the executive committee's resolution and reported that the National Longhouse meeting that year opened with a "very impressive memorial."[27] The December edition was prepared by the Indian Guides "tribes" of Fort Wayne, Indiana, where Harold and Martha Keltner had just attended the Indiana State Long House in September. As a result, it included an extensive history of Indian Guides, and Keltner once again told the stories about the origins of Indian Guides already shared in these pages. "Because Mr. Keltner gives Joe Friday, his Ojibway friend, much credit for the inspiration that brought Y-Indian Guides into being," *Long House News* reported, "we thought you would enjoy reading in his own words of their first meeting and his relation to the earliest tribe."[28]

In February 1956 the executive committee met in San Diego and received a report from members William Carmichael, Leo Fisher, and Cecil Foster about their attendance at Friday's burial ceremony, including "a series of Kodachrome slides." All assembled were "greatly moved, impressed, and inspired." At the committee's request, Keltner wrote the text inscribed on Friday's headstone, to which all Indian Guides "tribes" were asked to contribute.[29] The December 1957 edition of *Long House News* features a photograph of the marker placed at Friday's grave, which reads:

Joseph Friday (AHTIK)
Born November 10, 1887
Died February 10, 1955
Co-Founder of Y-Indian Guides
In our hearts as long as the rivers flow and the grass is green
Erected by
The National Longhouse of the Y.M.C.A.

Indian Guides
All Fathers and Sons

Friday's nephew sent a thank-you letter expressing gratitude "on behalf of our Chief, the Friday family, myself, and all my late Uncle Joe's
many friends from Bear Island and Temagami . . . for the erection of this
beautiful memorium."

Friday's grave is on a high bluff on the east end of Bear Island on
Lake Temagami.[30] While descendants of Friday's still live on Bear Island,
almost none had memories of him when we reached out in 2017. None
wished to comment on his association with Y-Indian Guides, or the fact
that his headstone refers not to his actual tribal affiliation, his business
dealings, or his political leadership in Canada, but to an oft-criticized
father-son program in the United States.

DOES GROWTH EQUAL SUCCESS?

From 1950 to 1958, Indian Guides grew exponentially, enlarging its
ranks from 943 to 9,644 tribes. From within the YMCA this work was
conducted or advised by 3,489 professional staff, 567 of which were
focused on youth.[31] Though many Indian Guides participants were also
counted as YMCA members, these numbers still tell us two things. First,
by 1958 the Indian Guides program was the largest YMCA youth development program as measured by the number of clubs, and the fourth
largest in terms of the number of youth enrolled. Second, as described
above, that success was largely the result of lay leaders' passion and dedication. YMCA staff with numerous other responsibilities could only
expend so much effort. It was fathers, recruiting their neighbors, serving
as longhouse chiefs, and meeting nationally to nurture the program,
who were the driving force behind the program's success and who, as
a result, had less affinity to and were less likely to be recruited by the
broader YMCA. These twin forces of growth and decentralization made
individual Indian Guides "tribes" less uniform, giving each the freedom
to harness, interpret, and caricature the Indian origin and themes of the
program as they wished.

In 1957 and 1958, still attempting to clarify the relationship
between itself and Indian Guides, the YMCA's National Council

continued to hope that "Indians" would become members of their succession of Y youth programs. At the very least they wanted older boys to "cast off some of the 'kid stuff,'" increase their level of physical activity, and "maintain the father and son relationship through such activities as weekend fishing trips, learning about guns, [and] going to sports events as a group."[32] When they sought input from Y staff and laymen on how to improve support for boys' work, one suggestion was the development of administrative practices within local Ys, giving both father and son "a sense of their membership relationship to the YMCA."[33] Strengthening this relationship was important, since in 1958 the Indian Guides' National Longhouse became a voting member of the National Council, elevating its influence within the YMCA movement.[34]

Indian Guides had arrived, not only as a full-fledged YMCA program but as a force to be reckoned with in many communities across the country. From September 12 to 18, 1960, for example, the Garden Court of Southdale in Edina, Minnesota, America's first fully enclosed,

Figure 21. "Y Indian Guide-A-Rama," a weeklong exposition held in September 1960 at Southdale Mall in Edina, Minnesota. *Long House News* 24, no. 2 (December 1960).

climate-controlled mall, hosted a weeklong "Y Indian Guide-A-Rama," putting Indian Guides in the community spotlight. The week culminated on the eighteenth with a two-and-a-half-hour program featuring Harold Keltner, Minnesota governor Orville Freeman, US representative Walter Judd, Minneapolis mayor P. Kenneth Peterson, and longtime WCCO radio personality Jergen Nash. The "conservatively estimated" crowd of five thousand was also serenaded by the Minneapolis Honeywell Band and Diversified Services Chorus. Though the Twin Cities area already boasted "some 275" Indian Guide tribes, event sponsors hoped to recruit many more into the fold under the imprimatur of state and community leaders.[35]

WE MUST STUDY THIS PROGRAM

In addition to its lack of clarity, the YMCA-Indian Guides relationship was also affected by decades of social change and breakthroughs in developmental and social sciences. As the father became less of a dominating and removed figure in society and the family, the understanding of the father-son relationship began to change. Questions increased about whether fathers needed to form similar bonds with their daughters, or whether mothers needed to have similar opportunities to bond with their children. African American fathers and sons also began to participate in Indian Guides, though in small numbers, bringing questions about whether National Pow-Wows would be integrated.

In 1959 and 1961, the YMCA's national board commissioned two studies of Y-Indian Guides. The first, conducted by Dr. Robert D. Hess of the University of Chicago's Committee on Human Relations, identified and evaluated the program's educational objectives and familial benefits.[36] Originating in the Chicagoland area, the study was supplemented with surveys in Portland, San Francisco, Los Angeles, Dallas, Kansas City, Milwaukee, Atlanta, Silver Springs, and Philadelphia. According to the study, the typical Indian Guides father was between thirty and forty and "very much over-represented in the professional and executive groups and under-represented in the skilled and unskilled workers category," a "pattern not too different from participation in the YMCA generally." After all, the ability to participate in Indian Guides was influenced by the size of one's home (able to host ten or more

guests), the presence of a stay-at-home mother who provided treats at
the end of the evening's meeting, and the ability to have some control
over one's working schedule.

Most members were Protestant, though twelve percent were Jewish
and nine percent Catholic. Unlike the average YMCA member, who
joined an organization designed as an auxiliary to the church (though
this association was waning), most Indian Guides fathers attended
services no more than once a month. Most had no exposure to the Y
before joining Indian Guides, and eighty-one percent participated in no
other Y program after joining, though eighty percent reported that the
Y supported them.

Two types of fathers entered the program: those happy with their relationship who nonetheless found it difficult to make time for their sons,
and those uncomfortable with their relationship who relied on Indian
Guides to create the time and space needed to improve the relationship.
Fifty-eight percent said they joined to spend more time with their families. More than half reported a change in the "pattern of interaction
outside of tribal meetings" constituting a beneficial "spill over" into the
rest of the family that improved their overall quality of life.

Most fathers believed their sons were typical, but almost two-thirds
thought their relationship with their sons was better than the one they
had with their own fathers. Regarding the motto "Pals forever," one camp
strongly supported the "pal" relationship, while the other felt it overem-
phasized equality. Lastly, fathers generally agreed that "ritual adds a good
bit to Y-Indian Guides," and "the Indian theme adds significance and
constitutes an essential part of the program." Praise for the Indian motif
was not universal, though in some cases fathers wanted more rather than
less of it. Some expressed dissatisfaction with the amount and types of
ritual employed. Dr. Hess presented his findings before the National
Longhouse, forecasting how the "changing roles in American life for
both men and women" might affect the development of the program.[37]
He thought it was awfully difficult to be a patriarch within a forty-hour
workweek. He saw the "do it yourself movement" as a father's response
to not knowing how to behave like a father when faced with a great
deal of leisure time. Moreover, Hess noted the demise of the historical
"patriarch . . . who is somewhat autocratic, who rules both his children

and his wife with a strong hand, who is at work most of the time and has very little opportunity for fun or play, a distant figure who is reserved and stern but essentially just."[38] Ironically, this was the very kind of patriarchy—not masculinity, but patriarchy—Indian Guides was designed to soften by promoting a kinder, more loving, playful father who was active in all aspects of family life. Hess was not alone in his belief that American masculinity was becoming, as sociologist Daniel Bell put it, "soft." A year prior, *Look* magazine ran a series of articles on "the decline of the American male," which would ultimately be published in book form. Historian K. A. Cuordileone traces this "crisis" to the anxiety of the Cold War and perceived forces of conformity that pushed men to adopt feminized roles that were directed toward others.[39]

While acknowledging the program's value, Hess claimed that Indian Guides was "missing the boat" in helping to preserve masculine identity, which he felt was under assault. Seeing the program and the nation at a crossroads, he offered two framing questions for consideration. First, what kind of emotional and social distance should there be between parents and children? Hess thought that fathers surrendered their "stature and dignity" when they became their sons' pals. Second, what kind of masculine model should be held up to the son? Hess saw Indigenous peoples as inherently masculine. He also felt that in recruiting for the program, the inadequacies and negative aspects of white fathers were "unnecessarily emphasize[d]."[40]

By way of answering those questions, a follow-up study was commissioned two years later. Authored by Professor (called "Mrs." in the report) Bess-Gene Holt of Purdue University, this new study expanded its inquiry beyond the father-son relationship of Y-Indian Guides participants to include the "need and desirability" of a father-daughter and/or mother-daughter YMCA program. Referencing the 1959 Hess study, which did not support an alternative for women and girls, Holt felt that the YMCA should create a separate father-daughter program so that Indian Guides could preserve its "masculine emphasis," noting that "the roles of males in our society are being changed and redefined. [Indian Guides] should offer clear, authoritative definitions of these roles." Unbeknownst to Holt, some local associations, as early as 1949, had already begun to form parent-daughter programs.

WHAT ABOUT THE GIRLS?

The involvement of women and girls in the activities of the YMCA is a story of incremental gains, one mirroring the nation as a whole. During the earliest years of the YMCA, several associations welcomed the presence of women at social events and prayer groups. Evangelist Dwight L. Moody, whose early career was with the Chicago YMCA, once commented that without women, YMCA events were "pretty dry prayer meetings." Yet as the YMCA expanded its presence into all aspects of their members' lives (education and physical work in addition to religious work), women were largely relegated to support roles: women's auxiliaries that offered hospitality, promoted the YMCA, and solicited funds for the organization. In 1943 the National Council conducted a constituency study in preparation of the global centennial of the movement. They discovered that women and girls represented ten percent of all members, with half of all Ys reporting female members. Clearly women and girls desired to participate in YMCA programs, including Indian Guides.

Figure 22. Mamie Sunley, left, of Huntington, Indiana, started the first Indian Guides "tribe" for girls in 1949, apparently at Joe Friday's suggestion. *Long House News* 14, no. 2 (November–December 1949).

In late 1949 Mamie Sunley told readers of *Long House News* about her role in starting the first known Indian Guides tribe for girls. Sunley met Joe Friday at the February 1949 Association of Secretaries conference, where "he asked me to start a tribe of Indian Girl Guides. That had been an ambition of his wife, who had passed away." As with

Harold Keltner, who had no sons, Sunley started a "tribe" though she had no daughters. She selected five girls from her swimming class who belonged neither to Girl Scouts nor took music, drama, or dancing lessons, writing personal invitations to each of their mothers. After the first meeting, all but one mother invited a friend and her daughter. The second meeting included "nine mothers, ten girls, and myself." The girls' program was similar to the boys', though "due to home circumstances all meetings were held in the 'Y.'" By November the response had been so enthusiastic that "we are going to have four groups." Another mother-daughter program was formed in 1951 in South Bend, Indiana. Shortly thereafter, actual "tribes" for mothers and daughters were organized in Torrance, California, by Alpha Rena, the branch's first female program director.[41] The increasing interest in reaching young girls was not shared in the national office, which had only tentatively discussed the possibility and appropriateness of sponsoring father-daughter or mother-daughter programs.

This new tension, in line with others covered in this chapter, was in part a byproduct of World War II, which had rapidly transformed common perceptions of women's roles in society. During the war, millions of women entered the workforce. At war's end, many were interested in keeping their jobs or at least not surrendering to the "cult of domesticity" that had reemerged in the postwar era as the United States reintegrated veterans into civilian life and emphasized the centrality of the family. Increasingly aware of these changes, YMCA youth work leaders met in 1954 to consider expanding the scope of Y-Indian Guides to include mother-daughter programs patterned after the father-son model. The National Committee on Youth Programs, concerned that these additions would detract from critical focus on the rapidly growing Y-Indian Guides movement, tabled the discussion.

Nonetheless, many local YMCAs worked with young girls; nearly three thousand clubs for junior high and high school girls are listed in the 1951 *YMCA Year Book and Official Roster*. At the national level, however, debate regarding the utility and desirability of such programs dragged on without resolution. In 1961 the National Committee on Youth Programs finally developed a set of principles related to the need for and desirability of a program for young girls similar to Indian

Guides. But once it had been discussed in earnest, the conversation quickly turned to its potentially negative impact on boys.

Informed by the Hess and Holt studies, the development of new principles for girls demonstrates only a modest evolution in the YMCA's thinking about the roles of fathers, mothers, and children. Parent-child and father-child language did begin to supplant the traditional father-son emphasis of the past. But even while opening the door to a mother-daughter program, Indian Guides leadership continued to reassert the supremacy of the father in the family. The committee discouraged a blended group of mothers, fathers, and children, citing the importance (though providing no examples) of allowing children to see fathers "doing things that mother cannot do." (As Holt stated in her 1961 study, children had "more opportunity to be with mothers than fathers; mothers meet more needs of children, and are preferred by children.") This doubling down on the primacy of the father and his parental needs is not surprising. The original intention of Indian Guides was to create opportunities (heretofore nonexistent, in the Y's view) for a father, a boy's first role model, to interact with his son(s). Yet, Hess and Holt's studies both asserted, American patriarchy and fatherhood were under tremendous negative pressure. In fact, these perceived pressures led to various plans to enhance the "masculine elements" of the program. One suggestion was to use Indian Guides as a space for youth to "identify themselves with adults" as they "go through the period of sorting out their feelings about men and women." (As this comment suggests, and as we will discuss shortly, boys were remaining in Indian Guides well past the original recommended age of nine.) Such discussions clearly would be conducted with a WASP heterosexual view, which suggests another imperative behind keeping boys and fathers separate from mothers and daughters: boys needed to aspire to masculinity and eschew femininity. Clearly, YMCA and Indian Guides leaders felt the ages targeted by Indian Guides were particularly vulnerable or malleable; boys in particular needed a strong masculine role model during these formative years. This position stands in stark contrast to the YMCA's programs for youth ages nine and older (Gra-Y, Junior Hi–Y, and Hi-Y), which were frequently co-ed by the 1960s, though these programs were not parent-child oriented. Ironically, the eventual inclusion of women and girls through Y-Indian Maidens (mother/daughter) and Y-Indian Princesses (father/daughter) in the early 1970s provided sorely needed membership during the last decades of the Y-Indian Guides programs, and these groups represent the bulk of the independent "tribes" active today.

Figure 23. A Y-Indian Princess father-daughter group, metropolitan St. Louis, October 1977. As father-son membership plateaued in the 1970s, father-daughter programs began to take off. Gateway Region Young Men's Christian Association (S0473).

"FIXING" THE PROBLEMS

By 1967 YMCA leaders had formed a series of task groups to evaluate problems within Y-Indian Guides that had remained relatively unchanged, despite all their previous studies, committees, and planning groups.

Though Indian Guides was "growing by leaps and bounds," popularity was not synonymous with effectiveness. Y leadership remained unclear about whether Indian Guides was in harmony with "Association

purposes, human needs, values desired, and benefit to individuals."
More studies were commissioned, conducted by child experts in consultation with seasoned Indian Guides participants. This time, they
hoped they would finally be able to create a responsible, uniform experience with measurable results that could be used to constantly improve
the program.[42]

One persisting concern regarded the appropriate ages for participation in Indian Guides. Even in the early 1940s there were tribes with
members in junior and senior high school.[43] A 1962 National Council
survey revealed that 526 of the 3,943 responding tribes (thirteen percent) had an older-boy tribe. Seventy-two percent of the older-boy tribes
were following the recommendations of a Y-Indian Guides executive
committee to "drop the kid stuff" and hold more outdoor activities.[44]
Standing in stark contrast to the national Y's expectation that boys
"age out" of Indian Guides, the prevailing wisdom of Y-Indian Guide
leadership (according to the 1960s task group) was that boys up to age
eleven could become an integral part of the National Longhouse. In
that same year, age ranges were removed from Indian Guides literature
and a chapter on programming for older boys was added to the manual. The YMCA now stated that a "tribe" should remain active as long
as the members wished. Indian Guides could help guide not only the
strengthening of the father-son relationship but also, in older boys, the
"wholesome separation of father and son."[45]

One suggested modification for the older boy groups was to adopt new
names, many of which were taken from existing older boys' groups. For
example, Y-Warriors in Minneapolis followed the traditional Y-Indian
Guides program with different terminology, a special emblem, a revised
opening ritual, and unique headdress. Foreshadowing the program that
ultimately replaced Y-Indian Guides, groups in New Jersey, Washington,
DC, and Illinois formed YMCA Adventure Guides for older boys.

For critics, the council's decision to allow boys to persist in Indian
Guides as long as they wished must have been a bitter pill to swallow.
Yet Indian Guides had experienced thousand-percent growth in membership from 1952 to 1962 (though numbers had plateaued between
1960 and 1962); it was hard to argue with that success. In 1964 there
were more than 14,000 tribes, with a total membership of over 200,000.

Exerting some measure of control and uniformity over the program was a second sore spot for the national YMCA. Y-Indian Guides' massive success, at least numerically, meant it was increasingly part of popular culture. Professional sports franchises often invited Indian Guides tribes to their games. The most "natural" connection was with the Atlanta Braves and Cleveland Indians (now Guardians) baseball clubs. A photo from 1959 shows Cleveland players, including catcher Hal Naragon and pitcher Herb Score, wearing faux Indian headdresses while standing in front of four little "braves." Mayors, governors, and other officials met with fathers and sons, even issuing official proclamations celebrating Y-Indian Guides. In 1961 San Antonio mayor Raymond Telles declared October 8–15 Y-Indian Guides Week; Senator Jacob Javits of New York received a petition from regional chief John J. Geier and his two sons supporting the declaration of a National American Indian Day—a bill Javits sponsored.[46]

It should be noted that Y-Indian Guide Week involved far more than a mayoral or gubernatorial proclamation. The 1970 national Y-Indian Guide Week kit, for example, distributed by the YMCA national board, provided insight on how to create the most effective and active committee for promoting Indian Guides; potential scripts for fifteen-second, thirty-second, and full minute radio and TV spots; and advice on how to work with the media and curry favor with public officials. An ambitious week's worth of activities was laid out: Sunday should include a YMCA open house with a special family swim and picnic with booths and displays and a Sunday news release with pictures; on Monday the longhouse chief should host the "mayor, school adminis-trators, ministers, neighborhood leaders, and press, radio-TV reporters for luncheon" to initiate the week's promotions. Membership materials should be distributed to every school's first- and second-grade students, and fathers should meet for a final training session; Tuesday should feature a "coffee klatsch" with neighborhood mothers to explain and promote the program, a TV segment featuring an Indian Guides father and son, and "membership promotion and tribal organization meetings" in all neighborhood schools; Wednesday should involve a news release in all community newspapers describing the history of Indian Guides, a talk by the YMCA about the program at a "Service Club Luncheon," and more membership promotional activity; Thursday should include a meeting with the local Y board of directors to recognize outstanding "tribal" leaders, a radio or TV interview "with women's editor interpreting [the] family import of Y-Indian Guides," and a final night of membership promotion"; and Friday would feature a powwow and craft display at the local Y and a special program "recognizing the dignity of the American Indian," a news release promoting the history of Y-Indian Guides and a calendar of upcoming events, and a father-son visit with an "outstanding college or professional athlete or evening sports program." Saturday brought not rest but a "Y-Indian Guide Parade in neighborhoods close to large shopping centers"; a Y-Indian Guides Carnival at the YMCA for dads and sons, with the proceeds going to fund travel to the following year's National Longhouse; and a "Pancake Feed for the Whole YMCA Family," the profits being sent to "help an American Indian Reservation or Family."[47] While this suggested schedule seems both exhausting and unrealistic, the accomplishments mentioned above and below suggest that more than a few "tribes" put a great deal of thought and effort into such events.

On August 18, 1962, while visiting Fresno, California, President John F. Kennedy received an in-person invitation to that year's National Longhouse. Its prose conveyed more whimsy than gravity: "President Kennedy, Great White Father, HOW! Great nation of Indian braves wishum you to come to twenty-sixth Annual Y-Indian Guide National Long House. Pow wow lastum three days, February 8, 9, and 10, in

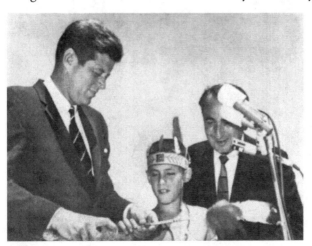

Figure 24. President Kennedy receiving an invitation to the 1962 National Longhouse. *Long House News* 26, no. 2 (1962).

Figure 25. Minnesota governor Elmer L. Andersen receives a "tribe" of young "Indians" in his office, early 1950s. Kautz Family YMCA Archives, University of Minnesota Libraries.

village white man call Fresno. Givem you much good time. Many strong Indian youth (physically fit) and plenty father (maybe not so fit)." The same issue of *Long House News* that reported on the Kennedy invitation also reproduced a thank-you letter from astronaut John Glenn, who was named an honorary member of the Donelson (Nashville, TN) YMCA's Fox "tribe."[48] In 1966 Michigan governor George Romney declared the week of September 23 to 29 "Y-Indian Guides Week in Michigan, in recognition of the excellence of this program." Romney received a plaque from Charles Beadle and his son, second-grader "Chip," and posed for a picture in which the youngster placed a faux "Indian" war bonnet on his head. Pennsylvania governor William Scranton issued a similar proclamation. Oregon governor Tom McCall followed suit two years later.[49] (From the perspective of Y leadership, even more impressive than the publicity itself was the ability of Indian Guides fathers to gain access to political figures.) But the greatest exposure at this time came in the 1960 film *The Facts of Life*, in which Bob Hope played a father who participated with his son in the Indian Guides program. Any potential, however, for using the movie to its advantage was undermined by the scene's use only for comic effect. Hope, whose character has begun an extramarital affair with the also-married Lucille Ball, is kept from an adulterous rendezvous by an agonizingly long report on smoke signals read by another boy in the tribe.

Figure 26: Bob Hope hamming it up for the camera as he is made an honorary Y-Indian Guides chief. Hope starred in the movie *The Facts of Life*, in which he and his son are part of an Indian Guides "tribe," but his character's extramarital affair made the film a poor promotional vehicle for the Y. Kautz Family YMCA Archives, University of Minnesota Libraries.

The National Council, however, did not simply surrender to the wave of Indian Guides' popularity. In 1964 they aligned tribes with the YMCA's new regional, area, and state structures and expected them to coordinate their efforts with their local Ys. Growth of the Indian Guides' magnitude needed management and study, they argued. Looking back on the studies conducted in 1959 and 1961, and renewing their efforts to decode and harness the power of Indian Guides that many leaders neither understood nor believed, the council began a new era of study and evaluation.[50] This study would, however, be colored throughout by the frustrations of national and local Y leaders over what they saw as a one-sided relationship. Though Y staff focused on improving the youth development aspects of the program, they were often reminded that "tribes" were only loosely affiliated with the Y and could largely do what they pleased—and do it for as long as they wished. As grumbling persisted, Y-Indian Guides were increasingly seen as a drain on Y resources (at least by those with no staff who participated in the program), while some tribes saw the Y as intrusive and heavy-handed.[51]

This frustration—and an attempt to mitigate it—was evidenced in a new tribal registration system implemented on September 1, 1967. The ten-point plan announced that "Y-Indian Guides participants are first of all members of a local YMCA and are responsible for its support and direct services." Therefore tribes needed to register directly through their local Y and receive their individual membership cards, which would "designate local membership fees and policies." Each tribe was expected to pay a $5 registration fee to its Y and another $2.50 to the National Longhouse. The National Board would produce and distribute all required registration forms, charters, and seals for big and little braves, and the National Longhouse would print and distribute *Long House News* four times a year "on the basis of 8 per registered tribe." A "national plan for registering Y-Indian Guide groups" was sound and necessary, but would also be evaluated after five years. "Careful interpretation of this total program is primarily dependent upon local YMCA lay and staff leaders," the policy concluded, though with more aspiration than authority.[52]

Similar rhetoric, bold in statement and short on proof, is found in the *1972–73 Father & Son Indian Guides Manual of Practice*: "Y-Indian Guides are an important and integral part of the total Young Men's Christian Association. . . . Fathers and sons in Y-Indian Guides tribes should be considered as members of their local YMCA. Membership in Y-Indian Guides is based upon this principle." Later, with a different typewriter, another sentence was added: "This applies to parent-daughter participants also."[53]

Both the YMCA and Y-Indian Guides were shaped by and responded to societal changes, even while aiming to be a positive influence over them. The shifting family dynamics desired and facilitated by Y-Indian

Guides (a more playful and active father), feared by Hess (an emasculated American father), and sought by women (their own full participation) would accelerate during the civil rights movement. At the same time, as the YMCA movement grappled with its own history of segregation, Indian Guides leadership began to take a more earnest and less naive interest in both the culture and the rights of Native Americans. Ultimately, as imitation transformed into appreciation, the realization that the program had run its course became apparent to some, especially those in critical leadership positions. This awareness, along with a rising tide of protests, potential lawsuits, and a new focus on diversity, finally proved more compelling than the longstanding hope, never truly realized, that Y-Indian Guides would funnel legions of members, volunteers, and donors into YMCAs across the country. But the ultimate decision to phase out Y-Indian Guides would take another thirty years.

CHAPTER SIX

"The Real Feelings and Concerns of the Indian"
The Fracturing of Y-Indian Guides

BY THE 1940S, the first generation of Indian Guides' little braves were becoming men. Edward Cleino, director of music at Vanderbilt University, was a member of St. Louis' very first "tribe," the Osage. In 1941 he wrote to Harold Keltner, sharing how the program had shaped his life: "Indian Guide membership . . . helped my father and me really get to know each other. . . . Through the medium of making things together, exploring together, and the like, we really came to know each other. Mohawk and Swift Eagle will, as the result, never be separated." Indian Guides, wrote Cleino, not only forged a strong bond between himself and his father but transformed him from a selfish child into a broad-minded man. " 'I' was the most important word in the language to me. The world revolved around me, in my own mind. In the Indian Guides . . . I became interested in other people, and that interest has grown until my whole philosophy has been built up about it."[1]

This letter is an early example of a story told time and again: Y-Indian Guides was the formative experience in many father-son relationships, and the catalyst for developing a broader personal and world view.

For some, gaining a broader perspective meant growing closer to family, friends, and members of their community, and enjoying shared experiences. Fathers came down to their sons' level, and sons developed greater awareness of and interest in their fathers.[2] Norris Lineweaver remembers walking on a cold morning to a cafeteria where he worked as a busboy in the mid-1950s. He was wearing an unzipped jacket, "and here comes a former Y-Indian tribe father in his utility truck . . . [who] rolled down the window and said, 'Little Brave Running Crow, you need to zip up that jacket.' I didn't hesitate, I zipped up that jacket! I'll *never* forget that. . . . Fathers looked out for each others' sons, and you just didn't go walking down the street with a slumped shoulder. They were going to come up to you: 'Straighten up, young man.' "[3]

Two American Indian boys in their ceremonial dance costumes meet Father and Son Y-Indian Guides at the Abington Branch YMCA, Philadelphia. Jacob and Marvin Frague, Jemez Pueblo, New Mexico, have been guests of the Lenape Nation at Abington for the month of June. Big Brave Don Shapiro and Little Brave Bryan Shapiro of the Cedar Hook Tribe are admiring the costumes of the real native Americans. In the center is William Hepburn, National Longhouse Tallykeeper and active in the Lenape Nation at Abington.

Figure 27. Jacob and Marvin Frague, two Jemez Pueblo boys from New Mexico, display their ceremonial dance attire to William Hepburn, center, National Longhouse Tallykeeper and member of the Lenape "tribe" of the Abingdon YMCA of Philadelphia, and father and son Don and Bryan Shapiro. The Frague brothers spent June 1963 as guests of the Lenape "tribe." *Long House News* 27, no. 1 (1963) , University of Minnesota Libraries.

For a significant number of others, Indian Guides also became a vehicle through which they developed an interest in contemporary Indigenous peoples, a process that national leadership earnestly sought to cultivate. *Long House News* editorial staff shared factual (as best they could tell), or at least positive, depictions of American Indians. While one must acknowledge that Indian Guides was dominated by caricatures of Indigenous peoples, there are numerous examples of attempts to show native people as members of unique, individual tribal nations, not a monolithic group. By the 1940s there was a marked increase in reeducation efforts, including true-false quizzes on native "facts" (e.g., popular myth: "Indians were not tolerant of white men's ideas"; fact: "Indians always listened respectfully to the views of white men. Some ideas they accepted, others they did not. You have never heard them say 'the only good white man is a dead one"). *Long House News* denounced the word *squaw* as a name imposed by white men. After looking into several languages, they recommended "Ta."[4] The newsletter, however, never abandoned fictitious or stereotyped writings and, aided by a growing national appetite for westerns, fueled by television, film, and literature, slowly developed an almost bipolar narrative, simultaneously humanizing and lampooning American Indians.

Nonetheless, examples of positive if not always entirely accurate depictions of Native Americans and Indigenous culture in *Long House News* abound. From the March 1939 issue, a letter from a Chicago "tribe" included a photo of "Indian signposts"—trees that had been bent over as saplings by Indigenous peoples from the area to serve as directional markers. The following October issue includes a substantial discussion about how and when Indigenous peoples arrived in North America and how Pueblo Indians irrigated their crops, leaving canals followed a thousand years later by modern dam projects. A list of "New Books on Indians" was also provided, including titles published by academic presses.[5] A March 1940 article discusses the role of "six young Indian artists" who were covering the walls of "two large rooms" in Washington, DC's new Department of Interior Building with murals depicting "Indian cultural life and expression," while an April 1940 article sought to dispel negative stereotypes about Indians, often comparing their culture and practices to those of whites in a favorable light. For example: "Had the white men followed the Indian habit of catching only the fish he needed and killing only those animals that were necessary for food, or even following the sport of hunting on a reasonable scale, there would be abundant hunting for everyone today."[6]

But an interest in Indians, especially in the eyes of the YMCA in the 1930s, '40s, and '50s, was always subsumed under a white, American, Christian lens, even when inappropriate. Also included in the March 1939 *Long House News* was a "tribal prayer" from "Big Brave Rev. Keller" of Chicago's "Potawatomie Tribe," which concluded with a phrase making this lens painfully clear: "This we ask in the name of the great White Chief—Jesus Christ our Lord—Amen."[7] One might be tempted to explain this comment away as an innocent mistake made by a single individual; but this is the nature of colonization, no matter how innocent Keller's comments were. First, Indian Guides representatives freely associated Jesus as white, as one of their own, just as European artists had been doing for centuries. Second, they were comfortable connecting Jesus to a title that nineteenth-century US political and military representatives, as well as some Native American leaders, associated with the US government and its military, with forces that sought to subdue, relocate, and "civilize" Indigenous peoples. In essence, white fathers, who co-opted their sons into this caricatured expression of "Indian" identity, used ignorant stereotypes for their own amusement without considering the historical tragedies embedded in the language they employed.

Once American involvement in World War II commenced, *Long House News* began heralding the wartime contributions of Native Americans: "A larger number of American Indians (in proportion to their population) are serving in the armed forces and in the defense industries than from any other group," they declared, and "some four thousand Indian women are in war industries and many are in the WAVES, WACS, and SPARS."[8] Interest in highlighting real Indians persisted, however sporadically, beyond the war years. In 1949, for example, an appeal went out to help the Navajo of New Mexico, living "in a desert reservation in New Mexico that can hardly support half their number. Most of them—some 61,000—are bound to the reservation by illiteracy, lack of vocational training, and disease." The article sought to educate readers about the great need for hospitals and health education, irrigation, and educational opportunity. "The death rate among our 420,000 American Indian citizens," lamented the author, "is more than double that of the rest of the population. Tuberculosis and enteritis are the chief killers. Available hospitals can't begin to meet the need." Schooling was inadequate—though the author focused on "some kind of industrial training" that might help individuals leave the reservation—and irrigation so poor that only small herds of cattle or sheep could survive on "their denuded land." *Long House News* encouraged readers to contribute to the Association on American Indian Affairs, a group "organized to keep the American people informed about the interests and needs of the Indians and to bring pressure on Congress to improve living conditions for the Indian. . . . This is an opportunity for the 'Y' Indian Guide tribes to do something for the descendants of the people whose traditions and culture they are exploring."[9]

In 1958 the National Longhouse collected funds to contribute to Korczak Ziolkowski's Crazy Horse memorial. (The remaining funds raised for Joe Friday's headstone were also sent there.) By the mid-1960s they were lobbying Congress to create a national holiday to honor Indigenous peoples. They sent money, food, clothing, and gifts to reservations suffering from cold weather or natural disaster. They began to learn about poor conditions and slim opportunities on many reservations, and at least a few groups went to visit them.[10] Yet however noble in intent, by and large these acts were centered on the needs of Y-Indian Guides participants and affirmed their status as "privileged Whites who were providing charity, instead of acting as students and allies."[11]

In April 1970, *Long House News* began supporting American Indian efforts to gain full legal rights for themselves. But they also admitted that Indian Guides members had not always embodied the lofty ideals of the organization's founders: "One of the greatest tragedies in American history," they wrote that month,

> has been the way the white man has treated his red brothers. Stories of mistreatment, chicanery, disrespect, and second-class paternalism are rampant, and have brought great dismay to many genuinely concerned American citizens. . . . In recent years efforts have been made to involve the American Indian to some extent in

determining his own future. But still the white man has controlled the destiny of his red brothers. . . . Indian Guides have borrowed from the customs and traditions of the American Indian. . . . In the past few years tribes throughout the nation have become increasingly sensitized to the needs of the American Indian. However, like most Americans, Y-Indian Guides have not always been fully aware of the real feelings and concerns of the Indian. The power of the movies and TV in communicating an unreal image of the Indian has influenced every home.

This point was unintentionally driven home only one issue later. The Hekawi "tribe" of Evanston, Illinois, had made Forrest Tucker, star of the sitcom *F Troop*, an honorary chief. Rather than choosing a tribe that once occupied their region, the Hekawis named themselves after the fictional Indians on Tucker's show. The name itself was based on a derogatory joke. Lost in the wilderness, they exclaimed, "Where the heck are we?"[12]

As a young boy, Thomas Saylor participated in Indian Guides in Allentown, Pennsylvania. While his memories of the experience are vague, his mother still has the headband he wore. "My mom's not a keeper; she doesn't keep everything, but she kept that. So that tells me that there were some positive memories or value attached to it." Saylor is now a professor of history in St. Paul, Minnesota. From his perspective, the explosive growth of Indian Guides in the post–World War II era was really a part of a larger phenomenon. "As white people we've long had a fascination with the West. Look at the writings and earliest films from the twenties and thirties. It shows some kind of mystique of the West, of what it was like, how we imagined it to be . . . this sense of fascination with an idealized West and idealized Indians. . . . Also . . . we've lost all of this with this urban and suburban experience that's so heartless and soulless. And this is a way of getting back to nature and embracing those who were first here."[13] Indeed, in the postwar period no genre of books, television, or film had more mass appeal than the western. From Louis L'Amour, Zane Grey, *The Rifleman*, *Bonanza*, and *Gunsmoke* to *Shane*, *High Noon*, and *The Searchers*, American popular culture was awash in all things related to cowboys, rustlers, gunfights, wagon trains, settlers, and Indians. Though not always cast as an enemy to be feared, even when presented favorably (such as Tonto in *The Lone Ranger*), American Indians in the media were secondary or subservient to white protagonists. As Norris Lineweaver observes, "Most of the movies you went to see when I was a kid were the cowboy westerns, battling the fierce Indians and extolling the virtues of the Plains Indian warrior, and that made a very popular theme for fathers and sons. . . . Imagine if we were trying to invent a father-son program during the time when *Star Trek* came out, or *Star Wars*. We'd all be sand people."[14]

In addition to books, film, and television, another force fueling the stereotyping of Native Americans on a broader scale by the late 1940s was the proliferation of companies eager to supply groups like Indian Guides with costumes and handicraft kits. Items previously made by father and son, perhaps with the guidance of an article in *Long House News*, a book published by the Association Press, or in rare cases, entities like the Handicrafts Division of Macdonald College in the province of Quebec, were by this time mass-produced and sold to numerous youth programs with Indian themes. In 1944 *Long House News* shared that MacDonald College had released a pamphlet entitled *Indian Slippers That You Can Make*. One could choose to craft moccasins in the style of the Nez Perce, Penobscot, or Cree people. Anyone buying the pamphlet would have to make their own tools, create a pattern, and punch, sew, and adorn their work.[15] By contrast, the winter 1968 edition heralds the arrival of "Indian Trails Products, Inc.," a Costa Mesa, California, firm supplying craft project materials. Readers were encouraged to contact the company to procure kits to make "Indian shields, feather arm ornaments, arrowhead necklaces, wampum and medicine bags, breechcloths, and vests."[16] Indian Trails had contracted with the National Board of YMCAs, gaining permission to display the YMCA trademark on its products. Other businesses like the Grey Owl Indian Crafts Manufacturing Company of Jamaica, New York, the Lackawanna Leather Company of Hackettstown, New Jersey, and Indianland of Flagstaff, Arizona, competed for the Indian Guides' and other groups' business. Now "tribes" everywhere could maximize their mimicry with less individual effort, supported by a new, affordable, nationwide manufacturing, merchandising, and distribution system. Unfortunately, this also decreased motivation to learn about and emulate, however clumsily, the real Indigenous peoples who were once the sole occupants of the land that Indian Guides "tribes" now called home. Centralized, mass-produced "Indian" goods led to greater caricaturization, homogeneity, and unreality.

Figure 28. The advent of commercial enterprises designed to supply every type of costume or prop someone might desire while "playing Indian" exponentially broadened and deepened the potential for mimicry and caricature, as clearly illustrated by a "tribe" from the Euclid YMCA of Cleveland, Ohio, in 1962. YMCA of Greater Cleveland.

There is no doubt that the editors of *Long House News*, true YMCA believers who saw in Indian Guides a means to literally transform society, were interested in fostering a closer and more robust relationship between their membership and real Native Americans. But given the ongoing disconnection between the Y's expectations for the integration of Y-Indian Guides into the YMCA and its other programs, as well as the persistent desire of local "tribes" for autonomy and their pervasive disinterest in the Y, messages in *Long House News* fell on both fertile and fallow soil. Yes, some "tribes" found in their role-playing and nature activities a way to think more sympathetically, even if from a limited perspective, of real Indigenous peoples. But on the other extreme were those who took a more insular view, seeing Indians as abstractions they could employ as they saw fit, serving as a source less of inspiration than of invention, even parody, a mere means to an end. Of course, it was entirely possible for groups to move from one extreme to the other and back again over the course of their existence.

Distinctions such as these were meaningless to most Native Americans, and in the wake of the many upheavals of the 1960s and '70s, especially the rise of the American Indian Movement, they began to express more frequently their displeasure with white appropriation of Indian culture, no matter how well-intentioned. While it was still possible to find older Indians who had lived through worse times and who saw Indian Guides as a sincere attempt to dispel old and harmful stereotypes and think about Indigenous peoples more sympathetically, the tide was turning.

AFRICAN AMERICANS AND INDIAN GUIDES

While the vast majority of fathers and sons in Y-Indian Guides were white, and usually middle- and upper-middle class, the program also attracted African Americans and a small number of other participants of color. "Black Indians" were at least officially welcomed with open arms and posed no real philosophical or functional complications, unlike (for many) women and girls.

The YMCA's relationship with African Americans predates the Civil War and, therefore, the official death of the institution of slavery. Anthony Bowen, a former slave and the first African American to become a clerk in the US Patent Office in Washington, DC, heard about the YMCA from a white coworker, William Chauncy Langdon. Since all organizations were segregated at that time, Langdon gathered friends and aided the establishment of the first "YMCA for Colored Men and Boys" in 1853. By the 1860s similar associations had come to life in New York City; Philadelphia; Charleston, South Carolina; and Harrisburg, Pennsylvania. New York's E. V. C. Eato became the first Black delegate to attend a YMCA annual convention in 1867. The national YMCA created a "Colored Men's Department" in 1890, led by William Hunton, who in 1875 became the first full-time paid director of a "Colored" Y (Norfolk, VA). In 1910 Sears, Roebuck and Co. president Julius Rosenwald facilitated the proliferation of Colored Associations by promising $25,000 to any African American urban community able to raise $75,000 for a new facility.

While Colored Ys were segregated and had less attractive facilities than their white counterparts, they were also autonomous. They were normally on friendly terms and often received financial support from other metropolitan Ys, as well as programmatic and logistical support from the national office. Colored Ys became, as one Y leader put it, "educational and spiritual oases," places of safety and security where members could speak freely on important issues of the day, undaunted by the presence of white listeners. Black athletes, entertainers, servicemen, and other travelers often found refuge from the humiliations of segregation at the local Colored Y.

An acceptance of gradualism, both in the Y and society as a whole, kept the Y from making radical changes to its racial practices, as did the feelings of autonomy, identity, and safety that some Black Y members appreciated and wished to preserve. But the advent of Indian Guides coincided with a time in which a younger, better educated, and more socially mobile generation of African Americans rejected their elders' philosophy of gradualism, especially on college campuses. White YMCA workers trained and deployed to international posts during and after World War I were also frequently of a Social Gospel mindset, focusing on not only religious conversion but also social justice, reconciliation, and world peace.[17]

Integration into Indian Guides, or even the establishment of separate African American Indian Guides chapters, did not occur until the mid-1940s. Prior to that time, as was the case in the Pine Street "Colored" Y in St. Louis, some Black boys were initiated into the Friendly Indians program. In a January 1926 edition of the *Pine Torch*, we read that eight African American boys "were initiated into the National Order of Friendly Indians."[18] There was a Friendly Indians Indoor Baseball League, a party celebrating George Washington's birthday, a February 26 Parents' Night event featuring musical performances, "stump speeches," recitations, a "splendid 'good night' speech by Mr. Joe Friday" (who by this time must have been hired as a Y secretary), and a subsequent visit to a "big city-wide pow-wow of Friendly Indians" in Ferguson, Missouri, which planted the "seed for interracial good will which will doubtless blossom forth in the greater St. Louis of the future." Joe Friday led a similar event the following February at the Carondelet Y. In other words, Friday was making himself available for Indian-themed events with boys of various racial and ethnic backgrounds even before the first Indian Guides "tribe" was established in Webster Groves. While Indian Guides supplanted Friendly Indians throughout most of St. Louis, it is doubtful Pine Street ever started its own Indian Guides program or had boys who participated in one. Joe Friday was able to navigate between white and Black worlds in the birthplace of Indian Guides, but there is no evidence that African American boys and their fathers were ever invited into Indian Guides "tribes."

Figure 29. An Indian Guides initiation in Flint, Michigan, on February 19, 1944. Harold Keltner and Joe Friday stand at the center of the group. Two African American fathers and sons are bottom left, and another man, two people left of Keltner, is likely a "Colored Y" secretary. *Long House News* 8, no. 5 (May 1944).

African American participation in Indian Guides elsewhere can be traced back to at least February 19, 1944, when, with Harold Keltner and Joe Friday present, five new "tribes" were inducted in Flint, Michigan, including two African American fathers and sons and likely a "Colored" Y secretary. The Lenape "tribe" from Abingdon, Pennsylvania, including a Black father and son, were pictured decorating a Christmas tree on the front page of the December 1958 *Long House News*. Two African American fathers and sons from the Spring Street Colored Y in Columbus, Ohio, won the chance to attend the 1959 National Longhouse in Milwaukee, which meant that the event was integrated. In 1968 the first known Negro Indian Guides tribe was established in the South by James M. Houston, the youth program director of the Baranco-Clark Y in Baton Rouge, Louisiana. "Since crowded home conditions have prevented meetings in members' homes," tribal meetings were held at the Reddy Elementary School with the blessing of principal Sadie C. Keel. Meetings were filled with games and stories, and the fathers "have undertaken a project to insure tribe participation in the 31st National Long House in Dallas." A photo of the tribe showed eleven men and fourteen boys. In September 1969 African American mayor Carl B. Stokes joined his white counterparts in kicking off Indian Guide Week in Cleveland, Ohio. He even allowed himself to be dressed in a long, flowing "war bonnet" by two young African American "Indians."[19]

African American participation in Indian Guides continued, but always at a marginal rate. This did not mean that African Americans, like their white counterparts, were immune from the impulse to appropriate imagined Indian dress and symbols for their own purposes, even outside the auspices of Friendly Indians or Indian Guides. In October 1961 the Harlem YMCA newsletter the *New Sign* splashed a photo of members leading the year's membership campaign. It featured eleven African American adults, all wearing various forms of faux Indian headdress. "The kickoff and first report was a very colorful and exciting meeting. Everyone had on their Indian Headdress and war paint. The Indians had a good dinner, sang their favorite songs and enjoyed some good entertainment." Almost five years later the *New Sign* heralded the success of its Summer Boys and Girls Program. Its "Y" Ranger Day Camp "was characterized by its Indian theme. The day camps were organized into tribes with the leaders taking on Indian tribal chief names. Indian lore, crafts, games, songs and dances were part of the daily activities." One photo featured African American girls wearing headbands and weaving baskets (with the caption "Look like Indians to me"), and another showed boys, some bare-chested, wearing headbands and sitting in a circle around a stack of unlit firewood ("Ummmm! Heap much peace talk").[20]

By 1968, with social and political unrest creating concern across the country, the YMCA's National Longhouse announced its plan to make Indian Guides a force for "interracial advance." In January of that year a six-man committee of Indian Guides leaders, three white and three Black, engaged in three days of "intensive dialog and action-oriented meetings." They sought to emphasize "the positive forces in every community, such as the strong promotion of the father-son relationship for all American families, the inner motivation of the responsible Negro and white fathers, increasing YMCA professional and lay concern for understanding and action, good training of lay organizers, attractive promotion materials, influence of boys' peer groups, the ability of mothers to influence dads, and the growing awareness and concern of community leaders."

All the members of the committee vowed to go back to their home Ys and engage in some experiment designed to enlarge mutual understanding between the races. The crises of the times had "been given very high priority by the National Council of Officers," the report continued. And since the attitudes of parents had a direct impact on their children and therefore the attitudes of the next generation (yes, this was still the opinion within the Y in 1968), "Y-Indian Guides may be one of the most productive avenues of positive advance for the Young Men's Christian Association. It will call for genuinely concerned witness and self-examination by Y-Indian Guide tribal, nation, and federation officers throughout the nation." [21] An "Urban Action Report" formulated by the six-man committee was shared at the 1968 Annual Longhouse. It encouraged "local concerted efforts and experimentation by YMCAs to encourage inter-racial understanding and attitudes and to extend the program to inner city neighborhoods." But no great racial breakthrough was ever delivered through the YMCA's Indian Guides program—or any other. [22]

In 1970 the Y-Indian Guide National Longhouse met in Atlanta. The host committee invited Georgia's staunchly segregationist governor, Lester Maddox, to offer the welcoming address, much to the chagrin of many Indian Guides dads and YMCA staff. A memo circulated by the regional office acknowledged the difficult position in which this placed many members: "We've wondered how such a travesty can occur in our Movement at a time when so many exciting efforts are underway to make the Y credible to young people, women and minorities." The letter discussed possible strategies that had been voiced by various constituents, including boycotting the Longhouse, requesting the removal of Governor Maddox from the platform, demanding that the National Council "enact legislation controlling speakers at National Conventions," and staging demonstrations during the convention. All these options were deemed "far short of the ideal form of YMCA involvement." Attendance at the Longhouse was still encouraged, so it could be used as "an opportunity to get ourselves together rather than reinforcing the polarization of peoples throughout the Movement and nation." Staff held a meeting of Indian Guides staff and volunteers "to collaborate on strategies to eliminate racism in . . . the Longhouse in Atlanta."[23]

Two years later, at the Pittsburgh National Longhouse, a parent-child leaders' session was held on Y-Afro Guides, a program "for fathers and sons emphasizing black culture and identity." Little evidence of Afro Guides remains. The cover of a 1968 Dallas County Y-Indian Guides program held in the Kautz Family YMCA Archives at the University of Minnesota has "Y-Afro Guides" written across the top. Inside, only one page contains a few amendments: "Chief, Bow, and Bear" becomes "Chief, Spear, and Lion." "Braves" become "fathers and sons."[24] A brief, undated four-page synopsis of a Y-African Guides Program instituted in the West End Program Center in Cincinnati, Ohio—unexpectedly found alongside miscellaneous survey and financial data collected between 1991 and 2000—provides a purpose statement very similar to that of Indian Guides. Its slogan was "United Always." Most of its aims were similar, but included "to take pride in myself" and "to take pride in my heritage." Oaths pledged by both parents and children reflected assumptions that families enjoyed a less tranquil and agreeable home life than white fathers and sons in Indian Guides. Parents promised not to abuse, neglect, ignore, discourage, or curse their children, and to provide for, share with, encourage, inspire, and express their love for them. Children promised not to talk back to, bring shame to, be dishonest with, disobey, or talk about the personal affairs of their parents, and to respect, support, honor, appreciate, and express love for them.

In 1973 Jesse Alexander and Fred Hill, an unofficial ad hoc committee of two representing the Black and Non-White YMCA Secretaries

(BAN-WYS), listed their thoughts on future training programs their conference could offer. Among the past experience and research to build upon was a 1971 training conference held in Los Angeles that, among other programs, promoted Afro-Guides.[25] This iteration of African Guides, based out of the Southwest Branch of the Los Angeles YMCA and led by Reuben Davis, appears to have enjoyed several years of success. In 1974, as part of the national BAN-WYS conference, an African Guides manual was distributed.[26] While acknowledging that Y-African Guides was similar to Y-Indian Guides, the manual makes the key distinction that "it should be understood that as Afro-Americans we have a rich and wonderful culture of our own. We do not need to be like white or red people." Beyond the handful of local examples, African Guides never developed into a nationally supported program, though mentions of Y-Afro Guides persist into the 1990s.[27]

Figure 30. In the TV series *Julia*, actress Diahann Carroll plays a widowed mother whose son Corey wants to join Indian Guides. Kautz Family YMCA Archives, University of Minnesota Libraries.

In March 1969, the first television program to feature an African American female lead character, *Julia*, aired an episode called "Home of the Braves." Diahann Carroll, playing the title role, is a widowed mother to her young son Corey. In this episode, Corey wants to attend an Indian Guides meeting with his friend, but without a father he cannot. Julia's neighbor, Mr. Cooper, tells Mr. Bowman, a Black handyman (and father of six) bidding on a job to fix Cooper's roof, that he will hire him if he takes Corey to an Indian Guides meeting. Shortly after Bowman arrives, three other men appear, coerced by Julia's friends to serve as Corey's "father." When Julia takes the lot of them to a community center, hoping to find fatherless boys for all of the men to take for a one-time visit to Indian Guides, the social worker says she won't send them unless the men agree to become permanent Indian Guides fathers, which they do. The show ends with young Corey, face aglow, sitting amid a group of Black and white fathers and sons, loving every moment of his Indian Guides experience.[28]

Participation in Indian Guides and its related programs must have afforded African American fathers and children opportunities to reflect on the irony of whites—and themselves—appropriating and reinventing the identities of another culture. Dr. Mel Shelby, a gynecologist and surgeon living in Bloomington, Minnesota, participated in Indian Princesses with his daughter in the 1990s. While he enjoyed the fellowship with other fathers and daughters and felt strongly that the program strengthened his relationship with his child, he never shed his unease. "Here I am as a Black man bringing his Black daughter to a mostly white gathering on a regular basis. We're dressing up and making so-called Indian handicrafts, and I'm enjoying it, but every now and then I'm also thinking, 'Mel, what are you doing?' I mean, is this much different than if we were putting on a minstrel show?"[29] This kind of cognitive dissonance was hardly reserved to African Americans or even people of color, but it resonated at a unique frequency. Only a year after Indian Guides was established, Al Jolson appeared as a blackface performer in *The Jazz Singer*, receiving positive reviews from both white and Black critics. As with Indians, African American caricatures were rife in advertising and popular media. Black participants in Indian Guides would have had difficulty avoiding some consideration of how their participation was, at the very least, odd. Yet, as Rayna Green noted in chapter 3, part of this discomfort was mitigated by the fact that "playing Indian" allowed African Americans to escape "the conventional and often highly restrictive boundaries of their fixed cultural identities based in gender or race."[30] Shelby, a highly educated and successful medical practitioner, nonetheless dealt with racism his entire life. In the Indian Guides circle, race became moot: everyone was an "Indian."

Figure 31. Though their numbers were always comparatively small, African Americans did participate in Y-Indian Guides. Here we see the Hongo "tribe," date and location unknown. Another group, Y-Afro Guides, sought to affirm that "as Afro-Americans we have a rich and wonderful culture of our own. We do not need to be like white or red people." Kautz Family YMCA Archives, University of Minnesota Libraries.

DEPICTING "THE INDIAN"

In 1968, when the National Longhouse expected to make Indian Guides a force for interracial advance, other leaders began openly voicing concerns for the first time about how the program portrayed Indigenous peoples. They even wondered what actual Native Americans might think of them. Within a short span of years these concerns grew, inspiring nationwide conversation and, in some Ys, reconsideration, or even abandonment, of the program.

In February 1968 staff from the YMCA publishing house Association Press met to discuss and evaluate Y-Indian Guides resources. *Twenty Teepee Tales*, a resource of long standing (and one scrutinized and found wanting in chapter 3), was retained. It was even suggested that one of the authors, Douglas Monahan, write additional stories. As was the case with earlier tales, some members expected that a "deeper meaning" or a "spiritual education" be found in each tale—what one member described as "moral tales in an Indian frame of reference." By the same token, one note asked, "How authentic?" There were also suggestions to expand literature into broader areas of conservation or to rely on resources from the Bureau of Indian Affairs.[31]

In April 1968 Indian Guides received more food for thought from John Corbett, chief archeologist for the Department of the Interior's Office of Archeology and Historic Preservation. After perusing an Indian Guides manual and finding many program objectives "doubtless of considerable value," he found a section he deemed highly objectionable. Under the heading "Indian Relic Collection," Corbett read that "tribes" were encouraged to regularly visit Native American burial mounds to "dig for relics." In addition to noting that the remnants of prehistoric Indigenous peoples were "a valuable part of our national heritage" and "of incalculable worth to scientists," he added, "The Congress in 1906 passed the Federal Act for the Preservation of American Antiquities (34 Stat. 225; Public Law 59-209) which makes it illegal to appropriate, disturb, or destroy an object or feature of antiquity on federally owned or controlled lands, except for qualified scientists affiliated with recognized scientific or education institutions conducting investigations under permits and which provides for fines and imprisonment as penalty for violation. Additionally, most states have similar legislation protecting antiquities occurring on lands under their control."

The activities encouraged in the Indian Guides manual, therefore, were not simply culturally insensitive and scientifically deleterious but almost certainly illegal.[32] This letter, as well as numerous conversations at board and National Longhouse meetings, contributed to the creation and release of the 1972 memo "National Y-Indian Guide Long House: A Guide for Better Understanding of the American Indian." According to Charles ("Chuck") Kujawa, the National Longhouse consultant who signed the letter, it was from "an outline prepared by the Urban Indian Development Association of Los Angeles." The most dramatic, factual summary to date from the YMCA and a first step to understanding the problems of appropriation, the memo opens with an acknowledgment that programs "have drawn heavily on the culture and customs of American Indian tribes," and that participants at all levels need to "represent accurately and positively the American Indians' contribution to America's life and history."

Figure 32. Ferguson, Missouri, Y-Indian Guides induction ceremony by a lake, date unknown. As the YMCA's National Longhouse began to take seriously criticism of Indian Guides' cultural insensitivity, it stated categorically in 1972 that any misrepresentation of Indigenous peoples' languages, practices, or beliefs constituted a "grave injustice to the American Indian." Gateway Region Young Men's Christian Association (S0473).

The letter contained fourteen separate points considered essential for understanding American Indians and depicting them with respect. It was high time "tribes" asked themselves if their depictions, whether playful or meant as an homage, were really appropriate. After all, each Native American nation had its own beliefs, "which were evolved over many thousands of years." Each nation's cultural practices were "sacred and meaningful" and had "special meaning." Any misrepresentation of Indigenous peoples' languages, practices, or beliefs constituted a "grave injustice to the American Indian." Instead of using non-Indian words like "how" or "ugh" or "heap big," the memo suggested American Indians be depicted using the English language, since "each tribe spoke in its own dialect and took great pride in oratory." Using such caricatural language simply denigrated Native Americans. Using "Chief," "Squaw," or "Buck" as nicknames also degraded American Indians, who should be addressed or referred to with respect, using proper names. Any titles used in publicity needed to convey respect to "the Indian populace." Songs and dances often invented by Indian Guides "tribes" were also to be discontinued. "Whenever used, they should be authentic, with the meaning portrayed correctly." Likewise, written or visual materials discussing Native Americans were to be prepared "from the Indian point of view. His values should be considered; his traditions respectfully upheld. His interpretation of history should also be presented." The letter observed that Indigenous peoples were too often left out of the industries and activities that pretended to depict them. "Indian" handicrafts were manufactured and "Indian" roles on television and in the movies were played by non-Native American people. "The Indian has been alienated while his rich heritage is exploited. . . . Hollywood has a stereotyped impression of the American Indian which is grossly distorted." And this image, sold to the general public, was widely internalized as real. Programs sponsored by the YMCA to develop healthy relationships between parents and children should avoid at all costs further perpetrating such misinformation in their newsletters, activities, and public events.

Finally, the widespread stereotype of Indians as aggressors needed to end:

> It should be remembered that the white settlers and fur traders encroached upon the Indian, threatening his very existence, disregarding his hunting grounds and his rights as the original inhabitant of his homeland. . . . It was honorable to defend their homeland. . . . He should be known as the defender against the white intruder, who gave no consideration to the way and life of

the Indian. Many . . . films, TV series, and books indicate that the Indian is a savage race. This abuse of the Indian culture is not accurate, and it should cease.[33]

Next came "A Guide for Local YMCAs in Working with American Indian People," an eight-page typescript primer for "concerned YMCA lay and staff leaders" who sought to form sound relationships with Indigenous peoples.[34] This document reviewed the background of the YMCA's work with American Indians, including the Sioux YMCA (as it was called then) in South Dakota (a group rarely if ever mentioned in Indian Guides literature), and the founding of Y-Indian Guides through the "teamwork" of Keltner and Friday. "Some American Indian arts, crafts, customs, games, and stories," it noted, "were borrowed and used in developing local parent-child programs," but after 1950, while the program was expanding rapidly, "many tribes of fathers and sons inadvertently misused Indian terminology, customs and lore because of ignorance and limited efforts to seek authenticity in values, dress, ceremonies, and practices."

The guide stressed the diversity of native cultures and highlighted the plight of American Indian families who suffered from poverty, substance abuse, and lack of independence. YMCAs were encouraged to reach out to "Key National Organizations of American Indians" for appropriate guidance.[35] The guide had been assembled in consultation with the "American Indian Consultant Team," comprised of ten individuals, nine of whom had tribal affiliation.[36]

As this guide suggests, the national YMCA was once again at a cross-roads in its relationship with Indian Guides. While there was a growing sense of unease with the appropriated elements of the program, the belief was that the "Indian" in Indian Guides needed to be "fixed," not elim-inated. Yet the "Indian" programs are only cited by name once, in an apologetic tone, in the historical background section; elsewhere they are referred to as parent-child programs. Readers were discouraged from mis-using native dress, language, rituals, and artifacts, participating in parades that perpetuated stereotypes, and communicating a sense of paternalism toward or superiority over Indigenous peoples. Unsolicited service ef-forts, however well-intentioned, should cease. Instead, Guides members were encouraged to ask American Indian groups and leaders in advance what they actually needed and what kind of assistance they desired. The guide also suggested best practices for "developing sound relationships" with Native people, focusing on small-group, two-way exchanges and an awareness of the great diversity of Native American cultures.

The *Guide for Local YMCAs in Working with American Indian People*, released in 1973, ushered in a new era of emphasizing "awareness of" and "interpretation of American Indian Culture." The manuals for Y-Indian Guides and Y-Indian Princesses were revised in 1974 to do the same. The National Council also aggressively explored ways to leverage the explicit interest in American Indians held by Guides participants into an increased organizational capacity to serve Native American peoples. Following a successful campaign to establish a National Longhouse American Indian Fund, the *Guide for Local YMCAs in Working with American Indian People* was now included within YMCA fundraising literature, promoting their international projects. A second consultation team including American Indian members was formed to guide this work.

At the same time, literature for Y-Indian Guides programs, which now included Y-Indian Maidens (mother/daughter), Y-Indian Princesses (father/daughter), and Y-Trail Blazers (father/older son) increasingly deemphasized the long-lived "Indian" elements within the programs. A list of Y-Trail Blazers aims from 1974, for example, bears no "Indian" references.[37]

Program Tips for YMCA Parent-Child Groups, a manual released by the National Board of YMCAs in 1975, is nearly devoid of American Indian elements, except for the use of the terms *tribe* and *chief*. The two exceptions are a section containing "facts about American Indians" and an excerpt from *Tales of Running Deer,* a "popular and timely new resource for story-telling time at Y-Indian Guide tribal meetings."[38] *Program Tips*, in fact could have served as a primer for any generic outdoor, nature-based youth development program with a heavy emphasis on the sixth aim, "to seek and preserve the beauty of the Great Spirit's work in forest, field, and stream."

As some groups, particularly those aimed at older youth, began deemphasizing Native American themes, others sought to continue employing them, but more responsibly. In 1973 the YMCA attempted to summarize "Past YMCA Experience" working with Indigenous peoples. This document indicates a clear shift in emphasis by 1970 from a more paternalistic and unilateral relationship (inviting American Indians to camps, schools, learn-to-swim programs, and employment programs) to one of more partnership and self-awareness. Post-1969 entries, all focused on Indian Guides, were:

c. The declaration of support for American Indian human rights—1970.
d. Program workshops on understanding Indian culture—1971.
e. The involvement of American Indian leaders as consultants to local YMCAs in Minneapolis, Seattle, Pittsburgh, and Rochester—1969–73
f. The establishment of the National Y-Indian Guide Center in the Osage country near Bartlesville, Oklahoma—1972 [This center, which will be discussed below, was staffed by Native American college students.]
g. American Indian panel at the Pittsburgh Convention 1972 with the adoption of a "Guide for Understanding the American Indian."
h. Participation of a ten-person American Indian Consultant Team in the 1973 Estes Park Convention.
i. The development of "A Guide for Local YMCAs in Working with American Indian People" for the 1973 Colorado Convention focusing on a change of poor practices that may have emerged in YMCA parent-child programs.[39]

In February 1976 the National Board of YMCAs' Urban Action and Program Division announced the formation of a national YMCA American Indian consultant team, a group of eight to fifteen "people of native heritage" appointed for a two-year term to help the YMCA not only competently reach out to Indigenous peoples on reservations and "in urban or rural areas" and emphasize "creative program development, fair solving of problems, and intercultural education," but more specifically "assist the National Long House of YMCA Parent-Child Groups in program quality, authentic use of American Indian culture, family intercultural education, and program materials development."[40]

While it is clear that national leadership became increasingly sensitive to Native American concerns about how they were depicted and how Indian Guides' humanitarian efforts were being framed, their actions also demonstrate that the very abuses they articulated were widespread enough not only to gain the attention of Indigenous peoples and other concerned parties but also to necessitate the national Y's intervention. In significant ways, Indian Guides had spun out of control. Still, few questioned its overall validity. The assumption was that with some fine-tuning, closer consultation with sympathetic Indigenous leaders, and the cooperation of individual "tribes" who would clearly see the need for reform, Indian Guides could continue to be the force for improving parent-child relationships it had always been. This expectation, however, proved illusory. Indian Guides was a sprawling national program with many independent-minded members, generations of alumni with strong affections for and a sense of ownership over the program, and almost fifty years of inertia. The National Y had little authority over the day-to-day operations of local associations. Even so, beginning with Palo Alto, California, in 1975, a handful of individual YMCAs began to grapple with the problems of cultural appropriation, remaking Indian Guides into a program that retained its emphasis on close family connections while removing its use of symbols, images, and rituals deemed both inauthentic and offensive.

CHAPTER SEVEN

"We Couldn't Fix It"
Removing the "Indian" from Indian Guides

WOOLAROC

THERE WERE NO public signs of imminent decline or danger for Indian Guides in the early 1970s. Indeed, its continued ascendancy seemed assured. After all, in May 1972 Indian Guides devotees gathered within the sprawling 3,700-acre Woolaroc Wildlife Preserve near Bartlesville, Oklahoma, to dedicate the National Y-Indian Guide Center.[1] Owned and operated by the Frank Phillips Foundation,[2] Woolaroc (a portmanteau of *woods*, *lakes*, and *rocks*) was already home to the Western-Indian Museum (now the Western Art and History Museum), a wildlife preserve, and "an historic lodge." In conjunction with planning for the Y-Indian Guides Center, Woolaroc also established a mile-and-a-half-long walking trail following a creek flowing between Elk Lake, Indian Princess Cascades, and Thunderbird Canyon. In the southeastern quadrant of Woolaroc, straddling Longhouse Plaza to the east and Longhouse Terrace to the west, were Heritage Hall and the Talent Teepee. As described by a promotional pamphlet, Heritage Hall was "a two-story facility . . . provid[ing] a showplace for authentic Indian arts and crafts. . . . On the main floor, visitors may watch Indian youths producing crafts in the ways of their forefathers. There is also a 'trading post' where the crafted items may be purchased," along with an information desk, a library, lounge, offices, and "a special setting for photo-taking." The second floor was a "wide all-around balcony for exhibition of authentic Indian tribal items" and featured a large stained-glass window "symbolizing the themes of the Center and [the] Y-Indian Guide program." To the north of Heritage Hall stood the Talent Teepee, a 250-seat amphitheater where "dramatic multimedia productions are scheduled several times daily utilizing live action, light, sound, still photography and motion pictures to reflect the American

Indian's heritage, talents and achievements." It also held "a stage for live performances and is equipped with the finest projection, lighting and sound systems."[3] Brochures were available to inform visitors about Y-Indian Guides and other Y parent-child programs. One such brochure mentioned that Y-Indian Guides was "at the entrance-age level to a lifelong succession of rewarding Y activities." It further stated that "emulation of Indian customs and traditions" added "great recreational and educational value," since "the generally recognized traits of the American Indian—his dignity, loyalty, helpfulness and justice, along with his respect for the family and things spiritual—provide inspiration for families of today," as did his "appreciation of nature and his understanding of conservation." Providing descriptions of Y-Indian Guides, Princesses, Maidens, and Trail Blazers, it noted that handbooks for each were available at the Woolaroc trading post.[4]

The May 1972 "Inspection Fete" was attended by Harold Keltner, "more than 150 American Indian leaders," the trustees of the Frank Phillips Foundation, and numerous YMCA "lay and staff officers." Keltner's day was undoubtedly made when W. W. Keeler, chief of the Cherokee Nation, presented him with honorary membership in the Cherokee tribe. His speech gave primary credit to Phillips Foundation chair Paul Endacott and general manager William Blakemore, who were instrumental in the completion of the center. In fact, the idea for the center had originated with the Phillips Foundation, not the National Longhouse. Endacott had sons and a grandson who were "enthusiastic Y-Indian Guides members" in Lincoln, Nebraska. Robert Harlan, executive director of the National Council of the YMCA, gave his full support to the center, "which will attract millions of people in the decade ahead."[5] The director of the center was twenty-two-year-old Larry Daylight, a member of the Quapaw and Miami "tribes," a national champion traditional dancer, and a Roman Catholic. It would be his responsibility to staff the center every summer with Native American college students.

Whether Harlan's prediction of millions of visitors was sincere or hyperbole designed to please his hosts, there is no doubt that early plans to greet visitors were permeated by wild optimism. An unattributed memo to employees predicted the center would become "a showcase for the

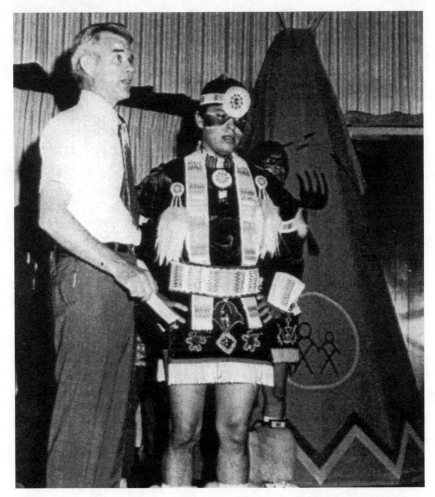

Figure 33. Larry Daylight, right, the first director of the National Indian Guide Center at Woolaroc, is introduced by William Blakemore, general manager of the Frank Phillips Foundation, in May 1972. *Long House News* 35, no. 1 (October 1972).

exhibition of handiwork and symbolic artifacts which typify authentic American Indian culture and heritage. However, even these attractions cannot deliver their full impact upon multitudes of viewers unless they . . . are superbly maintained and unless supplemental information about them is graciously supplied by knowledgeable and alert employees." The center's success would depend on the impressions left in the minds of the expected multitudes as they departed. Since there was no way to actually accomplish this, the author provided "hypothetical examples" of what he hoped might occur:

> I had never before realized the high degree of artistic and cultural development embodied in the authentic side of Indian activities and customs, as contrasted with presentations I often see and take for granted. . . . The genuine portrayals are more interesting than inaccurate ones, so I intend to learn more about the authentic. . . .
>
> I am only a young Indian boy. I want to learn to do all those things I saw at the Center. My sister wants to be like those people, too. . . .
>
> Until my time at the Center I never heard of Y-Indian Guides. I still don't know all I want to learn about them. Having both a son seven and a daughter eight, I can think of no better way to spend a little time with them than to join up with the Indian Guides and the Indian Princesses. . . .
>
> Being a free-lance writer for newspapers, magazines, radio, TV, and occasionally authoring a book, I envision a whole new approach to my treatment of American Indian subjects when I write. This will cause me to undertake a lot of reading on the subject, but this promises to be an enjoyable leisure-time activity on its own.[6]

Woolaroc also became the setting of a promotional film, *Blue Hill and Bobby*, produced by the National Board of YMCAs. The film features a boy, Little Cloud, whose father, Big Cloud, is too busy to uphold his promise to attend meetings. In a dream Bobby meets Blue Hill Townsend, an Indigenous man who shows him a special home dedicated to Indian Guides and the history of Native Americans. *Blue Hill and Bobby*, and Woolaroc generally, capture the various competing interests the YMCA was attempting to balance. The first tension laid out in the film's opening lament are the forces of modernity, driving wedges between family members: "When America was growing up, Sunday afternoon picnics in the park were something everybody enjoyed. Families spent a lot more time together then." Another is the programmatic aim of constructing masculinity in young boys. As Blue Hill explains to Bobby, "the finest deeds of father and son are in service to mother and home." Finally, the Frank Phillips Foundation, which financed the film and encouraged the establishment of the National Y-Indian Guides Center at Woolaroc, represents the men of means and influence the YMCA had long hoped to attract through the program.

Figure 34. A still from *Blue Hill and Bobby*, a film intended to promote the National Indian Guides Center at Woolaroc. Blue Hill Townsend, of Cherokee Delaware lineage, was a longtime Indian Guides supporter and member of a National YMCA American Indian consultant team meant to help the Indian Guides programs be more authentic and respectful. The stained-glass window seen behind Townsend was made especially for the center, and depicts a Native American man guiding a white boy and girl down life's path. Kautz Family YMCA Archives, University of Minnesota Libraries.

There are few mentions of the National Indian Guides Center in YMCA records. It served as a meeting place on rare occasion, and the National Advisory Council distributed promotional literature for it in 1976, but little else can be found. According to Woolaroc museum director Shiloh Thurman, the center was "heavily attended" for fifteen or twenty years. In fact, he remembers attending the center when he was in Boy Scouts. "It was quite the presentation that they would put on." But at a certain point, "Mr. Daylight started having trouble getting . . . Native American dancers to come out . . . and do the dances and do the sign language for him. So it kind of withered from there." But to this day, Thurman reports, people still come to Woolaroc and ask about it. "They remember it from when they were kids, or they remember taking their kids to it." The old Heritage Hall building was undergoing remodeling in 2021, and "one of the biggest questions was if we were going to be having Native American dancers back out there."[7]

While the themes from *Blue Hill and Bobby* resonated within Indian Guides from the beginning, American society, the family, relations between Indigenous and white Americans, and the YMCA itself had changed a great deal between 1926 and the early 1970s. The YMCA, in no small part out of a need to remain relevant (and solvent) and respond to social change, was moving away from work only with young men and boys, and focusing more on the entire family. This required a shift from single-gender or single-generation programs and toward "big tent" programs like Family Life or Y-Parent-Child.

The expansion into family life and the inclusion of mothers and daughters were also necessitated by a long-standing problem. For example, in 1974 the peak of Indian Guides membership was reached: 509,629. Yet despite these robust numbers, revenues were declining because fewer "tribes" were actually paying dues to the Y. As had been demonstrated for decades, these groups saw themselves as independent entities, not arms of YMCA youth development. A June 1975 report maintained that while the number of groups was continuing to increase (31,800 in 1973), the number completing national registration "has declined markedly since the 1970 peak of over 10,000 groups." A similar report observed, "A large proportion and growing number of groups have not been registered nationally . . . for a variety of reasons; special concern has been raised as to 'what do we get for our $5.00?'" In an era of stagflation, it was difficult for Y staff and volunteers to defend this fee, and the loyalties of "tribes" were fixed locally rather than nationally. "The current relevance and purpose of the National Long House structure and functions are frequently challenged and require examination. Substantial monies seem to some to be used for the operation of structure." At the same time, the report continued, "National Long House leaders have reflected internal dissatisfaction and frustration because many parent/child groups are not being registered," thereby benefiting from national services without paying for them.[8]

As a result, a decision was made in 1975: fees would be reduced and financial support for Indian Guides would come primarily from royalties earned from the sales of Y-Indian Guides program materials. This proved unsustainable, as it replaced one anemic source of revenue with one destined to grow even worse.

CRACKS IN THE WALL

In the mid-1970s, Larry Rosen was a program executive at the Palo Alto, California, YMCA. In 1974 or '75, a young woman named Princess Pale Moon reached out to him, saying she was a representative of the American Indian Heritage Foundation. She was concerned, she said, because she felt the Y-Indian Princess program was disrespectful to Indigenous cultures. "She wasn't in my face about this," recalls Rosen. "She laid out her concerns rationally and in compelling terms. It was impossible not to be sympathetic, especially after watching dads and sons treating the Indian theme with so little understanding or respect. I had her meet with a number [of] the leaders of our . . . program and they, too, saw the need to change."[9] With the message received, Palo Alto created a new father-daughter program called Y-Small World, retaining all of Y-Indian Princesses' parent-child bonding objectives, minus the cultural appropriation. Reconsideration of Indian Princesses led to a study of Y-Indian Guides as a whole, and in Palo Alto, Y-Indian Guides later became Y-Westerners. Both programs remained locally vibrant, though with a less avid constituency, twenty years later.

"A liberal university town during a period of social activism," Palo Alto "was uniquely receptive to this approach," remembers Rosen. Though some of his peers agreed with the rationale behind the change, no other Bay Area branch followed suit. In 1977 Rosen became an executive at the Torrance YMCA in Los Angeles, and found a Y-Indian Guides program he described as "a large, immovable object." Any changes to the program were limited to the realm of helping Guides be more respectful and authentic.[10]

In a bit of historical irony, Princess Pale Moon, who claims Cherokee and Ojibwe heritage, is in fact Rita Sentz, who infamously sang the national anthem for over a decade before Washington Redskins (currently the Washington Commanders) games and at two Republican

National Conventions. She is not enrolled in any tribe.[11] Rosen saw no need to question her authenticity at the time, having found merit in her words. In transitioning to Y-Small World and Y-Westerners, the Palo Alto YMCA discovered the mechanism that would ultimately end national support for Y-Indian Guides nearly thirty years later: personal intervention from American Indians, whether real or invented.

From nearly its inception, the popularity of Y-Indian Guides overruled any questioning of its propriety. And while Palo Alto, and the various Guides for Understanding, foreshadowed the eventual persuasiveness of the "moral" argument (that the appropriation Y-Indian Guides encouraged was wrong), that argument would only gain traction at the national level once enrollment and accompanying finances were in decline.

The Task Force on Y Parent-Child Programs met on Halloween 1979. Part of their agenda was a discussion of Indian Guides' noticeable decline. Their report listed several reasons, including a drop in the elementary school population; staff turnover; financial problems faced by local Ys; and a challenge in providing parent-child programs for older children with the resources at hand.[12] One window into this decline is found in merchandise sales:

	1975	1976	1977	1978	1979
Manuals	46,134	40,983	32,858	31,454	27,345
Headband	124,363	118,906	114,486	77,555	72,244
Emblem	97,020	97,560	95,068	78,624	52,503
Small Charter	16,071	21,727	20,240	22,150	18,021

This precipitous decline not only significantly reduced the amount of financial support the National Longhouse received, but also left them with an average overhead (in 1979) of $100,000 in unsold goods. By comparison, annual royalties netted National Longhouse only about $40,000.[13] These numbers demonstrate an ever-growing separation from, even disaffection with, the YMCA, which in turn exacerbated a disconnect between individual "tribes" and the National Longhouse's entreaties to consider their depictions of Native Americans with greater awareness and sensitivity.

What is striking, however, is that these declining numbers did not seem to give any of the Y's leadership entities serious cause for reconsideration of Indian Guides' purpose, operation, or appeal. In fact, the October 1979 minutes of the National Board asserted that oft-repeated yet long-disproven claim (with some exceptions) that simply refused to die: "Many, many families are introduced to the YMCA through Y-Indian Guides and its corollaries. Good initial experiences for parents and children attract members to support and leadership." Meeting minutes instead celebrated the ever-broadening circle of Indian Guides spin-offs: parent-daughter programs, Y-Trail Blazers for older children, and so on. The only problem discussed in 1979 meetings was finding a better way to enhance revenue through increasing program material sales.

The YMCA had found itself at a crossroads. Social and economic changes were forcing the institution to move its focus away from youth development toward family development. The YMCA National Board's minutes from this time captured this shift when it stated, "The family, not the individual, is the real molecule of society, the key link in the social chain of being" (a quote ascribed to American sociologist Robert Nisbet). This shift, however, was still in its infancy. Only a few months earlier, after "vigorous discussion," the Indian Guides' Middle Atlantic Region Council rejected a recommendation to rename Indian Guides the National Parent-Child Council.[14]

While staunch advocates of Indian Guides were able to fend off the first attempt to dissolve the National Longhouse, the die had been cast. Y-Indian Guides, Y-Indian Princesses, and the other programs were eventually aggregated administratively into Y Parent-Child Programs.[15] While ostensibly including all Guides programs as foundational familial experiences, these programs also began to include other methods for reaching into family life.

To facilitate this transition, the national office created a National Family Life program whose charge was to identify which social issues the YMCA should address in the 1980s. For program members this task required a careful assessment of changing family dynamics: "The

Figure 35. This photograph, taken in Portland in 1979, suggests that Y-Indian Guides had become a highly diverse and integrated program. National statistics suggested otherwise. Kautz Family YMCA Archives, University of Minnesota Libraries.

changes of the past four decades affecting American family life have been enormous and swift, forcing families to struggle, bend, separate, reconstitute, and alter lifestyles and relationships. The nuclear family, the extended family, the one-parent family, the two-parent working household, the couples without children, the communal family are examples of the growing pluralism in American family life."[16]

As YMCA leaders saw it, the post–World War II era created, or accelerated, a constellation of forces that threatened the American family. Postwar suburbanization and urbanization moved young people away from extended family networks (a foundational concern for the YMCA). Television and mass media promoted materialism and idealized new family norms, pushing mothers into the workforce to supplement family income. The women's rights movement also provided more opportunity for women to do more than stay at home or work in a relatively narrow list of fields: teacher, nurse, secretary, flight attendant, waitress. All of these factors put new stresses on spousal relationships and isolated children from their parents by placing them in childcare. These changes also led to increased feelings of loneliness, despair, distrust, and fear, which in turn exacerbated rates of divorce, separation, runaway youth, and drug dependency.

If the success of Indian Guides had rested on the relatively stable white middle- and upper-middle class family where Dad worked and Mom stayed at home, how would it grow in this new culture of more diversely composed families?

While urban youth and young adults (overwhelmingly male) were a key client of the Y from its earliest years, by the 1980s the YMCA had become a far more suburban entity. This change centered the family as its main clientele, and family cohesion became its main goal. Increasingly, the YMCA emphasized its parent-child programs as an "integral part of the National YMCA thrust toward strengthening family life," calling on "YMCAs to improve the quality of family relationships and strengthen the development of family members."[17]

Citing (perhaps overzealously) the Y's long history of working with families, they traced this shift toward families back to the post–World War II era.[18] The YMCA laid out seven goals for the National Family Life Thrust. Significant to Indian Guides was the fifth, "Strengthening Family Life," and the seventh: "The National Board will have assisted Member YMCAs to increase Y-Parent Child group membership and to enrich Y-Parent-Child programs through increased staff training, lay leadership development, parent education . . . and creative program development."[19] This set the stage for a greater acceptance of the inclusion of mothers and daughters, which, factoring in the decline of father/son enrollment, undoubtedly allowed the Y-Indian Guides programs to persist longer than they would have otherwise. Similar in intent to Y-Indian Guides (the strengthening of parent-child and familial bonds), Y-Indian Princesses (father/daughter) and Y-Indian Maidens (mother/daughter) were like Y-Indian Guides with one key difference: father-daughter dances, the highlight of the year for many Y-Indian Princess tribes.

As Robert Eilenfeldt recalls, "the biggest event of the year for our nation was our Sweetheart Banquet, [held on] the Thursday of Valentine's week. Every year we would take over the Arlington Convention Center, which is in . . . the largest suburb of Dallas. . . . They would take a room and there'd be 500 dads and their daughters and the dads would be in their best suits or tuxedos, the daughters would be in their best dresses, and we would have a DJ come in and do a dance and lead the dancing." As with Y-Indian Guides, for many families Y-Indian Princess programs created lifelong memories. "Butterfly Kisses," a favorite song of Mr. Eilenfeldt and his daughter from the Sweetheart Banquet, was their first song at her wedding years later. But for years Eilenfeld, his daughter, and their comrades were unaware of any problems created by the program in which they participated.

The Dallas YMCA, under the direction of Jerry Haralson, vice president for operations and program, took the lead in attempting to turn around Y-Parent-Child Program membership in decline. Representing a cohort of true believers that continued to see Guides as the solution to society's ills, despite evidence to the contrary the Dallas Y, as others had done in the past, re-emphasized Y-Indian Guides' role as a "basic YMCA program for working with families and strengthening the quality of family life."

However enthusiastic, Ys like Dallas were increasingly in the minority. Recognizing this tension, the Y acknowledged that "although Y-Indian Guides and its accompanying program formats have had significant success in the past, the present and the future present a formidable challenge to insure growth, maintenance, and enrichment of thousands of YMCA families in the 1980's."[20] The YMCA desired that its Y-Parent-Child programs, primarily the Guides programs, be a "viable and powerful family life development program," but maintained the stance, now more fantasy than attainable reality, that the program had not reached its full potential in leadership or participation. National Longhouse and Guides members hoped the national thrust would be a shot in the arm, effecting program resurgence at all levels. Supporters were, however, honest about the issues Indian Guides faced and understood that the YMCA and Y parent-child programs needed to respond to social change while maintaining fiscal sustainability. Without addressing critical structural issues, staffing, financial resources, professionalism, and program quality and consistency, Y-Indian Guides and related programs would face continued decline.

By the mid- to late 1970s, growing criticism of Indian Guides was slowly chipping away at the YMCA's long-held and exaggerated image of the program as a source of ardent Y members and leaders. This image was further eroded by the National YMCA's long inability to exert influence on or collect annual dues from individual "tribes." Passionate Indian Guides defenders and advocates remained, but their numbers were diminishing. Even so, as they were able to solicit the support of enthusiastic, wealthy, or well-connected individuals, their influence remained potent.

Figure 36: In November 1975, at eighty-two, Harold Keltner was honored by the National Association of YMCA Program Directors for his outstanding contribution to YMCA activities (that is, Y-Indian Guides). Presenting the award is DeWitt Smith, then the leader of Indian Guides for the Metropolitan St. Louis YMCA. By this time it was estimated that more than seven million fathers and sons had participated in the program. Keltner died in August 1986, more than thirty years after Joe Friday. Gateway Region Young Men's Christian Association (S0473).

On August 2, 1986, Harold Keltner died at the age of ninety-three, predeceasing Martha, his wife of more than sixty-seven years. While his obituary in the *St. Louis Post-Dispatch* celebrated him as the founder of Y-Indian Guides, it also captured the decline of the once ubiquitous program, noting that its current membership was "more than 200,000," a precipitous drop from its late 1960s, early 1970s heyday. An Indian Guides museum had been named in his honor at Sunnen Lake, the article noted, but it was "being renovated." Keltner had retired in 1954. While he was still an important symbol and speaker within the Indian Guides movement, he had long since relinquished any influence over it. He lived more than thirty years longer than Joe Friday, but sought to keep his friend's memory alive whenever he spoke at Indian Guide events.

"WE CAN FIX IT"

In 1994 Barbara Taylor moved from her position as child care and program director for the Lansing, Michigan, YMCA to take on the role of associate director for family programming at Y-USA. Lansing's Parkwood Branch had a popular Y-Indian Guides program, and to Taylor's knowledge, it was not controversial. When she moved to Y-USA, the transition in nomenclature from Indian Guides to Y Parent-Child Programs was well underway. As Taylor sat in on various meetings and training opportunities, Indian Guides would "often come up, and people would want to discuss it. . . . We had activists within the YMCA who wanted to have these conversations. I don't think we were questioning whether we, as YMCA staff and volunteers, were true and authentic. I think we just knew that Native Americans felt disrespected." But even before external criticism became sharper and louder, developments within the YMCA were making its association with Y-Indian Guides more problematic. According to Taylor,

> the number of Ys offering Y-Indian Guides was declining. Ys struggled to get African American or Hispanic families to take part in Indian Guides because they had their own culture [and] they didn't quite understand why we had glorified this Native American culture. The program didn't work for them. We also had seen a surge in single parent families and the traditional dad with a daughter or dad with a son program wasn't working for many families. The YMCA Maidens for mothers and daughters and Braves for mothers and sons never really took off in many Ys.

In addition, by the mid-1980s "dads were playing a more significant role in raising their children and that same need to set aside one-on-one time and to be very intentional about spending quality time together wasn't as prominent."[21] The executive director of St. Louis's South Side Y, Mary Ann Zirkle, made similar observations in an interview she gave to *South Side Journal* in 1985. Y-Indian Guides may have originated on the

South Side, she observed, but "it very quickly became a more suburban-oriented program." The working-class South Side never seemed interested in Indian Guides, "despite a long push to re-establish it in the 1960s." This disinterest was a "residual effect of suburban flight." Besides, Zirkle added, the YMCA nationally was now focusing on the whole family.[22]

Throughout the 1990s, regional differences between Ys offering Indian Guides became more pronounced. In the South and parts of the Midwest (Michigan, Ohio, and Illinois) the program remained strong or even grew. On the East Coast and in Indiana and Wisconsin the program was floundering, and in the Dakotas, Wisconsin, and Minnesota, Ys found they could no longer "relate to the Indian theme" and replaced Indian Guides with the Y-Voyagers.[23] The Minneapolis YMCA, originator of Y-Voyagers and home to a large urban population of American Indians, had been informed by the United Way that funding was at risk unless they created a "non-Indian theme program."[24]

In 1991 the Lattof YMCA in Des Plaines, Illinois, conducted a survey of YMCAs known to have Y-Indian Guide Programs. The survey showed that roughly a quarter (522) of YMCAs offered the program, with a total youth participation of 106,287.[25] Sixty percent of the participants came from just six states: Pennsylvania, Illinois, Ohio, North Carolina, Texas, and California. Reflective of the divide, in those six states 404 Ys used the Indian theme (6 did not), and only 62 Ys saw a need for a non-Indian theme in the program. Finally, at the national level, Dave Mercer, president and CEO of the national YMCA, called "for a redirection of energy toward family and parent-child programs." The National Advisory Committee (NAC), he said, could benefit from expanding its scope into "alternative parent-child programs that complemented the already successful Y-Indian Guides-Y-Indian Princess Program."[26]

A restructuring of funding streams enacted in 1975 to support the program through sales of manuals and materials failed to provide sufficient revenue to maintain the National Longhouse and had become a drain on the national YMCA.[27] Quality concerns, which in the 1930s amounted to doubting the ability of lay volunteers to instruct youth, were now an imminent threat to the program. In a 1991 memo to YMCA executives with Y-Indian programs, Bob Telleen, associate director of the Program Services Division of Y-USA, wrote that the program was "under assault in at least two areas."[28] The first assault came from the "parts of the country which tolerate alcohol." Camp hosts had been complaining "for years," wrote Telleen, that "they cannot control Y-Indian Guides fathers who insist on drinking at night after their children are in bed."[29] These incidents were taking a toll on the YMCA's reputation. Telleen recounted two egregious complaints to underscore the issue. The first came from a woman who insisted she would never bring campers to any site that hosted Indian Guides retreats, "even if assured that there will be no Guiders in residence on her proposed event weekend." The second complaint came from an "irate military base which threatens never to let YMCA program events onto their base again after three successive weekends of 'out-of-control' Y-Indian fathers and children, several of the graphic alleged violences to the peace and tranquility of the base which were alcohol consumption related."[30] In 1993 eastern chief Jerry Williams reported that he had sent a letter to program executives and staff because "there have been problems with alcohol at campouts. A YMCA staff person should be at all campouts. This is the wave of the future because of risk management." Western chief Jeff Guzzardo agreed that "alcohol and authenticity issues should be moved to the beginning of these training sessions since these are a major issue and concern."[31] In 2021, when California-based former YMCA executive Larry Rosen spoke with three friends, all former Y executives,

> each one of us could recount too many stories about how [alcohol] was abused routinely, and how drunken fathers who abandoned their sons at camp-outs for too much beer was one of the major problems with the program. A lot of staff time was concentrated on trying to keep guys from being falling-down drunk. . . . The vast majority of dads were responsible and good with their sons, but I saw some of the ugliest father-son incidents in my life at camp-outs with guys getting shit-faced while their sons were hanging on their pant legs crying, "Daddy, Daddy!" and the dad would be swatting away at him because he was drunk as a skunk. I mean, there was some really brutal stuff.[32]

The second assault Telleen described was the "insensitivity to the truth about American Indians."[33] Particularly for metropolitan associations with large numbers of American Indian residents, the images connected to Indian Guides had become an embarrassment. Many felt the need to distance themselves from the theme and avail themselves of new programming options. Indian Guides leaders came to view these alternative programs, especially Voyagers, as an existential threat. They believed acceptance of Y-Voyagers "as a competing program to the existing Y-Indian Guide programs may begin as a small crack . . . but may eventually lead to a loss in the Indian name and theme."[34] Furthermore, the statement claimed, Voyagers, a "thinly veiled Y-Indian Guide look-alike," might be more offensive than Indian Guides, which "give[s] full credit to Native Americans for use of the Indian culture, values and love of nature," whereas Voyagers made only superficial reference.[35]

Telleen hoped to neutralize many of the protests against Indian Guides by partnering with the still-developing National Museum of the American Indian (NMAI) in Washington, DC. With the substantial input of national chief Dave Connelly, Telleen disseminated resolutions on April 28, 1991, encouraging the NAC "to promote, encourage and support sensitivity and authenticity with respect to the Native American cultural heritage in all aspects . . . of Y-Indian Guides Programs" and to work closely with the Smithsonian on development of the NMAI "for mutual benefit." In a May 17 memo, Telleen explained, "

> This is a collaborative plan whereby the YMCA will help promote family memberships in the newly developing [museum]. . . . In return, the YMCA will receive use of the vast Smithsonian resources to help us further sensitize our program materials, develop new program resources and gain access to authoritative American Indians who might be enlisted to help us further authenticate our regional Y-Indian programs and advocate for the needs of the American Indian the way the State of Florida Y-Indian Guide Longhouse and the Seminole Indians now collaborate."[36]

The NAC's July 9 minutes reveal the folly of Telleen and Connelly's proposal. NMAI director W. Richard West Jr. was reported to have had a "very negative" reaction to the Indian Guides' "Pals Forever" manual and their suggested collaboration, which would have included the Smithsonian providing material on various tribes and nations.[37] West's reaction: "I don't play White Man, why are they playing Indian?"[38] Even so, organizational energy remained focused on reforming the program and finding ways to more authentically honor, promote, and learn from Native American cultures.

In response to these two perceived threats, the YMCA of the USA's Program Services Division released a set of minimum standards in 1993 to address these and other issues. Part of the standards state that "the Y-Indian Guide program at all levels should be sensitive to the traditions, culture, and religious beliefs of the Native American Indian without violating any of those values."[39] They also stated that drugs and alcohol should be banned from all functions.

Even as the National Advisory Committee struggled internally with criticisms concerning Indian Guides, two articles in the YMCA magazine *Perspective* revealed evolving attitudes in professional circles. In August 1994, Palo Alto YMCA associate executive director Debbie Garver discussed the need to update Indian Guides now that the program was almost seventy years old. "Much has changed" since 1926, Garver observed, "including the development of a strong sensitivity and awareness of the diversity of people and their cultures in this country." As Larry Rosen reported above, she noted that the Palo Alto Y had replaced Y-Indian Princesses with Y-Small World in the late 1970s, utilizing "a more universal and acceptable theme."[40]

In April 1995 Thomas Heck, outdoors program director at the Community Services YMCA in Asheville, North Carolina, published the first open condemnation of Indian Guides by someone within the Y. Asheville, he reported, had voted the previous fall to discontinue the program "based on the belief that it is demeaning to Native American people." Having spoken to many other YMCA personnel on both sides of the issue, Heck raised six recurring arguments supporting Indian Guides and responded to each one. To the first—that Y-Indian Guides had to be a good program because it had begun in 1926 and was still around—he said that by that logic, women should never have been given the right to vote, since they had been disenfranchised for so many years. To the second—that since Joe Friday had helped establish Y-Indian Guides, its continuance was justified—he countered that no one member of any group could speak for everyone in it. To the third—that the large number of people involved in Indian Guides proved its success—he pointed out that child labor had been widespread for many years, but was finally abolished when people exposed its immorality. To the fourth—that if Indian Guides was wrong, the national YMCA would have said something—he responded that YMCA management was site-based, not nationally imposed, and thus change would have to happen locally. The fifth argument was that there was no reason to change Y-Indian Guides unless it was openly attacked. Given that Native Americans comprised one percent of the national population, and many lived on reservations, Heck thought they had enough challenges in their lives already without having to personally convince every white person not to engage in appropriation; thus, lack of protest did not justify Indian Guides' ongoing operation. And finally, to the argument that Y-Indian Guides was fine if done respectfully, authentically, and in collaboration with Native Americans. Heck asked readers to imagine a scenario in which Y-Indian Guides became Y-Hasidic Jew Guides, and let it play out to absurd and degrading detail. "I contend," Heck concluded, "that Y-Indian Guides goes beyond the study of Native American culture and offers, in many cases, a mockery of it. We must not degrade the lives and cultures of others in our efforts to create a positive and lasting relationship with our children."[41]

The discussion, often started but then tabled, had found new life. "It was hard to ignore," remembers Barbara Taylor, "because Ys across the country read *Perspective* magazine." Taylor called Heck to better capture his thoughts, then went to the National Advisory Committee to share these. Since she was based in Chicago, Taylor reached out to a woman on the Native American Affairs faculty at the University of Illinois. "I said, 'Across the country our YMCA Indian Guide programs are being criticized for their portrayal of Native Americans. We really want to hang on to this program. It has an impressive history in many YMCAs. We want to be sensitive, we want to be more authentic, we want to be respectful. What can we do?' . . . She said to me, 'You need to change the name.' " Taylor took this message back to the NAC, but found insufficient support to effect the change. For the next few years, Taylor says she lived with the sense that, "Okay, we can't change the name or the program, but we'll fix this; we'll make it work." As in the 1970s, the NAC issued another document, "The Responsible Use of the Native American

Theme," which caught the attention of Y staff, but likely made nary a dent with most "tribes." When Taylor spoke to "tribe" leaders, she heard the same common refrains: "I'm not doing anything wrong. What we're doing is respectful, we're honoring this culture. Native Americans should be honored that we've recognized the role they play in raising their children, and we want to be like them." At the same time, Taylor heard increasingly from Native American activists whose message was loud and clear: "This is offensive to my children. Nobody's living this lifestyle that you're celebrating and emulating. . . . You're writing about Hollywood's portrayal of Indians and that's not who we are, or who we were or . . . how we want people to remember us." Though Indian Guides leaders claimed to be educating children about Native American culture, many Native Americans responded that they were either teaching them wrong or inaccurate things or perpetuating harmful stereotypes. If someone was going to teach white kids about Indians, they argued, it should be Indians themselves, not self-appointed intermediaries.

MAN OF THE HOUSE

Even as the YMCA was fighting a battle on multiple fronts to "fix" Indian Guides, it participated in the production of a film that ultimately helped unmask the increasingly out-of-step ethos of Y-Indian Guides and bring it under broad public scrutiny and wider repudiation by the national Y: 1995's Disney film *Man of the House*. Ironically, the Y provided significant input and had some control over the finished product, but grossly misjudged how the public would receive the movie and in what light it would cast Indian Guides.

As then Hollywood YMCA CEO Norris Lineweaver recounts, in the late 1980s two producers from New York City flew to Los Angeles to pitch an idea to Disney executive Michael Eisner. The pitch was interrupted, however, when Eisner abruptly excused himself. When the producers asked Eisner's secretary to explain his sudden departure, she revealed that he had a Y-Indian Guides meeting with his sons. Upon their return to New York City, the producers learned about Indian Guides and why it was so important to Eisner. Abandoning their original idea, they returned with a script proposal for a comedy based on Indian Guides. Eisner liked the idea, and *Man of the House* was released in

1995, starring Chevy Chase, whose Indian Guides name was "Squatting Dog." The movie is about a nine-year-old boy (Jonathan Taylor Thomas) trying to drive away the new man in his mother (Farrah Fawcett)'s life by signing up for Indian Guides, "thinking the 'rinky-dink' program will be sheer torture and drive the man away."[42] Instead, the two form a close bond. Y-USA was very supportive of the project, believing at the time that the movie's depiction of Indian Guides would create a groundswell of new enrollments. Even so, says Barbara Taylor, "I remember [director of Program Services] Lynn Vaughn saying, 'They're going to do this with or without us. If we're at the table, at least we can try to influence the script.'" "We thought [Indian Guides] would be more central to the story than it actually was," recalls Carmelita Gallo, a Y-USA executive in the mid-1990s and early 2000s. "I think we got carried away and overestimated what exactly would happen."[43]

Entertainment Weekly magazine described *Man of the House* as "borderline amusing for the one or two scenes in which it seems to recognize that the Indian Guides are a suburban embarrassment." It describes the "film's low point" as a "skin-crawling montage in which everyone does a rain dance to the pumped-up beat of 'Gonna Make You Sweat.' I'd be hard-pressed to say whom this sequence insults more: Native Americans, who've been trying to outrun these tribal-kitsch cliches for years, or fathers and sons, who—according to 'Man of the House'—have no hope of bonding apart from their shared eagerness to act like degraded idiots."[44]

To its credit, the national YMCA did attempt to curb the more egregious elements of the movie. It is unclear, however, whether the attempts were born from a genuine concern for the depiction of American Indians or for the YMCA brand. In a November 1992 conference call, for example, associate Y-USA Program Services Division director Bob Telleen expressed concern. "We have problems in particular areas of the US in reference to the Native Americans. We don't know if they are going to reference the YMCA in the movie. We also don't know how the Whittier, CA tribe is run, which is where Michael Eisner is from. We don't want to defeat but we must be careful that we don't get criticized."[45] There had been previous discussions in 1991, likely for the first time, by the Program Committee of the National Board on whether the Y

Figure 37: When the National YMCA sought to discourage Disney from using a war bonnet in its film *Man of the House*, the Y was informed that Disney had purchased such an item, like the ones seen on this father and son, from the Westside Hollywood YMCA. Kautz Family YMCA Archives.

should take a "static vs pro-active stance" on the use of American Indian themes following that year's World Series, which featured the Atlanta Braves and their fans' overzealous display of the "Chop." Though the Y attempted to restrict the use of "war bonnets" in Indian Guides, *Man of the House* producers purchased said items from the Westside YMCA in Los Angeles. Another point of contention involved a scene where Chevy Chase's character creates a cutout of Custer and throws an ax at it. The Y won the concession that no children would throw axes and that it would be made clear that the cutout was the character's idea and not a standard Indian Guide activity. A final point of disagreement involved the depiction of American Indians and their language. The Y lobbied for a greater role for Leonard Red Crow, the American Indian lawyer in the movie who learns of and assists the tribe, teaching them the rain dance that *Entertainment Weekly* called "skin-crawling." The Y wanted Red Crow to have more lines, though the bulk of his performance is during a montage where he teaches the boys and fathers "native ways," legitimizing their efforts (and by extension Y-Indian Guides). The Y also objected to a scene referred to as the "Lakota Story" in which Chase's character tells a fictitious parable of Pain-in-Butt and his father Takes-Too-Long-on-Can. The producers reminded the Y that they had previously agreed to the inclusion of the scene and had been assured by their technical adviser, Chief Leonard George, that the script had been reviewed by "other Native American representatives" who deemed it "harmless entertainment."[46] What is most striking about this episode is that the YMCA reviewers' critiques of the movie script were not reflected back on Indian Guides itself. For decades "tribes" wore "war bonnets" during their meetings; from the outset they had concerns about older boys participating in a program ostensibly intended for six-to-nine-year-olds. And lastly, as described throughout this book, there were factions within the Y that lamented the appropriation and lampooning of American Indian culture. The concern now appeared to be that programmatic deficiencies had been highlighted and magnified through the medium of the silver screen.

Producers of the Disney movie reached out to a variety of American Indian groups, including the Assembly of First Nations / National Indian Brotherhood, Old Raven Consultation, LTD, Haida Corporation, Native American Casting, and American Indians in Film.[47] All thanked the producers for seeking their perspective, claimed that there was no harm in the script, and, overall, thought that if anything the movie showed how ridiculous white stereotypes of native cultures were. This tracks with efforts from individual Ys who reached out to local Indigenous groups.

The Tempe, Arizona, YMCA, for example, connected with the Multicultural Resource Center of the Tempe School District 3 for consultation following a "situation regarding the recruitment of participants for the Indian Guides Program" at a local elementary school. The center offered four suggestions, all indicating that many programs had begun to move away from the American Indian theme and they should as well, given the need to be culturally sensitive to native cultures.[48] Tempe leaders failed to take the hint, and later claimed that the situation was "turned into positive feelings." But Tempe served as a bellwether that the long-simmering issue of "authenticity" was reaching a breaking point.[49] There were certainly Ys, such as those in Florida, who sought and received support for their programs, in Florida's case from the Seminole.[50] But as scholars such as Danielle Endres have shown, when programs like Y-Indian Guides seek permission, they put those tribal nations in a double bind that places "upholding sovereignty and resisting racist stereotypes" in conflict.[51] American Indians possess both a racial and legal identity (sovereignty).[52] On the one hand, by granting permission, tribes reinforce ownership over their culture (including name, language, religious practices, and objects); on the other, the granting of permission is seen by many as reinforcing colonialism by condoning the commodification of one's culture.

ONE FINAL STUDY

By the late 1990s, sufficient concern had been raised both within and outside of the YMCA that there was no longer any doubt that meaningful action was required. Norris Lineweaver, aka Little Brave Running Crow in his late 1940s Oklahoma Y-Indian Guides "tribe," had pursued a career in the YMCA, and was serving on the National Membership and Program Committee in the late 1990s. As he remembers, several prominent issues began to raise the stakes of the discussions concerning Y-Indian Guides. First, as the internet came into popular use in the mid- to late 1990s, Native American communities wanted to register their domain names. The Seneca tribe, for example, went to register the Seneca name and found

> it happened to be an independent web site of a Y-Indian Guide group somewhere, and they had songs and stuff in it . . . that were really enlightening to the Seneca tribe. . . . And of course, the Seneca . . . have tremendous investments in casinos and entertainment parks and so forth, and they thrive on that [name]. They take it very seriously. So with the advent of the internet . . . came a lot more exposure with these, if you will, rogue Indian Guide groups who had a very limited relationship with their local Y and hardly felt accountable to the Y's concern about the character in which a local group would carry the [Indian Guides] theme.

Indeed, the host of a website called Blue Corn Comics reported on an Indian Guides website he visited in 2000. Among the more blatant stereotypes he found on the site were an emphasis on Plains Indians and "'camping out,' with technology no more sophisticated than 'making crafts.' (Have the Indian Guides ever heard of Chaco Canyon, Cahokia, or Tenochtitlán?)"; Tonto talk, with phrases like "How how"; strict male-female roles with men as hunter-gatherers and women as stay-at-home "princesses"; and ritualistic songs so clearly silly that they mocked rather than honored Native Americans.[53] According to Pam Atkins, a longtime Y staffer in Dallas, Texas, some Ys "had taken 'Indian' out of the actual name, and it was just Guides, for the very reason that if anybody decided to Google 'Indian,' the Y wasn't the first thing that popped up. According to what I had been told . . . [this was] kind of how we got on the hit list."[54]

A second concern centered on the Y's fastest-growing initiative at that time, after-school programs. Their success depended on continued access to public schools. If the YMCA ran afoul of the law or even public opinion, it stood to lose a great deal.

Thirdly, Y-Indian Guides had always been an overwhelmingly white, suburban program. It simply didn't work in the inner city and attracted only minuscule numbers of people of color. As the YMCA sought to better engage and serve communities of color, Y-Indian Guides did not seem to send the appropriate message to those communities. Carmelita Gallo recalls that Y CEOs in places like Seattle (Neil Nicoll) and Minneapolis (Harold Mezile) were hearing from their Native American communities that Y-Indian Guides was offensive and needed to change.[55] Vernon Bellecourt, leader of the Minneapolis AIM chapter, said it was impossible to simply "reform" Y-Indian Guides and its related programs. People were so caught up in playing Indian, he said, that they totally ignored "the holocaust that claimed at least 16 million of us." He called for the elimination of "racist images" that he deemed "a cancer on American popular culture."[56] As Gallo recalls, "We were espousing this very inclusive, respectful strategy called the [YMCA National] Diversity Initiative." Central to the initiative was "the platinum rule": treat others not just as you would want to be treated but as they want to be treated. "Once that became utilized and known by local YMCAs, there started to be an inner conflict with the way some YMCAs portrayed Native cultures in the program." Native American community newspaper articles in Oklahoma, upstate New York, Washington State, and elsewhere began to write about and criticize Y-Indian Guides. "The [National YMCA] Board of Directors decided that we really needed to look more into this and establish a Task Force [which reported to the National Board's Program Committee] to study what was going on." Their desire was certainly to preserve vibrant father-son and mother-daughter programs, but "really moving away from the focus on native cultures."[57]

The Association Resources and YMCA CEOs Task Force, established in May 2001, began to carefully study the situation and make recommendations for change. Norris Lineweaver chaired the task force and appointed its members. Pam Atkins, a third generation YMCA employee from Dallas, Texas, had watched her father and younger brother go through the Indian Guides program together. She went on a few campouts, but "was very much not welcomed as the only girl." In Dallas "the program was always very, very strong," she recalls. "I know my dad always went to his Guide dads first as he started looking for board members, as he started looking for fundraisers." The goal now was not to attract boys into youth development programs but to bring in the whole family for swimming and other physical fitness programs. Guides was, however, an exclusively suburban experience. By the mid-1990s, says Atkins, "they had taken out the use of 'Ugh' and 'How' . . . That was a Hollywood thing. . . . No Indian tribe ever used those words. . . . [But just] because they took it out on the program level, that did not necessarily mean that the volunteers took it out. I always joked that some of my dad volunteers were really theater kids that never got the chance to perform, and so being able to go in a comfortable place and dress up to the nines and get a persona was part of the love of the program. And so the 'Ugh' [and] the 'How' didn't go away as much as it should have."

(While several current and former YMCA officials bemoan "rogue" Y-Indian Guides "tribes" that made changes to the officially issued handbook—engaging in their own brand of outreach, performing "rituals," dressing in attire, and designing websites—which caught the attention and ire of critics, it is fair to point out that even an "orthodox," uniform approach done exactly as Harold Keltner and Joe Friday intended would still have been deemed problematic by critics.)

When Y-USA formed the National Task Force, Atkins was sent to Chicago to represent the Dallas YMCA "to save the Indian." While she was aware that other Ys had been "hit hard" by criticism from their communities, "Nobody was calling [Dallas] on the carpet, nobody was boycotting the program, nobody was questioning what we were doing." Bruce Klunder and Bob Eilenfeldt were two volunteer leaders who accompanied Atkins to Chicago. They had heard rumblings about a need for change, and they were dead set against it. Eilenfeldt, one of the NAC's five regional chiefs, said all five had "talked ahead of time to kind of agree that we were going to stand tough on this. So we went in prepared, because we knew what they were going to want to do."[58] Barb Taylor accompanied Eilenfeldt and Klunder on the El to dine downtown, and she told Klunder in no uncertain terms that "the Y was going to go on with us or without us. What did we want to do?"[59]

Figure 38: Bob Eilenfeldt and his daughter, "Proud Pawneees" of the Airport YMCA (Dallas), preparing for the 1996 Kachina Festival in Fort Worth, Texas. Eilenfeldt was an ardent participant in and supporter of the Y-Indian Guides and Indian Princesses programs, becoming a regional chief and then a member of the National Advisory Council. After receiving pointed feedback from Native American representatives in Dallas and at a national meeting in Chicago, Eilenfeldt and other volunteer leaders like Bruce Klingman made the difficult decision to support the YMCA as it moved to phase out the program's Indian theme. Photo courtesy Robert Eilenfeldt.

When the meeting convened the next morning, remembers Eilenfeldt, "we still stood tough, we still said no, this isn't disrespectful and it's a very important program to the parent-child relationship and we can't support [a change]." But a prominent part of the meeting was input from Native Americans who found the program offensive. "I wasn't ready for what we heard there. I evolved" over those discussions, recalls Bruce Klunder.

> We had several natives come talk to us about how our appropria-
> tion of things that are sacred to them—you know, pink and green
> feathers that we stuck in our daughters' hair—was heretical to them
> and man, I never understood that. I mean, in one of the programs
> in Dallas, we had a full-blooded Choctaw Methodist minister . . .
> from a community in Oklahoma, come to our things. . . . We had
> him give our camp fire talks and everything. . . . But what these
> people were saying was really was heartfelt and they said, "Hey
> look at what you're doing." So I said okay.[60]

Listening to the variety of perspectives shared around the table, Atkins decided, "Okay, I've got two degrees in education. Dallas can keep the Indian. We're going to make it educational. . . . I'm going to figure out who I need to talk to and we're going to make it authentic, and it'll be an educational program. We won't offend anybody because we're just going to fix it. I can do this."

After checking in with her constituencies, Atkins got to the work of "saving the Indian" for her YMCA. She reached out to Dallas's American Indian Chamber of Commerce and had a very positive meeting with its then president, who promised she would set up a meeting with members of the chamber and Y-Indian Guides staff and volunteers. The president's grandson had participated in the program, so Atkins felt surely a reasonable, inoffensive solution could be found.

One of those invited to this fateful meeting was Peggy Larney, who describes herself as a full-blooded Choctaw Indian. Born in Macalester, Oklahoma, and educated at Haskell Institute (now Haskell Indian Nations University) in Lawrence, Kansas, Larney came to Dallas as a young adult. (Under the 1956 Indian Relocation Act, numerous Indigenous peoples were moved to Dallas. In the ensuing years many chose the city as a place to start their professional lives.) "This was just the beginning of the Indian community here in Dallas," she remembers. A pianist at her Indian Methodist church, she became secretary of what is now the Urban Inter-Tribal Center of Texas, which partnered with a local "white church" to create the American Indian Center, which established preschools for children and provided job training for adults.

By 2001 Larney had been working for many years as director of American Indian education programs in the Dallas Independent School District. She and her staff "had been going to schools talking about unwanted stereotyping of American Indians, and just before that I had campaigned for removing ten American Indian mascots. . . . We were able to do so internally and very peacefully."

As Larney recalls, she was contacted by the head of the American Indian Chamber of Commerce about attending a meeting with representatives of the YMCA's Indian Guides and Indian Princesses programs. "And I said, 'Well, you know where I stand. I don't really want to work with anybody or anything that has stereotyping'—and at that time stereotyping was the popular word we used—'against American Indians.' And she told me, well, that was all right, and so I went."[61]

On the appointed day Atkins arrived with her boss, the Dallas Y's COO, two program directors from two of the area's biggest "tribes," and two volunteer members of the NAC. True to her word, the chamber president had brought representatives from "at least nineteen different tribes" to the table.

The meeting began pleasantly enough. One gentleman noted that Dallas's curriculum included an "Indian" story that was essentially a reworked version of "Goldilocks and the Three Bears." He could share any number of authentic Native American stories. Why not use them instead? "Great," replied Atkins. Things were off to a fine start. Others brought craft projects that were legitimate for use in the program. Wonderful. But there was a Choctaw representative sitting at the end of the table who, as Atkins remembers, "didn't look as happy to be there as everybody else."

Indeed, as Larney recalls, she grew frustrated that no other members of the chamber seemed critical of what the YMCA was doing. Just weeks before the meeting, she recalls, she had seen an article about a YMCA program where a white father was calling himself the chief of a particular nation and his daughter was an Indian princess. "The title of chief," she told the Y representatives, "is not handed to anybody in a tribal nation. . . . Each nation has its own way of choosing chief. But for a white person to go and call himself chief of . . . something that calls itself an Indian name, that is very, very disrespectful." Daughters, too, Larney continued, had to go through a sacred ceremony to receive an Indian name. "I said that is totally disrespectful what the white people or the Y is doing to the American Indian, especially for that to be in the newspaper. And so my presence with the group that day was just to tell . . . the Y what they were doing was not acceptable. You just don't go doing that."

As Atkins, recalled, still moved in the retelling of the story, "As you can see, I'm a pretty emotional person, and I was like, 'That's not our intent! How do I fix it? I don't want to be offensive! Please help me.'" Larney replied,

> "I'm sorry . . . I'm not going to tell you that you can't do it, but there is no way for you to do this program and it not be offensive to somebody." And then she started to educate us all. . . . "There's too many different tribes; you do this and it doesn't even exist. . . . You say you're honoring us by building the relationship between the dad and the child and in some tribes it's the matriarch that's the [head of the family]"—you know, just educated us. So she said, "Thank you. I applaud you for trying the way you're trying, for reaching out. You are the *first person* since all of this started. . . . *Nobody* has ever asked us anything."

As Larney left, Atkins remembers thinking, "I've still got this." But then other tribal representatives "kind of changed their tune," acknowledging the validity of Larney's critique. The meeting came to an unceremonious end, but Atkins and her Y colleagues were allowed to remain in the room. Once she and the other Y representatives were alone, remembers Atkins, "I burst into tears . . . and I turn around and I'm not the only one in tears. . . . [They] all looked at me and went, 'We're going to change, aren't we?' And I was like, 'Do we have a choice?' . . . 'What are you going to do?' they asked." Atkins replied, "I don't know. I don't know."[62]

Bob Eilenfeldt, who was also in attendance, remembers that "when I heard [Larney] speak passionately about how our program was disrespectful I went home that night and prayed. I'm a Christian and deeply involved in our church, and I pray, and the Holy Spirit said, 'It's time to support changing the program.' And I contacted Barbara and told her that." His decision did not come without cost. For example, he was driving through Oklahoma on business when a man he did not know called him, identifying himself as an Indian Guides participant. "And he got really upset with me when I said I want to be part of the solution instead of part of the problem, and he said, 'You sound like a Nazi.' . . . I was quite hurt by that. That ended the conversation, needless to say."[63]

It became clear to everyone on the task force that "the Indian" could not be saved. The program could not be "fixed." Their work turned to finding a way to preserve the essential elements of the program without relying on an Indian theme. In September 2001 the YMCA's national board received and accepted the task force's recommendation to "change the name and thoroughly review the Y-Indian Guides Program." Until the review was complete, programs would simply be called "Y Guides," "Y Princesses," etc.[64]

In December the task force met to begin its work. One great source of help was the Santa Clara YMCA, its CEO, Dave Thornton, and its staff. An ardent supporter of the YMCA's diversity initiative, Thornton offered to pilot a new framework for what became Adventure Guides. Members of the task force, consulting with staff and volunteers from across the country, began the arduous task of preparing for this massive change. "Then Y-USA went into full program development and dissemination mode," says Barbara Taylor. "We created a transition guide, a rollout kit, and new marketing materials. We wrote two new manuals, developed new training, and we started a website. I mean, we put a lot of resources into trying to make sure this succeeded." But success was a long way off, and complete success—having a program that neither offended nor caricatured Indigenous peoples—simply unattainable.

As Lineweaver recalls, "We spent a lot of time in the early discussions . . . [asking] what was really core to the experience of Y-Indian

Guides that we want to keep? We might have listed seven or eight virtues of the program, and we retained seven out of the eight. . . . The eighth one was extolling the virtues of Indian culture. Many people believed in that, but that wasn't really what Native American activist groups" found acceptable.[65]

As Pam Atkins recounts, the task force invested considerable discussion in trying to find a new theme for the program. What would allow groups to dress up, have different names, earn patches, create community? "Pioneer Guides" led right back to encounters with Indians. So did "Cowboy Guides." "Pirate Guides" didn't exactly promote ethical, healthy living. Finally, says Pam Atkins, "it was decided, 'We're not going to come up with a theme. We are not going to tell people what to do. We're going to be Adventure Guides. That way, people can figure it out. Well, you've got some people that are like, 'Sweet!' and other people [saying] 'I don't know what to do! I don't know how we're going to handle it!'"

In the spring of 2002 Y-USA distributed a forty-seven-page transition plan to all YMCAs still sponsoring Indian Guides. Signed by Barbara Taylor, it announced a new program launch for the fall of 2003. The exceedingly thorough document gave painstaking instructions for local Ys and thoroughly reviewed the reasons for the impending change and the outcomes of the task force's deliberations. It provided leaders with copious amounts of material on how best to address the removal of the Indian theme with different constituents who might be at different places on the "change adoption curve." It included a sample presentation and a list of frequently asked questions, concluding with a collection of comments provided by Native Americans and other individuals who had reviewed the program. One anonymous source, for example, commented, "The bottom line is that Indian people are generally offended when you pretend to be them. . . . It makes no difference whether you try to make the program more 'authentic.' There is no way to make it palatable. It is racist and demeaning. I choose such harsh words very carefully, because I know you are not a racist organization. But this program is, and will always be, a cancer that eats at the very integrity of every thing else good you seek to do."[66]

A *Chicago Tribune* article in the fall of 2002 suggested that plenty of Y-Indian Guides participants would reject this criticism outright. One interviewee who'd been in the program for twelve years opined that Y-USA was underestimating the backlash that would ensue from the removal of the Indian theme and assumed that some would go along with the change, but others would "develop their own theme or break away." A second fifteen-year participant said, "People are evaluating their options . . . but I would not be surprised to see people move away from their Ys entirely."[67]

Y-USA and the task force were united in their confidence that they were doing the right thing. From Atkins's perspective, the transition should not have been that difficult. When she spoke to Indian Guides dads resistant to change, "They were very diehard about spending time with their child. . . . Okay, that has nothing to do with an Indian. 'We want to dress up. It's fun and the kids['] . . . faces light up when we are in front of the campfire and we're all dressed up.' I'm like, 'Could you dress as something besides an Indian and get that same effect?' . . . 'Well, yeah.' . . . [They found] their vest . . . and their head bands . . . in the lockbox and it brought back all these memories. . . . But none of that is Indian. And their nicknames were hugely important. Again it's a nickname. If you don't have an Indian name and you call it a nickname, guess what? You still got it, as long as you don't try to offend anybody. . . . When I asked the right questions, it was not Indian. That was not the piece of it that was really important to them."

But things were not that simple. First, many people were not even willing to have the kind of conversation that Atkins had with Peggy Larney or with those worried about the transition. To them, what they were doing was an homage to Native Americans. Their intentions were pure and their actions were simply misunderstood. Second, as Atkins makes clear, the task force could not find a straightforward way to replace the theme. Harold Keltner and Joe Friday had harnessed and the YMCA had helped disseminate something they never fully understood and certainly never completely controlled. "Playing Indian," an impulse older than the United States itself, was a powerful force not easily supplanted. The camaraderie between fathers, the warm intimate relationships between parents and children, were to Indian Guides proponents all a result of the Indian theme. They could not be so easily disassociated. As Stephen Hanpeter recalls, the change was "pushed on us. . . . Adventure Guides has nothing. . . . Of course, I rejected it. . . . Not having the theme there . . . made me not take it seriously."[68] Jim Wotruba was chief of Indian Guides and Indian Princesses "tribes" in 2001 when the change was announced. "For *my* nation [the Comanche], it was about 100% against changing it. . . . So we [named ourselves after] the Comanche River. The Mohawks . . . became the Missouri Hawks and that was shortened to MO Hawks. We actually sat in meetings to try to preserve names." While their YMCA staff insisted only the name, not the program, was changing, Wotruba's group wasn't buying it. "We are like, 'Everything comes from this: Native Americans and the way they have respected the land and respected each other. So if you take that away, everything is changed.' It ruined it all." Understanding that the YMCA would provide no programmatic support to a group calling itself "Indian Guides," Wotruba and the other fathers did everything they could to avoid alienating their groups while complying with the YMCA's directives. Ultimately change occurred, but grudgingly. "We did . . . [a] ceremony to say out with the old in with the new, and as nation chief I . . . announce[d] that we were doing this transition. People stood up and booed. . . . The Y changed the name and it changed the patches, but every one of my kids consider themselves Indian Guides." Yet even as he shared difficult memories, and perhaps given the passage of time between those events and the present, Wotruba acknowledged, "In fairness to the Y, at least in my experience, I do think it was only a name change. . . . All the good they do and everything that I like best about it never changed."[69]

In 2003 the Y stopped producing and distributing materials for Indian Guides and instead promoted programs like Adventure Guides, which retained the programmatic goals of strengthening the parent-child bond while being less likely to alienate Ys from their broader communities. That November Barbara Taylor sent an update to the "Adventure Guide Program Network" that included a note of congratulations from YMCA national executive director Ken Gladish. Acknowledging the many years of listening and learning it took for the YMCA to finally make this momentous change, Gladish addressed those still resisting it. "Those who cry out 'political correctness run amok' simply do not understand the need for listening, for common courtesy and for respect. Your action embodies those traits and the YMCA will be better for it now and in the future."[70] The update also featured an excerpt from the *Dallas News* featuring Vicki Yellowfish, a Native American mother of four, and Peggy Larney, the leader of Indian Citizens against Racial Exploitation who had spoken so candidly to Pam Atkins and her colleagues a few years earlier. When American Indian groups visited local schools, said Larney, "Sometimes the little kids will ask us if we live in a teepee. They'll say, 'Do you still shoot people with arrows?' Because that's what they see on TV. . . . To me, [participants in the Indian Guides program] were playing out a fairytale; like Indians aren't real, but they are real. You can play-act Cinderella—that's a fairy tale—but not a people who still exist."[71]

Ultimately the YMCA could not escape the reality that American Indians are people who still exist. Throughout Y-Indian Guides' more than seventy-five-year history, there were many within the Y who questioned the program's appropriateness and utility for youth development, as well as the potential harm it posed to the YMCA's relationships with communities and to its organizational identity. Despite those reservations, the YMCA retained a program about which it always had a variety of concerns, but kept because it was popular and had the potential to win over influential members like Michael Eisner. To its credit, by the late 1960s the national YMCA had begun to take seriously the harms caused by the program. The nature of the YMCA's federated structure, however, limited their ability to influence local YMCAs, local "tribes," and their supporters.

Ardent backers of the program frequently point to Joe Friday's role in the founding of Y-Indian Guides to not only legitimize the use of American Indian culture but demand it. Much has changed in American culture, however, during Y-Indian Guides' tenure, not least of which is the evolution of masculine norms and the regaining of political voice by Indigenous peoples. Simply put, Y-Indian Guides failed to adapt to the times, and in many cases chose to double down on its more egregious elements. In renouncing Indian Guides, the YMCA was reminded how little control it had over the program, and how passionately some of its adherents would resist. Though far from peak participation in Indian Guides, today many families continue to don feathers, beat the drum, and become pals forever through "rogue" groups and a breakaway organization called National Longhouse.

EPILOGUE

ONE WOULD BE hard-pressed to find an individual in the early twenty-first century more dedicated to Indian Guides than Greg Measor. A participant in the former program beginning in 1993, Measor had three children—two daughters and a son—who all went through a combined Indian Guides and Princesses program. Like many others, the Bedford, Ohio, "tribe" never had a graduate-out age. As he became more involved and more entranced with the program, which had suffered decline in the preceding decade or two, Measor and some of his friends decided to "build it back up." As many predecessors have noted, he observed: "Volunteers were key to really making those programs happen. A lot of the Ys . . . had a staff member that was responsible for [Indian Guides], but . . . that was a small part of what they were supposed to take care of. . . . They basically would give us help when we asked for it." As he and his friends began the process of rebuilding, they "just got infected by it." They started reemphasizing the Six Aims, tribal meetings, and the Indian theme "because those were the things that were so unique and special about it." The annual rituals at campouts and other activities became beloved by children and fathers alike. "My own kids . . . still rave about it." Each child adopted an "Indian" name and created a corresponding symbol, "and they've seriously talked about having those symbols tattooed on themselves."[1]

Measor and his friends developed "a keen interest" in Indian culture, visiting local libraries as well as Indigenous powwows in the region. "Once in a while, we'd actually have Native Americans come to us. And one time we had a group of them perform and do some traditional dances for us at a campout." During a service activity helping collect and load relief supplies for the Pine Ridge Reservation in South Dakota, which was in distress after a severe winter, the driver told Measor's group he knew a Native American who lived nearby.

> And so we ended up meeting this lady. Her twin sons . . . were hoop dancers. . . . She also had a daughter who did traditional grass dancing. . . . When they came to our event, their grandmother happened to be down from Pine Ridge, and she came, too . . . and she talked to the kids a little bit. So it was a very tender moment to be able to meet folks like that . . . and know they were open about their culture. . . . Sometimes you meet folks who are like, "That's not white man's culture, that's ours." But if you want to slam the door shut, you'll never have cultures want to interact and understand each other. . . . I've met a lot of Native folks who are very open to that whole thing. Better to share the cultures and let them engage a little bit. . . . Okay, yeah, we all misuse each other's cultures a little bit. But to what end? Indian Guides was always meant to be a positive use of it.

When Y-USA announced that it was decommissioning Indian Guides, "That just really kind of tore me up inside. . . . You're really willing to walk away from this whole Indian theme? How are you ever going to replace some of that stuff we did around a campfire using the Indian theme? How are you ever going to make it that unique?" During this same period he became involved in a small regional Y-Indian Guide Program support group composed of many individuals who had been part of the program for many years and were dedicated to its continuance. They understood the external pressures bearing down on the YMCA at the time, but thought, as Barbara Taylor and Pamela Atkins and other YMCA executives once had, that with some tinkering and consultation, Indian Guides could be saved. Unlike Taylor and Atkins, Measor had never been confronted by someone like Peggy Larney who might have disabused him of that notion. "Let's meet at the table and talk about this a little bit more," was the sentiment of the group. "How do we uplift this rather than just keep it under the table for the rest of time?"

Why was retaining the Indian theme so important? "I think that goes all the way back to the foundation of it," he says. "When Harold met

Joe, he found that Indian culture was a natural element to allow fathers
and children to relate to something together. . . . You've got to remember that Harold Keltner . . . [believed] it was divine intervention that
brought him and Joe together by happenstance. . . . [Indian Guides]
lasted for all these years because there was a unique aspect to it that
allowed them to make a connection."

When it was clear the die had been cast, several "tribes" in the Ohio
area and elsewhere "basically revolted and said, 'No, we're not doing
that. If you think you're going to force us to do that, we'll just go
away.'" He thinks Y staff were hoping they would relent over time or
just quit, but as the three-year transitional period was elapsing, many
remained intent, as Pam Atkins once had, on "saving the Indian." Two
of them were members of a Christian outreach organization called
Lighthouse. After approaching the organization's leadership about
preserving Indian Guides outside the auspices of the YMCA, on April
15, 2002, the parties approved the official establishment of National
Longhouse, Ltd., a "new national, Christian, Indian-themed parent-
child program." A quick succession of planning meetings in the region
helped forge the program's basic structure. Early volunteers David
Garberson, Jim Advent, and Measor were soon joined by Don Bittala
and Brian Jemmi. In less than a year, National Longhouse created
"Native Sons and Daughters Programs" that included the whole family.
As the National Longhouse website states, "To prevent similar mistakes
from occurring as in the past, National Longhouse developed strong
national guidelines. It . . . is committed to receive input from the First
Nation people." There are National Longhouse chapters in Alabama,
California, Florida, Indiana, Michigan, Ohio, and Tennessee.[2] (There
may be other groups not listed on National Longhouse's website, and
there are certainly a few "independent" tribes, even a few still sponsored
by local YMCAs.)

Part of this process of creating Longhouse International involved
reaching out to descendants of Harold Keltner and Joe Friday for their
blessing. Charles Keltner Shanks, Keltner's eldest grandson, responded
quickly, pleased to know that there were still people wanting to continue his grandfather's legacy. He joined the new National Longhouse,
attending and speaking at several of its earlier annual meetings. (When

interviewed in 2015, Gene Keltner Cannon made it clear she had no part in her grandson's "blessing.")[3] A small delegation, including Measor and his son, contacted and visited Joe Friday's descendants on Bear Island, staying in cabins owned by Friday's grandniece. Friday's niece, June Friday McInnis, was among those who received them. As Measor recalls,

> The most thrilling aspect of that whole trip was that those folks were so open to us and welcoming to us. I mean, there's a Tribal Band Office . . . there on Bear Island. And we were invited to go there, and they had a library and kind of a historical collection and things, and they basically just opened it all up to us. . . . The family started out in the 1890s [from the St. James Bay area] and then . . . they stopped on Bear Island and [Joe's father] died. . . . Another one of the elders on that island took them in, and again, it was that divine intervention that caused that all to sort of happen. Because if that wouldn't have happened, Harold wouldn't have met Joe. . . . I can't believe it was all happenstance. You have to believe there was definitely a plan in place somehow.[4]

Having secured the blessings of at least one individual from the Keltner and Friday families, National Longhouse, Ltd. moved forward, and by June 2007 separated from Lighthouse. By that time, the organization had developed the expertise to stand on its own two feet as a nonprofit 501(c)(3) organization. In addition, recalls Measor, the programs did not attract as broad a cross-section of families as Lighthouse had hoped. "Like it or not, this program model is really not built for underprivileged families. There's a cost to doing it, and sadly so."

Many early leaders have remained involved with National Longhouse since its inception. Along the way Greg Measor has become a collector of all things Indian Guides–related. His activities are "part obsession, part quest, part just fun." He has shared his resources, and in fact has revealed more to the authors about Joe Friday's history than they were able to obtain from Friday's descendants. Some of National Longhouse's most exciting acquisitions came when they contacted Woolaroc to ask about the National Indian Guides Center. By the early '90s, Measor recalls, interest in the center had waned and the YMCA stopped promoting it, so Woolaroc staff removed the displays and put them in storage. "We found out about this, so we made some inquiries to Woolaroc, and sure enough, they knew that they had these things, so . . . they shipped it to us and said, 'Okay, if you guys want to be caretakers of this, sure, take it.'" A number of these articles were displayed prominently at National Longhouse annual meetings and other events for years.

Measor is just one of numerous individuals interviewed for this book who cannot understand what was so wrong about Y-Indian Guides. To these people, the program helped develop a genuine interest in and respect for Native Americans. "I was in awe of them," remembers a former Y-Indian Guides "chief" from the Twin Cities area. Their admiration is so intense, their intentions so sincere, and the program's visible benefits so great that it is inconceivable to them that anyone could take offense if they truly understood what the program was about. As we have seen, a number of Native Americans, including Kwaquilth Indian Ronn Wilson, were devoted to the mission and vision of the Y-Indian Guides programs. In Wilson's view, misuse of Native American culture was rare and more a function of well-intentioned ignorance than an expression of neocolonialism. Yet Wilson also observed, "Just the overall concept of any group . . . trying to re-create Native culture is inherently offensive because of the history of what happened to Native people. . . . It doesn't matter how sincere you are. If you don't understand the culture, you cannot understand the offense." Wilson felt he was providing Indian Guides members with the cultural competence necessary to avoid giving offense to Indigenous peoples. Yet, curiously, he remembers telling groups on several occasions, "Here is what the coup feather represents and why you do not ever wear it in public. In your private gatherings, okay, but if you're going to portray a cultural context, do it right and pay very close attention to those symbolic items that could cause offense." Wilson tried to draw a bright line between what was acceptable in private and offensive in public, but it was a line he could not regulate once its interpretation was left to others.

As Philip Deloria, Shari Huhndorf, and others have shown, playing Indian or going native is a long-standing practice in the United

States. As Karl May has shown us, it is not even a practice reserved
to our shores. While claiming to pay tribute to Indigenous peoples,
non-Natives have often become lost, as Michael Chabon has noted,
not in an imaginary world of Indians but in a world of imaginary
Indians. This world was powerful and profound, even to many of those
responsible for separating the YMCA from it. Barbara Taylor says she
never questioned the impact of Indian Guides. "The testimonials from
kids who participated with their dads, and dads who participated with
their children, were extremely powerful. . . . I think if there was a stick-
ing point, it was always why does it have to be this Indian theme."[5]
Pam Atkins recalls the story of a divorced father who found a way to
preserve his relationship with his daughters through Indian Princesses.
"He could give a speech that would bring me to tears, talking about
if he hadn't had this program . . . then he would not have had the
relationship with his girls. . . . One dad talked about how he learned
to braid hair at a campout, because his daughter had long hair and
they were all sitting in a circle braiding, and he got in the circle and
learned."[6] Despite playing a central role in the decommissioning of
Y-Indian Guides, Norris Lineweaver, aka Little Brave Running Crow,
can still speak ardently of its positive influence. "Joe Friday described
the relationship between father and son as a spiritual relationship and
taken very seriously. . . . It was right on. . . . I've talked to other colleagues who went through Y-Indian Guides and they expressed some
of the same views, how impactful it was to be so close to other fathers.
There was just no other program like that. . . . I really truly understood
the passion that people had resisting what we were doing later in the
'90s . . . I mean, I was a part of it." But for the sake of the YMCA and
out of respect for the rising tide of criticism, Lineweaver has no qualms
about the choice he made.

As Thomas Heck showed in 1995, there are at least six consistent
arguments for preserving Indian Guides:

1. It endured for decades, so it must be good.
2. It was founded by a First Nations person, Joe Friday, which
   makes it OK.
3. It was widely popular.

4. The National YMCA never told us it was wrong until Native Americans started complaining.
5. If no one protested in our area, we shouldn't have had to change it.
6. It can be successful if done with respect, authenticity, and in collaboration with Native Americans.

As shown in chapter 7, Heck also provided effective rebuttals to each of these arguments. For a small number of true believers, including Measor and Charles Keltner Shanks, there is a seventh reason: it would never have happened if God hadn't orchestrated it. Many, though certainly not all, of those who spoke glowingly about Indian Guides did so in spiritual or mystical terms, though not to the degree expressed by Measor. As Barbara Taylor remembered, "Program leaders and participants really believed the Native American theme was the magic and the thread that tied it all together. They didn't believe that the program could survive without that magic." Dave Lehleitner affirmed that Indian Guides was very much a Christian movement when he was a boy in the 1940s. "Faith was always a big factor." With a decline in church attendance over the last several decades, Indian Guides provided an outlet for spiritual inquiry. If men didn't want to affiliate with a specific Christian denomination, perhaps they could, "like an Indian," at least believe in a Great Spirit who was the author of nature.[7] Stephen Hanpeter went through Indian Guides with his father, lived in Japan for seventeen years, and married a Japanese woman before returning to the St. Louis area. She was not interested in allowing their two sons to attend church. "I thought [Indian Guides] is based on Christian values. . . . I thought that was a good way for us to at least touch on values, touch on ritual, touch on Christianity even though it was very much downplayed for them. And for me, it was kind of a replacement for church since we couldn't go there. . . . With Indian Guides, those values are in my eyes just totally core. It's almost like religion. I mean, the religion *is* the values."[8] For some, Indian Guides provided a ritual, one might go so far as to say a liturgy, otherwise missing from their lives.

Figure 39: Promotional image of a young boy kneeling before a man in Native American dress. The mystique or "magic" of the Indian theme in Indian Guides is, to its adherents, irreplaceable. Kautz Family YMCA Archives.

Christians often speak of their faith springing from the gratitude they have, knowing that God sacrificed himself out of love for them. What Indian Guides ultimately promised and often delivered to fathers and children was love. In 2015 seventy-two-year-old Les Neal Jr. of St. Louis noted that even though his son was forty, "We're still Pals Forever and he hasn't forgotten it." When asked how that manifested itself, Neal replied, "Not only does my son tell me that he loves me at least once a week, when we get talking about different things, he brings that model up that we are Pals Forever, which I think is kind of cool."[9] For most Indian Guides apologists, this miracle of sorts was so precious that messing with the formula, so to speak, was simply too dangerous a proposition to contemplate.

To Larry Rosen, this sentiment comes from a different, if still well-intentioned, place. Participants in Y-Indian Guides or most other programs experienced in youth or with their children fall in love with "the way it was when I joined." The thing they love the most, the thing that attracted them and hooked them is the thing they want to perpetuate—and for every good reason: "This meant so much to me, this meant so much to my sons, so much to my family. This changed our lives for the better. I want this for everybody." Nobly motivated, but in love with yesterday's answer to a world that has changed dramatically in the generations since that love affair began. . . . Helping people bridge from that joy to how we're going to bring joy to another more diverse generation in another time with different realities is the artwork of the leadership of a nonprofit.[10]

But even apart from the controversies surrounding the misappropriation of Indigenous cultures, says Rosen, the Y-Indian Guides program had run its course. "It died of natural causes, as programs are wont to do." Indian Guides "worked beautifully," but almost exclusively for middle- and upper-middle-class suburban whites. It relied heavily on the contributions of stay-at-home mothers, who picked up a lot of the slack at home so that Dad could "run from work to a meeting." When women joined the workforce in larger and larger numbers beginning in the mid-1970s, Rosen observes, "*that* more than anything was the death knell for that type of programming."

If all seven of the above reasons to preserve Indians Guides fail to convince critics, there is always an eighth, less diplomatic, rationale: we have a constitutional right to express ourselves as we wish. While this argument is very rarely expressed, it nonetheless operates as a tacit, functional argument. In this context, "You don't understand, we're honoring Indians" can very easily sound to critics like "I won't listen to you. You can't make me change."

So who gets to decide what actually honors and conveys respect to Indigenous peoples? If one professes admiration, even awe, for American Indians, and a significant number of them express anger, dismay, even pain, regarding the ways in which that "admiration" is expressed, what is the appropriate response? Is it to lean on the opinions of Indians who aren't offended, or at least who view this form of expression as less offensive than others? Or is it to listen and to change in order to convey the very respect one professes to hold? The former response suggests that, as this book has argued, Indian Guides was not really about Indians and conveying respect for them. It was about using the Indian as a means to develop better relationships between fathers and children. This it did effectively, though only for a narrow and relatively privileged cross-section of the population, and at a significant cost. That cost was detailed in part by a resolution against the use of Native American-themed mascots passed by the American Psychological Association (APA) in 2005. Broad research showed that the continued use of mascots, symbols, and personalities has a negative effect on all students, but especially Native American students, because it restricts the ways they see themselves. The APA summarized its findings in five points, arguing that the use of mascots is harmful because it:

- Undermin[es] the educational experiences of members of all communities—especially those who have had little or no contact with indigenous peoples. . . .
- Establishes an unwelcome and often times hostile learning environment for American Indian students that affirms negative images/stereotypes that are promoted in mainstream society.
- Undermines the ability of American Indian Nations to portray accurate and respectful images of their culture, spirituality, and traditions. . . .
- Presents stereotypical images of American Indians. Such mascots are a contemporary example of prejudice by the dominant culture against racial and ethnic minority groups.
- Is a form of discrimination against American Indian Nations that can lead to negative relations between groups.[11]

To take this assessment, and the opinions of millions of Native Americans, seriously is to choose the latter option, to surrender control over something that one doesn't truly own out of respect and concern for the welfare of others. As Peggy Larney observes, "White people need to [understand] the word 'decolonization' or 'colonization' . . . especially over American Indians, because there are so few of us when it comes to the census. Our Indian people are very quiet. Most of them . . . won't say anything. It's just a fact that white privilege and the very concept of playing like they think they have the power over Indians or any minority [is wrong], and that is something that they really need to learn."

The authors understand and respect the difficulty of a decision like this when so many years of fond memories and strong relationships were forged in the program. But we also believe that the decision to remove the "Indian" from Indian Guides was correct, and should have happened earlier. By the late 1960s the editors of *Long House News* already recognized the great chasm separating the "Indian" being portrayed in their program and genuine historical and contemporary Native Americans. By the mid-1970s numerous attempts were being made to "correct" abuses and regularize practices that even in their best state would still have been offensive. The Palo Alto YMCA quickly and effectively transformed Indian Princesses and Indian Guides into Y Small World and Y-Westerners, precursors to Adventure Guides. Larry Rosen recalls making numerous speeches to his professional colleagues predicting the imminent and inevitable decline of the Indian Guides programs. One in particular stands out in his memory. In the mid-1980s he was speaking to "a couple hundred" YMCA staff in Houston, Texas, "from my experience over the previous fifteen years with the program, forecasting its doom and its demographic death, and how YMCA staff had enabled that fatal condition by [failing] to look at the changing landscape of diversity, the expanding roles of women outside the home, and the over-scheduled family." A prominent executive stood up in the back of the room and yelled, "This son of a bitch is full of it! Greatest program ever! Don't listen to him!" And most YMCAs with an Indian Guides program didn't listen for another fifteen years. Owing to the Y's federated structure, Larry Rosen was allowed to facilitate the changes made in Palo Alto in the mid-1970s. Other Y leaders were free to stand pat, whether because they truly believed in the program, or because they feared the backlash that would ensue from local "nations," from numerous alumni, or from a prominent board member or donor who loved the YMCA because of its Indian Guides program.

That real love for the program and our efforts to depict Y-Indian Guides and its related programs in a positive light in this book will undoubtedly frustrate some. In our efforts to understand the programs, however, we must acknowledge that we see and understand why they were so dear to so many for so long. Without question, the Y-Indian Guides programs strengthened countless families. We hope, though, that those who benefited from the programs will also see the real harm those programs caused, and can carefully and compassionately examine what was so problematic about them, and understand why they needed to end. Perhaps, upon reflection, participants will see that they too were negatively affected through their participation that made them unintentional accomplices to the forces of colonialism. This kind of difficult but important rumination was done not only by adults.... like Norris Lineweaver, Barbara Taylor, Pam Atkins, Bruce Klingman, and Bob Eilenfeldt but also by children like nine-year-old Christina Bohmfalk of Foothill Ranch, California. In the spring of 2001 Christina's father, Dave, asked her: If she knew some of the things they were doing in the program "actually kind of bothered" American Indians, should they change the theme? "Change it," she replied. "But I would miss being a Shoshone."[12]

In the final analysis, Americans of all backgrounds must acknowledge that "playing Indian" largely ignores a central fact of our nation's history. The story of Indigenous peoples is inextricably linked to centuries of efforts by European and European American settlers to exterminate them, whether physically or culturally, from the continent. Playing Indian almost always involves a process by which European Americans erase this uncomfortable truth from that narrative.

It's okay to admire Indigenous peoples, study their history and culture, buy their art, even invite them to speak to your group, so you can better understand them. If they invite you to participate in an activity, so much the better. But imitation, in this case, is not the highest form of flattery. It is, in fact, a harmful practice best left in the past.

NOTES

INTRODUCTION

1. David Treuer, *The Heartbeat of Wounded Knee: Native America from 1890 to Present* (New York: Riverhead, 2019), 1.

2. "Y-Indian Guides Initiate Action Planning for Interracial Advance," *Long House News* 31, no. 2 (Spring 1968): 1.

3. Danielle Endres, "American Indian Permission for Mascots: Resistance or Complicity within Rhetorical Colonialism?" *Rhetoric and Public Affairs* 18, no. 4 (Winter 2015): 175.

4. Bryan McKinley Jones Brayboy, "Toward a Tribal Critical Race Theory in Education," *Urban Review* 37, no. 5 (December 2005): 425–46.

5. Danielle Endres and Mary Gould, "'I Am Also in the Position to Use My Whiteness to Help Them Out': The Communication of Whiteness in Service Learning," *Western Journal of Communication* 73, no. 4 (2009): 419.

6. Steve Long-Nguyen Robbins, "Someday They Will See," *Do Diversity Right!* (official weekly newsletter of the Woodrick Institute for the Study of Racism and Diversity, Aquinas College, Grand Rapids, Michigan) 2, no. 7 (February 2002). This article was reprinted in a YMCA Parent-Child Programs transition packet sent to YMCA CEOs by Barbara Taylor, Spring 2002, 43–44. Copy provided by Barbara Taylor.

7. Jennifer Brooks, "State Senators Try to Slash Minnesota Historical Society's Budget over Sign at Fort Snelling," *Minneapolis Star Tribune*, April 25, 2019.

8. Treuer, *Heartbeat of Wounded Knee*, 1, 10.

9. Treuer, 15.

10. Philip Deloria, *Playing Indian* (New Haven, CT: Yale University Press, 1998), 7.

11. Deloria, 31.

12. Shari M. Huhndorf, *Going Native: Indians in the American Cultural Imagination* (Ithaca, NY: Cornell University Press, 2001), 2, 6, 8, 14.

13. Harold Keltner, unpaginated, undated typescript, scanned copy in the author's possession.

14. Huhndorf, *Going Native*, 8.

15. See Michael Kammen, *Mystic Chords of Memory: The Transformation of Tradition in American Culture* (New York: Vintage, 1991), 185.

16. Huhndorf, *Going Native*, 23–24.

17. Huhndorf, 26–27.

18. Robert Rydell, *All the World's a Fair: Visions of Empire at American International Expositions, 1876–1916* (Chicago: University of Chicago Press, 1984), 24.

19. Alan Trachtenberg, *The Incorporation of America: Culture and Society in the Gilded Age* (New York: Hill & Wang, 1972), 7, 8.

20. Huhndorf, *Going Native*, 38–39.

21. Quoted in Curtis M. Hinsley, "The World as Marketplace: Commodification of the Exotic at the World's Columbian Exposition, Chicago, 1893," in *Exhibiting Cultures: The Poetics and Politics of Museum Display*, ed. Ivan Karp and Steven D. Lavine (Washington, DC: Smithsonian Institution Press, 1991), 347.

22. Huhndorf, *Going Native*, 48–49. See also Tony Bennett, *The Birth of the Museum: History, Theory, Politics* (London: Routledge, 1995), 60–61, 66.

23. Huhndorf, *Going Native*, 33–34.

24. Huhndorf, 33, 34.

25. Deloria, *Playing Indian*, 183.

26. Scott B. Vickers, *Native American Identities: From Stereotype to Archetype in Art and Literature* (Albuquerque: University of New Mexico Press, 1998), 1–4.

27. Jason Edward Black, "The 'Mascotting' of Native America: Construction, Commodity, and Assimilation," *American Indian Quarterly* 26, no. 4 (Autumn 2002): 607.

28. John Keilman, "Indian Guides, Princesses Must Drop Indian Theme or Leave YMCA," *Chicago Tribune*, September 19, 2015. The LaGrange program chose to leave the YMCA rather than give up their Indian theme.

29. Lewis Kamb, "Y Sheds Indian Trappings Now Deemed Racist," *Seattle Post-Intelligencer Reporter*, April 25, 2003.

30. Stephanie Houston Grey, "The Tail of the Black Snake," in *Decolonizing Native American Rhetoric: Communicating Self-Determination* (New York: Peter Lang, 2018), 227–28.

31. Casey Ryan Kelly and Jason Edward Black, eds., *Decolonizing Native American Rhetoric: Communicating Self-Determination* (New York: Peter Lang, 2018), 9.

CHAPTER ONE

1. Susan Curtis, "The Son of Man and God the Father: The Social Gospel and Victorian Masculinity," in *Meanings for Manhood: Constructions of Masculinity in Victorian America*, ed. Mark C. Carnes and Clyde Griffen (Chicago: University of Chicago Press, 1990), 67–78.

2. J. E. Hodder-Williams, *The Life of Sir George Williams* (London: Hodder and Stoughton, 1907), 3.

3. Clyde Binfield, *George Williams and the Y.M.C.A.: A Study in Victorian Social Attitudes* (London: Heinemann, 1973), 11.

4. Hodder-Williams, *Sir George Williams*, 21.

5. Binfield, *Williams and the Y.M.C.A.*, 15. The word *evangelical* refers to a cluster of Protestant Christian denominations that believe in the inerrancy of scripture, the deity and vicarious atonement of Jesus Christ, the need for a personal conversion or "born again" experience, and the need for constant evangelism, that is, sharing the Christian message with those outside the faith.

6. It should be noted that there was, for many decades, an ongoing tension within the YMCA regarding its religious and its social programs and purposes. Older, often more

conservative members often complained of overreach by their more progressive counterparts. Conservatives tended to emphasize saving souls and building up the strength of believers, while progressives tended to focus more on social ministry for its own sake, using the Sermon on the Mount, the parable of the Good Samaritan, and expectations of the return of Christ to motivate their ministries. Conversely, internationally the work of the American YMCA in foreign nations that were not historically Christian was to be in support of existing missionary activities and not to establish new Christian communities.

7. Harald Fischer-Tiné, Stefan Huebner, and Ian Tyrrell, eds., *Spreading Protestant Modernity: Global Perspectives on the Social Work of the YMCA and YWCA, 1889–1970*, Perspectives on the Global Past (Honolulu: University of Hawai'i Press, 2021), 215–16.

8. C. Howard Hopkins, *History of the YMCA in North America* (New York: Association Press, 1951), 202. Ellen Brown of the Buffalo YMCA is often heralded as a pioneer in this work.

9. L. Doggett, *Life of Robert R. McBurney* (New York: Association Press, 1925), 247. The Springfield Training School exists today as Springfield College.

10. *Year Book of the Young Men's Christian Associations of North America, 1920–1921* (New York: Association Press, 1921), 217.

11. Hopkins, *History of the YMCA*, 203.

12. Hopkins, 205; Eugene A. Turner Jr., *YMCA Camping: An Abbreviated History* (Chicago: YMCA of the USA, 1984), 15.

13. Turner, 15, 21.

14. *Encyclopedia of Chicago*, online ed., s.v. "Playground Movement," accessed July 2, 2015, http://www.encyclopedia.chicagohistory.org/pages/976.html; Paul Hillmer, *The Cleveland YMCA: Reflections on 150 Years of Service to a Community* (Cleveland: Herwell, 2004), 52.

15. Minneapolis YMCA, *Annual Report, 1910–1911*.

16. For more on Muscular Christianity, see Clifford Putney, *Muscular Christianity: Manhood and Sports in Protestant America, 1880–1920* (Cambridge, MA: Harvard University Press, 2003).

17. William George Escott, "The Need for Boys Work in the YMCA," graduation thesis, 1900, George Williams College theses and dissertations, box 17, Kautz Family YMCA Archives, University of Minnesota Libraries (henceforth Kautz Archives).

18. Paula Lupkin, *Manhood Factories: YMCA Architecture and the Making of Modern Urban Culture* (Minneapolis: University of Minnesota Press, 2010).

19. Hopkins, *History of the YMCA*, 26–27.

20. As the YMCA's 1859 Articles of Confederation stated, "Any difference of opinion on other subjects [than the basic Christian affirmation of unity], however important in themselves, but not embraced by the specific designs of the Associations, shall not interfere with the harmonious relations of the Confederated Societies." Hopkins, 51–52.

21. Hopkins, 84–98.

22. Robert Lancaster, *Serving the U.S. Armed Forces, 1861–1986* (Schaumburg, IL: Armed Services YMCA of the USA), 1–19.

23. Taft quoted in Frederick Harris, ed., *Service with Fighting Men: An Account of the Work of the American Young Men's Christian Associations in World War* (New York: Association Press, 1922), vii.

24. *Summary of World War Work of the American YMCA*, internal report for private distribution, International Committee of Young Men's Christian Associations, 1920, 2.

25. *Summary of World War Work*, v.

26. "When Pershing Arraigned the Association," *Association Men*, July 1917, 543.

27. *Summary of World War Work*, 26.

28. "When Pershing Arraigned the Association," 544.

29. *Summary of World War Work*, 26–27.

30. William Howard Taft, *Service with Fighting Men: An Account of the Work of the American Young Men's Christian Associations in the World War*, 2 vols. (New York: Association Press, 1922), 1:115.

31. *Summary of World War Work*, 28–29.

32. Taft, *Service with Fighting Men*, 2:51.

33. "Africana Age," Schomburg Center for Research in Black Culture, New York Public Library, http://exhibitions.nypl.org/africanaage/essay-world-war-i.html, accessed July 10, 2015.

34. Hopkins, *History of the YMCA*, 499–501.

35. Daniel Okrent, *Last Call: The Rise and Fall of Prohibition* (New York: Scribner, 2010) 239.

36. Hopkins, *History of the YMCA*, 555. Many YMCA schools would ultimately become community colleges.

37. Ezra Pound, from "Hugh Selwyn Mauberly," part 1 (1920), http://www.poetryfoundation.org/poem/174181, accessed July 24, 2015.

38. Minutes of the Society for the Promotion of Social Service, session 3, October 19, 1906 Industrial Work Records, box 13, Kautz Archives.

39. Proceedings of the YMCA's National Convention, 1907, Washington, DC, 122–24.

40. Bryan was much less interested in punishing the substitute biology teacher John T. Scopes, who stood accused of illegally teaching evolution in a Dayton, Tennessee, school, than he was in defending the idea that humans were creations of God himself. Embracing evolution would, Bryan feared, lead the church down the path of \social Darwinism\ and strangle their impulses to help the poor.

41. Hopkins, *History of the YMCA*, 550.

42. Owen Pence, *The YMCA and Social Need* (New York: Association Press, 1939), 143.

43. Harold Keltner, unpaginated, undated typescript, scanned copy in the author's possession. Ms. Cannon was in possession of many other artifacts, including minutes from the very first Indian Guides tribe, and a binder containing letters of thanks and congratulations from numerous Y officials for his role in establishing Indian Guides. Given the limited amount of time she had available, not all the pages of the manuscript were scanned. Ms. Cannon died in April 2015.

44. A digital copy of Keltner's application, accessed January 19, 2016, can be found at http://cdm16122.contentdm.oclc.org/cdm/ref/collection/p15370coll2/id/15374.

When asked what the object of the YMCA was, he answered, "To uplift men." When asked about the relation between the YMCA and the churches, he said, "Cooperative, uniting the different denominations."

45. Keltner, typescript; *South Bend Tribune*, May 6, 1934.

46. Keltner, typescript; Lansing Smith Papers, box 191, YMCA biographical files, Kautz Archives.

47. Keltner, "Tribute to Joe Friday," *Long House News* 19, no. 2 (December 1955): 3.

48. Keltner, typescript. By the time Indian Guides began to take off, Cheley was in Colorado and Smith in New York City.

49. Keltner.

CHAPTER TWO

1. Robert S. Tilton, *Pocahontas: The Evolution of an American Narrative* (Cambridge, UK: Cambridge University Press, 1994), 174.

2. S. Elizabeth Bird, ed., *Dressing in Feathers: The Construction of the Indian in American Popular Culture* (Boulder, CO: Westview Press, 1996), 2.

3. Harold Keltner, unpaginated, undated typescript, scanned copy in the author's possession.

4. Keltner.

5. Bill McGoogan Jr., "Fathers and Sons Are 'Pals Forever' When They Join the Y-Indian Guides," *St. Louis Globe-Democrat*, November 19, 1948.

6. "Woodcraft History," Ernest Thompson Seton Institute, https://etsetoninstitute.org/woodcraft-history/, accessed September 10, 2015.

7. Philip Deloria, *Playing Indian* (New Haven, CT: Yale University Press, 1998), 108–11.

8. Keltner, "Tribute to Joe Friday," *Long House News* 19, no. 2 (December 1955): 3.

9. Keltner, typescript.

10. Adele Starbird, "The Start of the Indian Guides," *St. Louis Post-Dispatch*, July 16, 1953.

11. *Herald and Presbyter* 93, no. 47 (November 1922): 14. Phillips and his wife returned to Poplar, Montana, in May 1964 to visit three Indian Presbyterian churches they had served "for several years" until leaving in 1953 to serve "in another area of Dakota work" until they retired in 1957. "Dr. H. Phillips Will Speak at Services," *Poplar (Montana) Standard*, May 8, 1964.

12. Starbird, "Start of the Indian Guides," states that six fathers signed up with Keltner to form the first tribe.

13. H. S. Keltner, "Origin and History of the Indian Guides—Father and Son Movement of the YMCA," July 1946, Histories and Research on Indian Guides and Father and Son Movement, box 16, Boys Work Records, Kautz Archives.

14. These aims were introduced one by one in a series of typed, illustrated, and mimeographed newsletters distributed between October 1933 and May 1934. YMCA Indian Guides Records no. 801, box 1, Western Historical Manuscripts Collection, University of Missouri–St. Louis.

15. Young Men's Christian Association, *The Father and Son Y-Indian Guides* (New York: Association Press, 1954).

16. Of one binder in particular, Ms. Keltner-Cannon recalls, "Daddy told me I should keep very close. He said it was very important because it proved that he was the founder of Indian Guides." It was filled with letters of congratulations from YMCA secretaries and grateful fathers from across the country. Written on the cover of the minute book: "Osage Tally 1st Ind. Guide tribe in World. 2 yrs 1926–1928." Though the first minutes in the folder are from November 17, there is reference in the minutes to a previous October meeting that may have been an organizational meeting for men only, to help prepare for this first gathering with both fathers and sons.

17. The listing of members comes from Osage Indian Guides minutes, November 17, 1926. The quotes within parentheses come from Keltner, "Origin and History," 5. In the latter account, Keltner mentions "Prof. O.B. Badger, of Columbia University Extension Work, with his two boys," but they are not mentioned in the original minutes.

18. Keltner, "Origin and History," 4.

19. Keltner, typescript.

20. Keltner presided as "Chief Lone Wolf" for the Osages' first several months, but when elections for offices were held in April 1927, he stepped aside and urged the election of Hefelfinger. "In electing a new chief," the minutes from April 27 stated, "the members all felt as though it would be impossible to carry on without Chief Lone Wolf in the chair and feel sure he would have been elected in spite of his protest if he had not promised to council and help new chief."

21. Keltner, "Tribute to Joe Friday."

22. Starbird, "Start of the Indian Guides."

23. "Negaunee Speaks," *Long House News* 10, no. 2 (November 1945): 2.

24. "Stay Close to That Boy," *Long House News* 6 (1942): 7.

25. Osage Indian Guides minutes, February 14, 1927, courtesy Gene Keltner Cannon.

26. Robert Berkhofer, *The White Man's Indian* (New York: Alfred A. Knopf, 1978).

27. The authors made repeated attempts to contact Friday's descendants. While we wish we could have learned more about him, we respect the wishes of his family and community not to engage with this work.

28. This information was taken from a Friday family tree (labeled "no. 10 Wabima'k'wa Friday") sent to us by Greg Measor, who visited the Friday family on Bear Island in 2006.

29. Information courtesy of Greg Measor, one of the founders of National Longhouse, who was given it by members of the Friday family.

30. Andrew Holman, "Telling Stories about Indigeneity and Canadian Sport: The Spectacular Cree and Ojibway Hockey Barnstorming Tour of North America, 1928," *Sport History Review* 43, no. 2 (2012): 192.

31. Patricia Jasen, "Native People and the Tourist Industry in Nineteenth-Century Ontario," *Journal of Canadian Studies* 28, no. 4 (1993–94), 21.

32. Holman, "Telling Stories," 181, 185, 192.

33. Holman, 185.

34. According to Holman, the distinction between Cree and Ojibwe was essentially meaningless; they frequently intermarried and "considered themselves virtually one people: *Anishinaabe*." Holman, 185.

35. Holman, 181.

36. Arch Wilkinson Shaw, "Grasping the Opportunity," *System: The Magazine of Business* 17, no. 4 (April 1910): 408–9.

37. George W. Lee, "Ontario's Railway Owned by Province, Run by Commission," *Toronto Globe*, January 3, 1928.

38. Jocelyn Thorpe, "Temagami's Tangled Wild: Race, Gender and the Making of Canadian Nature," PhD diss., York University, 2008, 250.

39. Jocelyn Thorpe, *Temagami's Tangled Wild: Race, Gender, and the Making of Canadian Nature* (Toronto: UBC Press, 2012), 77–79.

40. Thorpe, 88–89.

41. Thorpe, "Temagami's Tangled Wild," 269.

42. "Joe Friday," *Long House News* 9, no. 1 (October 1944): 3–4.

43. Thorpe, "Temagami's Tangled Wild," 275.

44. This portrait was painted by Keats Petree and presented to Keltner in 1970 by the Atlanta Longhouse of Indian Guides.

45. Gene Keltner Cannon, interview by Paul Hillmer, May 24, 2015.

46. Keltner, typescript.

47. Keltner.

CHAPTER THREE

1. Philip Deloria, *Playing Indian* (New Haven, CT: Yale University Press, 1998).

2. Jason Edward Black, "The 'Mascotting' of Native America: Construction, Commodity, and Assimilation," *American Indian Quarterly* 26, no. 4 (Autumn 2002): 605–22.

3. Rayna Green, "The Tribe Called Wannabe: Playing Indian in America and Europe." *Folklore* 99, no. 1 (1988): 30–55.

4. "Introduction to the First Edition," in *American Indian Stereotypes in the World of Children: A Reader and Bibliography*, ed. Arlene Hirschfelder, Paulette Fairbanks Molin, and Yvonne Wakim, 2nd ed. (London: Scarecrow Press, 1999), xiii.

5. Kevin Gover, address to members of the Saint Paul & Minnesota Foundation, October 30, 2018.

6. Rebecca Tsosie, "Reclaiming Native Stories: An Essay on Cultural Appropriation and Cultural Rights," *Arizona State Law Journal* 34 (2002): 310.

7. Eric Lott, *Love and Theft: Blackface Minstrelsy and the American Working Class* (New York: Oxford University Press, 1993), 3–6.

8. Rebecca Tsosie, "Reclaiming Native Stories," 323.

9. "Summary of the APA Resolution Recommending Retirement of American Indian Mascots," American Psychological Association, https://www.apa.org/pi/oema/resources/indian-mascots.

10. Erik Stegman and Victoria Phillips, "Missing the Point: The Real Impact of Native Mascots and Team Names on American Indian and Alaska Native Youth," Center for American Progress, https://www.americanprogress.org/issues/race/reports/2014/07/22/94214/missing-the-point/.

11. Sara L. Schewebel, *Child-Sized History: Fictions of the Past in U.S. Classrooms* (Nashville, TN: Vanderbilt University Press, 2011), 35–70.

12. C. Howard Hopkins, *History of the YMCA in North America* (New York: Association Press, 1951), 210.

13. *Year Book of the Young Men's Christian Associations of North America for the Year 1895* (New York: International Committee, 1895), 30–31.

14. *Year Book.*

15. Robert D. Hall, "Progress Made by the Indian," *Association Men*, August 1911, 488.

16. Hall, 488.

17. Katie Johnston-Goodstar, "Decolonizing Youth Development: Re-imagining Youthwork for Indigenous Youth Futures," *AlterNative: An International Journal of Indigenous Peoples* 16, no. 4 (2020): 378–86. G. Stanley Hall's theory of recapitulation states that as youth mature into adulthood their minds recreate the evolution of the human species, rising from primitive to civilized.

18. Hall, "Progress," 488.

19. *Indian Guides*, brochure, n.d., box 52, Boys Work Records, Kautz Family YMCA Archives.

20. Mary Gloyne Byler, "Introduction to American Indian Authors for Young Readers," *American Indian Stereotypes in the World of Children* (Lanham, MD: Scarecrow Press, 1999), 47–54.

21. Theodore Whitson Ressler, *Treasure of American Indian Tales* (New York: Association Press, 1957), dust jacket. The Indian Guides publication *Long House News* contains ads for the book and describes Ressler as an experienced Y-Indian Guide story teller. Unpaginated insert in *Long House News* 23, no. 1 (October 1960) .

22. Whitson, *Treasure*, x.

23. "Karl der Deutsche," *Der Spiegel* 16 (September 1962): 73.

24. Richard H. Cracroft, "The American West of Karl Mai," *American Quarterly* 19, no. 2, pt. 1 (Summer 1967): 250–52.

25. Cracroft, 253.

26. Werner Mahrholz, "Karl May," *Das literarische Echo 12* (November 1918), 136–37.

27. Cracroft, "Karl Mai," 258.

28. Harold Keltner, "Eric among the Savages," master's thesis, 1915, Springfield College Archives.

29. William Hefelfinger, "Soundness of Using Indian Background in Indian Guide Program," *Long House News* 10, no. 2 (November 1945): 2.

30. The Raggers program dates back to 1914 and is still present at many YMCA camps. It is a progressive program designed to bring youth closer to God and conforms to other YMCA Christian citizenship programs of the early twentieth century.

31. Abigail A. Van Slyck, *A Manufactured Wilderness: Summer Camps and the Shaping of American Youth, 1890–1960* (Minneapolis: University of Minnesota Press, 2006), 10.

32. Van Slyck, xx.

33. Van Slyck, 189–90.

34. Harold Keltner, editorial, *Long House News* 1, no. 1 (January 1935): 1 (emphasis ours).

35. The article was found in a file of clippings in the YMCA Indian Guides Records no. 801, box 1, folder 3, Western Historical Manuscripts Collection, University of Missouri–St. Louis. There is no visible date, but references to the upcoming "pow-wow" suggest the article is from February 27, the Sunday preceding the event.

36. "How 'Y' Makes Good Indians," *St. Louis Globe-Democrat*, December 8, 1935.

37. Keltner, editorial, 2.

38. Arthur Martin, "What the Indian Guides Mean to Me," *Long House News* 4, no. 4 (March 1939): 2.

39. "The Indians," *Long House News* 14, no. 2 (December 1950): 4.

CHAPTER FOUR

1. H. S. Keltner, "Origin and History of the Indian Guides—Father and Son Movement of the YMCA," July 1946, Histories and Research on Indian Guides and Father and Son Movement, box 16, Boys Work Records, Kautz Archives.

2. "A Report on Y-Indian Guide Developments," May 26, 1967, Indian Guides Papers, 1960–1969, box 52, Boys Work Records.

3. Between 1926 and January 1938, the following "tribes" were formed: Osage (1926), Algonquin (1927), Kaw (1934), Iroquois (December 1930), Capaha (February 1931), Ojibwe (December 1930), Otoe (January 1931), Seminole (May 1933?), Sioux (February 8/34), Mohican (February 7, 1934), Shawnee (February 7, 1934), Cherokee (February 7, 1934), Chickasaw (February 7, 1934), Navajo (December 1932), Mohican (South Bend, IN, February 12, 1934), Pottawatomie (South Bend, IN, February 12, 1934), Miami (South Bend, IN, February 12, 1934), Cheyenne (Charleston, MO, February 13, 1934), Seminole (November 28, 1934), Chippewa (Webster Groves, January 22, 1935), Mandan (St. Louis, March 1935), Mohawk (St. Louis, April 35), Pawnee (Kirkwood, May 1922, 1935), Algonquin ([Granite?] City, IL, May 1922, 1935), Osage (Charleston, MO, June 21, 1935), Cheyenne (KC, MO, May 3, 1936), Shawnee (Flat River, May 18, 1936), Okaw (Belleville, IL, February 16, 1937), Arapahoe (KC, MO, March 1, 1937), Mohican (Webster Groves, March 12, 1937), Shoshone (Webster Groves, March 12, 1937), Winnebago (University City, March 12, 1937), Arapaho (Webster Groves, March 25, 1937), Delaware (Webster Groves, March 1937), Osage (May 37), Onondaga (May 1937), and Blackfoot, Kopaha? (January 1938).

4. National Council of the YMCA, "A Criticism of the Indian Guides Idea," *Christian Citizenship* 9, no. 9 (November 1930): 3.

5. "Mad Moon," as-yet-unnamed Indian Guides newsletter, 1933, YMCA Indian Guides Records no. 801, box 1.

6. "Start of the Indian Guides," *St. Louis Post-Dispatch*, July 16, 1953.

7. At a summer campout for the Kirkwood "tribe," for example, "Corn Planter told about guarding a munitions dump while the Germans were trying to find their range to blow it up. Leather Snake [J. L. McKay] told about getting two hundred children out of a river just as a four-foot wall of water swept down the mountain and out to the sea." "Pow Wow of Kirkwood Tribes at Camp Skull-Bones in the Woods," *Long House News* 1, no. 7 (October 1935): 3. McKay's name is listed in the December 1936 issue of *Long House News*, p. 2.

8. Keltner, typescript, n.d.

9. Keltner, "Origin and History," 6.

10. St. Louis YMCA, *The Indian Guides*, program manual, 2nd ed., 1933, 12–13.

11. "3rd Sun, Snow Moon, 1938," minutes of the Chickasaw tribe, YMCA Indian Guides Records no. 801, box 1, folder 5.

12. A letter from Abel Gregg to J. E. Sproul does, however, indicate that Rickey accepted chairmanship of the second National Hi-Y Congress. Gregg to Sproul, January 10, 1938, Correspondence, 1938–1941, box 50, Boys Work Records.

13. Pam Atkins, interview, July 30, 2021.

14. St. Louis YMCA, *Indian Guides*, 17.

15. St. Louis YMCA, 19–20. The manual also provided many suggestions for indoor and outdoor activities, camping, field trips to historical sites, and a collection of books on a wide variety of related subjects. It listed and described various hobbies, games, and collections, and in fact borrowed pictographs from Ernest Thompson Seton to show boys how they could create "Indian-themed" invitations. One could also find suggestions on how to choose an Indian name, a list of tribes and where they resided, and many suggestions to chiefs on how to run successful meetings. Finally, space was provided in the back to list the names and addresses of all the members of the tribe.

16. Jim Wotruba, interview, 27 June, 2014.

17. C. Howard Hopkins, *History of the YMCA in North America* (New York: Association Press, 1951), 549–55. By the 1920s, YMCA leaders, such as Abel Gregg, were increasingly advocating the use of "natural social groups" for youth development and other YMCA character development programs.

18. Hopkins, 549–55.

19. Osage Indian Guides minutes, July 6, 1928; "The Tale of the Chickasaws," n.d., YMCA Indian Guides Records no. 801, box 1, folder 5.

20. "The American Indian," *Long House News* 1, no. 1 (January 1935): 3.

21. "Lansing Smith," *Long House News* 2, no. 2 (May 1936): 3.

22. Greg Norman, interview, March 18, 2016.

23. Stephen Hanpeter, interview, June 27, 2014.

24. National Council of the YMCA, "A Criticism."

25. "Indian Guides Adopted as National Program for Boys at International Convention of YMCA in Niagara Falls, October 24, 1935," *Long House News* 1, no. 8 (December 1935): 1. While no specific tie between Keltner and Gray can be easily established, both men grew up in Indiana (Gray in West Lafayette, Keltner in South Bend) and served in World War I, though Gray was living in Cook County, Illinois, when he enlisted.

26. Greg Measor, e-mail exchange, November 22, 2016. Measor attributes this story to Charles Keltner Shanks, Harold Keltner's grandson. The account can be found at http://www.nationallonghouse.org/about-programs/basic-info/joe-friday-bio/.

27. Harrison S. Elliott to members of the National Boys' Work Committee, May 13, 1935, Correspondence, 1925–1935, box 56, Boys Work Records.

28. H. S. Keltner, "Origin and History of the Indian Guides—Father and Son Movement of the YMCA," July 1946, Histories and Research on Indian Guides and Father and Son Movement, box 16, Boys Work Records.

29. "Indian Guides Adopted," 1.

30. "Indian Guides Adopted," 1, 3. See also minutes of the eleventh annual meeting of the National Council of the YMCA, Niagara Falls, New York, October 24–26, 1935, 24, Kautz Archives.

31. Keltner, "Origin and History."

32. *The Indian Guides Father Son Program* (pamphlet), c. 1935, Papers, 1947–1963 (misfiled), box 16, Boys Work Records.

33. "HOW to Hunt Wampum," fundraising card, Papers, 1930–1937, box 52, Boys Work Records.

34. "As the Exhibit Draws Near," *Long House News* 3, no. 4 (February 1938).

35. "Indian Guides Wampum Hunt," general bulletin no. 3, January 23, 1936, Papers, 1930–1937.

36. J. A. Urice to John Manley, February 8, 1934, Correspondence, July 1934–1935, 1936–1939, box 50, Boys Work Records.

37. Jay A. Urice to Charles Russell, August 26, 1937, and John Manley to Jay Urice, July 30, 1937, Correspondence, July 1934–1935, 1936–1939.

38. Keltner, "Origin and History."

39. Tracy Redding, "What's in a Name?," n.d. (c. 1937), Boys Work Historical Summaries, 1900–1953, box 57, Boys Work Records. Redding's name was not a part of the original manuscript, but someone wrote his name in pencil under the title.

40. Andrew A. Santanen, "Why Indian Guides?," n.d. (c. 1937), Boys Work Historical Summaries, 1900–1953.

41. Gregg to Sproul.

42. National meeting of Council of Indian Guides, South Side YMCA, St. Louis, MO, March 5, 1938, National Longhouse Convention, 1938, box 15, Boys Work Records.

43. "Ed" [J. E. Sproul?] to Abel Gregg, March 23, 1938, Correspondence, 1938–1941, box 50, Boys Work Records.

44. "Boys Work Projects from May 1939 to September 1939," July 12, 1939, Correspondence, 1938–1941.

45. Report from Abel Gregg to J. E. Sproul, "Principle Tasks for 1939 and Enterprises ahead for 1940," November 24, 1939, Correspondence, 1938–1941.

46. "Joe Friday 'Ahtik' Ojibway Indian," undated flyer, provided by Ms. Debbie Redmond of the St. Louis YMCA, who found it while removing artifacts from the old South Side Y building in St. Louis.

47. Joe Friday to Abel Gregg, January 31, 1940, Joe Friday Letter and Publisher Letter, 1940–1970, box 57, Boys Work Records.

48. "Tribal Trails in Missouri" and "Joe Friday," *Long House News* 9, no. 1 (October 1944): 2, 3.

CHAPTER FIVE

1. "What the Guides Mean to a Boy," *Long House News* 4, no. 4 (March 1939): 2.

2. Ibid., 2. Martin was a member of the Osage tribe and principal of McCoy School in Kansas City, Missouri.

3. *Long House News* 13, no. 3 (January–February 1949): 2.

4. "General Douglas MacArthur Knows What Fatherhood Means," *Long House News* 6, no. 7 (1942): 1.

5. "Letter from A. A. Miller, National Chief of Indian Guides," *Long House News* 9, no. 1 (October 1944): 1.

6. Dr. Milton Towner, "Stay Close to That Boy," speech delivered at the fifth National Long House meeting, May 23–24, 1942, Chicago.

7. *Long House News* 9, no. 1 (October 1944): 2.

8. Harrison S. Elliott to chairman of Boys' Work Committee, "American Boys and the War," undated memo, Correspondence, 1938–1941, box 50, Boys Work Records, Kautz Archives.

9. "Publicity Suggestions for the 25th Anniversary of Father and Son Y-Indian Guides," Indian Guides Papers, 1950–1959, box 58, Boys Work Records.

10. "Publicity Suggestions."

11. "National Y-Indian Guides Reservation Now Officially Named," *Long House News* 14 no. 4 (May–June 1950): 1.

12. "'Negaunee Reservation'—W. H. Hefelfinger Discusses Development of National Y-Indian Guides Project," *Long House News* 14, no. 1 (October 1949): 1, 4.

13. Ledlie to Sproul, December 14, 1950, Indian Guides Papers, 1950–1959.

14. "A Proposal for the National Indian Guides Reservation," Indian Guides Papers.

15. "Break Ground for Y-Indian Guide Museum," *Long House News* 25, no. 3 (February 1962): 1.

16. Report of Boys' Work Committee Department, n.d., Correspondence, 1938–1941.

17. Young Men's Christian Association, *Y-Indian Guides*.

18. David Lehleitner, interview, June 27, 2015.

19. Minutes of the Midwest consultation of members of the National Council Committees related to Boy's Work, February 13, 1948, Midwest Consultation on Youth Program, 1948–1963, box 57, Boys Work Records.

20. The committee minutes do not disclose what the fundamental requirements are, but a 1949 manual, *The Marks of Good Boy's Work: A Procedure for the Administration of National Standards for YMCA Boys' Work*, cites the "Purposes of YMCA Boys' Work," developed at the 1944 Cleveland Assembly on YMCA Boys' Work, as the source of these objectives. Boys Work Correspondence and Reports, 1948–1950, box 56, Boys Work Records.

21. Midwest consultation minutes, February 11, 1948.

22. Midwest consultation minutes.

23. "Little Running Bear Visits Forest Home of Joe Friday," *Long House News* 17, no. 4 (April 1954): 1, 4. The popular song "Running Bear" was not released until 1959.

24. "Joe Friday Biography," National Longhouse, https://www.nationallonghouse.org/about-programs/basic-info/joe-friday-bio/, accessed August 19, 2021.

25. St. Louis YMCA Board minutes, S0835-YMCA Addenda, 1853–2003, box 22, folder 395, Western History Archives, University of Missouri–St. Louis.

26. National Longhouse executive committee minutes, February 18, 1955, box 56, Boys Work Records. Friday's nephew is unnamed in the minutes, but he sent a letter of thanks that was quoted in the December 1957 edition of *Long House News*.

27. "Memorial to Joe Friday," *Long House News* 18, no. 4 (May 1955): 1.

28. "Smoke Signals from the First Big Chief, Harold Keltner," *Long House News*, 14, no. 2 (December 1955): 3.

29. National Longhouse executive committee minutes, February 17, 1956, box 56, Boys Work Records. Indiana seems to have played an outsize role in representing the executive committee on Bear Island, whether because the meeting prior to the service was held in South Bend, because of those who had visited him the previous year, or because of Indiana's closer proximity to Lake Temagami and the efficiency of sending three representatives from a single airport. Carmichael and Fisher were from South Bend and Foster from nearby Mishawaka.

30. *Long House News* 21, no. 2 (December 1957): 2.

31. *YMCA Year Book and Official Roster* (New York: Association Press, 1959).

32. Midwest consultation minutes, February 8, 1957.

33. Midwest consultation minutes, February 21, 1958.

34. McCollem to Dudley Armstrong, February 10, 1958, Indian Guides Papers, 1950–1959.

35. "Minneapolis Y-Indian Guide-A-Rama," *Long House News* 24, no. 2 (December 1960): 4.

36. "The Y-Indian Guide Program of the Young Men's Christian Association," Y-Indian Guides, Study + Suggestions, 1960, box 46, Boys Work Records.

37. "The Y-Indian Guide Study," Indian Guides Papers, 1950–1959.

38. Ibid.

39. K. A. Cuordileone, "'Politics in an Age of Anxiety': Cold War Political Culture and the Crisis in American Masculinity, 1949–1960," *Journal of American History* (Bloomington, IN) 87, no. 2 (2000): 515–45.

40. "The Y-Indian Guide Study."

41. Larry Rosen, interview, August 20, 2021.

42. "Task Group IV—Principles of Program with 9–11 Year Olds," Indian Guides Papers, 1960–1969, box 52, Boys Work Records. The first mention of Y-Adventure Guides notes that the group has functioned in the east, primarily in Burlington County, New Jersey, and Rochester, New York. The group is described as a successor for Indian Guides, and a proposal to the continued problem of youth not wanting to grow up.

43. "Task Group IV."

44. J. A. Ledlie, "A Study of the Extent, Location, Organization, and Program of Older Boy Tribes in the Y-Indian Guide Program," February 1962, Indian Guides Papers, 1960–1969.

45. Young Men's Christian Association, *Y-Indian Guides*.

46. "Y-Indian Guide Week in El Paso" and "National American Indian Day," both from *Long House News* 25, no. 1 (October 1961): 2. The proposed holiday was not designed to promote Y-Indian Guides but to celebrate the history and contributions of Native Americans.

47. "National Y-Indian Guide Week Kit, 1970," 14–15, box 57, Boys Work Records.

48. "Y Indian Guides Week in Fresno," *Long House News* 25, no. 1 (October 1961): 2; "National American Indian Day," *Long House News* 25, no. 1 (October 1961): 2; "Fresno Y-Indian Guides Deal Directly with President Kennedy," *Long House News* 26, no. 2 (1962): 1.

49. "Two Governors Proclaim State Y-Indian Guide Weeks," *Long House News* 30, no. 1 (Fall 1966): 1 and 6; "Oregon Governor Feted for Y-Indian Guide Week," *Long House News* 31, no. 1 (Winter 1968): 4.

50. "Reorganization of the Regional Structure of Y-Indian Guides," memo, May 11, 1964, Indian Guides Papers, 1960–1969.

51. Don Reap, "How to Relate Y-Indian Guides Closer to the YMCA," Indian Guides Papers.

52. "New Tribe Registration Plan Instituted," *Long House News* 30, no. 4 (Fall 1967): 1.

53. Charles Kujawa, ed., *Father and Son Indian Guide Manual* (New York: Association Press, 1976), 23.

CHAPTER SIX

1. Edward Cleino, "Indian Guide Membership Has Helped Me," *Long House News* 6, no. 2 (1941): 3. (In this same issue it is announced that the first Indian Guides tribe of the Deep South has been established in Birmingham, Alabama.) Cleino was born in Rolla, Missouri, on January 29, 1917, and grew up in St. Louis. Before graduating from high school he had already established a reputation as a fine tenor soloist and was principal timpanist for the St. Louis Philharmonic Orchestra at age seventeen. After earning a master's degree in music at George Peabody College, now a part of Vanderbilt University, he taught for both institutions. He enlisted during World War II in 1942 and ended his service in 1946 as a captain in the US Army Air Corps, having earned the Bronze Star. After his military service Cleino returned to Nashville, earning a doctorate at Peabody. In 1949 he accepted a position at the University of Alabama, where he spent the rest of his career. According to his obituary (he died in 2015 at the age of ninety-eight), he "left behind a legacy of students who were deeply impacted by his care, thoughtfulness, and dedication to their growth and success." https://www.legacy.com/obituaries/tuscaloosa/obituary.aspx?n=Edward-Henry-Cleino&pid=174571478, accessed 28 February, 2019. A year before his death he was the subject of a doctoral dissertation written by the University of Alabama's Beth Ann Davis.

2. Cleino, "Indian Guide Membership," 3.

3. Norris Lineweaver, interview, July 14 and December 19, 2017.

4. "True and False Questions on Indians," *Long House News* 5, no. 4 (April 1940): 3; "No One Likes the Word 'Squaw,'" *Long House News* 5, no. 3 (March 1940): 3.

5. "An Interesting Letter from Our Chicago Braves," *Long House News* 4, no. 2 (March 1939): 4; "How Did the Indian Get Here?" and "The Indian and Engineering," *Long House News* 5, no. 1 (October 1939): 3. According to the second article, "Coolidge and Roosevelt Dams and the Yuma project now irrigate approximately 575,000 acres. But the canals follow in many instances the contours established by the old Pueblo Indians of the desert 1000 years ago."

6. "Indians and Art," *Long House House News* 5, no. 3 (March 1940): 3. "It is a matter of real interest that the war motif plays only a minor part in these paintings. The real theme is around Indian cultural life and expression." "True and False Questions on Indians," *Long House News* 5, no. 4 (April 1940): 3.

7. "Our Tribal Prayer," *Long House News* 4, no. 4 (March 1939): 2.

8. "Tribal Trails in Missouri," *Long House News* 9, no. 1 (October 1944): 2, 3. Also interspersed in this issue are comments like "The earliest colonists would have perished but for the generosity of Indians"; "All Indians born in the United States are citizens but in a few states they are not allowed to vote!"; and "Swearing in the form of blasphemy was practically unknown among Indians."

9. "Help Needed for Navajo Indians," *Long House News* 14, no. 2 (November–December 1949): 4.

10. For example, "Y-Indian Guides Visit Navajo Land," *Long House News* 22, no. 2 (December 1958), describes the "Crow Tribe" from Long Beach, California, visiting a Navajo reservation in Window Rock, Arizona, the previous July and planning to take a larger group the following year. In 1969 a "tribe" from Seattle's East Side organized 650 Indian Guides members to help with flooding caused by a broken dike. "Y-Indian Guides Respond to Emergency," *Long House News* 32, no. 2 (September 1969). Other articles discuss the possibility of "tribes" visiting nearby reservations, but no actual evidence of their doing so exists.

11. Endres and Gould, "'I Am Also in the Position,'" 419.

12. "The American Indian Calls for Full Status and Treatment," *Long House News* 32, no. 4 (April 1970): 1; "Forrest Tucker Honored," *Long House News* 33, no. 1 (May 1970): 3.

13. Thomas Saylor, interview, July 7, 2014.

14. Lineweaver, interview.

15. "Make Your Moccasins," *Long House News* 9, no. 1 (October 1944): 4.

16. "Indian Trails Products," *Long House News* 31, no. 1 (October 1968): 3. While other examples of these companies come from undated advertisements, the authors were able to locate similar ads, at least for the Grey Owl Indian Craft Leather Company, in issues of the Boy Scouts magazine *Boys' Life* going back to at least 1948.

17. Nina Mjagkij, *Light in the Darkness: African Americans and the YMCA, 1852–1946* (Lexington: University Press of Kentucky, 1994). *Light in the Darkness* offers an excellent general history of the African American YMCA experience from 1852 to 1946, when the national office ended the practice of racial descriptions in data collection and reporting.

18. "Friendly Indians Initiated," *Pine Torch* 5, no. 16 (January 1926): 2.

19. *Long House News* 8, no. 5 (May 1944): 4; "Merry Christmas! Braves and Families," *Long House News* 22, no. 2 (December 1958): 1; "Popcorn Profits Send Dads to National Longhouse," *Long House News* 23, no. 1 (October 1959): 3; "Baton Rouge Tribe Scores a "First," *Long House News* 31, no. 2 (Spring 1968): 4; Paul Hillmer, *The Cleveland YMCA: Reflections on 150 Years of Service to a Community* (Cleveland: Herwell Press, 2004), 130–31.

20. "Membership Workers Set Record," *New Sign* (Harlem YMCA), October 1961, 1; "The New Sign," "1021 Boys and Girls in Summer Program," *New Sign*, September 1966, 2–3.

21. "Y-Indian Guides Initiate Action Planning for Interracial Advance," *Long House News* 31, no. 2 (Spring 1968): 1.

22. "Max M. Spencer Presides at 1968 Annual Executive Committee," *Long House News*, 31, no. 4 (Autumn 1968): 3. An undated, typewritten manuscript (with a penciled date: "1973?") describes "new program thrusts," including those "that foster interracial and inter-cultural understanding, programs with minority families and inner city families," but there is no evidence that the Y made any significant headway in these areas. "Basic Facts on YMCA Parent-Child Programs," National Longhouse Papers, 1970–1973, box 58, Boys Work Records, Kautz Archives.

23. Region I staff to "Y" Indian Guides dads and YMCA staff, 27 March, 1970, National Longhouse Papers.

24. "Over 700 to Attend Pittsburgh Convention," *Long House News* 34, no. 2 (March 1972): 1; "Dallas County YMCA Indian Guides, How!" Ronald Kinnamon Papers, box 112, YMCA Biographical Files, Kautz Archives.

25. "Thoughts on the Future of BAN-WYS Training Program," December 1, 1973, box 1, folder 14, Jesse Alexander Papers, Kautz Archives, digital file accessed August 19, 2021, https://umedia.lib.umn.edu/item/p16022coll416:2162.

26. *African Guides*, manual distributed by the National Conference of Black and Non-white Secretaries (BAN-WYS), Notes and Miscellaneous Records, BAN-WYS, box 1, Jesse Alexander Papers, Kautz Archives, digital file accessed August 19, 2021, https://umedia.lib.umn.edu/item/p16022coll315:1720.

27. Untitled description of Y-African Guide program, YMCA Child and Family Programs & Indian Guides Surveys, 1991–2000, box 59, Boys Work Records. For example, associate director Bob Telleen in a May 17, 1991, letter to "Executives with Y-Indian Program" mentions that several groups are interested in establishing "Y-African Guides" programs. Parent-Child Indian Program—National Advisory Committee, 1989–1993, box 59, Boys Work Records.

28. From the script of "Home of the Braves," dated January 16, 1969, written by Harry Winkler and Harry Dolan. A copy was kindly provided by the Moving Image section of the Library of Congress.

29. Dr. Melridge R. Shelby, interview, June 13, 2014.

30. Rayna Green, "The Tribe Called Wannabe: Playing Indian in America and Europe." *Folklore* 99, no. 1 (1988): 30–55.

31. Planning Session for Y-Indian Guide Resources, February 26, 1968, Indian Guides Papers, 1960–1969, box 58, Boys Work Records.

32. John M. Corbett to James Bunting, April 12, 1968, Indian Guides Papers, 1960–1969.

33. "National Y-Indian Guide Long House: A Guide for Better Understanding of the American Indian," memo, 1972, National Longhouse Papers, 1970–1973.

34. "A Guide for Local YMCAs in Working with American Indian People," typescript, National Longhouse Papers, 1970–1973.

35. These groups included the American Indian Historical Society, American Indian Movement, Americans for Indian Opportunity, American Indian Press Association, National Congress of American Indians, National Council on Indian Opportunity, National Indian Women's Association, National Indian Youth Council, and the National Tribal Chairman's Association.

36. The nine Native members represented the Creek, Colville, Kickapoo, Tonawanda, Montauk, Choctaw, Osage, Delaware, and Comanche nations.

37. Those new aims were: "1. To strengthen the bonds of companionship with my father (son); 2. To increase in fitness, physical skills, and body development; 3. To grow in wisdom, intellectual curiosity, and independence; 4. To develop reverence for the Creator, spiritual understanding, and a faith for daily living; 5. To serve others—young and old—who are in need, sick, or lonely; 6. To gain in appreciation, love, and support of my family." Charles C. Kujawa, ed., "Program Guide for Father and Son Y-Trail Blazers," 5, box 57, Boys Work Records.

38. National Longhouse 1975, "Program Tips for YMCA Parent-Child Groups," National Longhouse Papers, 1974–1976, box 58, Boys Work Records.

39. "Work with the American Indian," April 24, 1973, National Longhouse Papers, 1970–1973.

40. National Board of YMCAs Urban Action and Program Division, "Commission to the National YMCA American Indian Consultant Team" (dated "Feb 1976" in pencil), National Longhouse Papers, 1974–76. Original members listed were: Betty Beaver, Aberdeen, SD; Maria Davalos, New York; Reginald Elgin, Santa Rosa, CA; Valerie Elgin, Salt Lake City, UT; Carol Gardner, Muskogee, OK; John Kasaske, Landover Hills, MN; Chuck Kujawa (YMCA staff), New York; Francis Lee, Dupree, SD; Beeman Logan, Basom, NY; Karla Miller, Phoenix, AZ; John D. Parker, Washington, DC; Kathryn Red Corn, Norman, OK; Rose Tonepahhote, Quakertown, PA; Blue Hill Townsend, Bartlesville, OK; Elmer Winnerchy, Lawton, OK.

CHAPTER SEVEN

1. "Welcome to the National Longhouse," National Longhouse Papers, 1970–1973, box 58, Boys Work Records, Kautz Archives.

2. Frank Phillips was the founder of the Phillips Petroleum Company.

3. *National Y-Indian Guide Center: A Living Link to America's Indian Heritage*, undated pamphlet (c. 1972), National Y Indian Guide Center—Woolaroc, 1965–1976, box 59, Boys Work Records.

4. "Y-Indian Guides and Other YMCA Parent-Child Programs," WOOLAROC Highlight Series, booklet no. 10, provided by Woolaroc museum director Shiloh Thurman.

5. "New National Y-Indian Center Opened," *Long House News* 35, no. 1 (October 1972): 1, 3.

6. "Objectives of the National Y-Indian Guide Center Which Impose Special Responsibilities upon Every Center Employee," National Y Indian Guide Center—Woolaroc.

7. Shiloh Thurman, phone conversation, August 23, 2021. The authors made numerous attempts to speak with Mr. Daylight. On one occasion he called one of us at an inopportune moment. Arrangements were made to connect the following day, but Mr. Daylight never reconnected. His late wife called shortly after his death to say he had intended to speak with us, but never did.

8. National YMCA Task Force on Group Registration, Report and Recommendations, June 6, 1975, 1, National Longhouse Papers, 1974–1976, box 58, Boys

Work Records; Task Force on Group Registration, n.d., National Longhouse Papers, 1974–1976.

9. Larry Rosen, email to authors, August 18, 2021.

10. Larry Rosen, interview, August 20, 2021

11. Leonard Shapiro, "Princess Pale Moon Draws Special Note," *Washington Post*, November 3, 1991, accessed online November 3, 1991, https://www.washingtonpost.com/archive/sports/1991/11/03/princess-pale-moon-draws-special-note/d3a1ddc2-8909-4266-b531-cf1cf2c798e7/.

12. National Board of YMCAs Urban Action and Program Division, "Task Force on Y-Parent-Child Programs, 10/31/1979," National Longhouse Reports, 1972–80, box 16, Boys Work Records.

13. National Longhouse executive committee minutes, April 24–25, 1980, and National Council of Chiefs minutes, September 21–23, 1979, both in Y-Indian Guide Documents, 1973–1983. While the National Council of Chiefs mentions that average annual royalties totaled $40,000, a November 5–6, 1980, National Longhouse report to the Urban Action and Program Division (Parent and Child Programs, 1959–1980, Kautz Archives) states that "program sales" were $22,695 in 1977 and only $16,740 in 1979. It is possible that "program sales" did not include other income generated from "royalties."

14. "Task Force on Y-Parent-Child Programs"; National Longhouse executive committee minutes, May 3–4, 1979, 13, Y-Indian Guide Documents, 1973–1983.

15. National Board of YMCAs Urban Action and Program Division, "IG Parent Child Programs 1959–1980A," November 5–6, 1980, Parent and Child Programs, 1959–1980, Kautz Archives.

16. "National Family Life Program Goal, 1979–84," Parent and Child Programs, 1959–1980.

17. "National Family Life Program Goal."

18. "National Family Life Program Goal."

19. "Models for Progress," Parent and Child Programs, 1959–1980.

20. National Board of YMCAs Urban Action and Program Division, "Task Force on Y-Parent-Child Programs."

21. Barbara Taylor, interview, July 26, 2021.

22. Ken Walk, "Indian Guides Lore Reveals South Side Founder Wished to Combat Delinquency," *Southside Journal*, September 18, 1985, 13.

23. Annual meeting minutes, YMCA of the USA Indian Guide/Princess Programs National Advisory Committee (NAC), April 25 and April 26, 1991, Parent-Child Indian Program—National Advisory Committee, 1989–1993, box 59, Boys Work Records.

24. NAC minutes, December 17, 1990, Parent-Child Indian Program.

25. "Y-Indian Guide Programs and Their Concerns" (survey), 1991, YMCA Child and Family Programs & Indian Guides Surveys, 1991–2000, box 59, Boys Work Records.

26. Ibid.

27. Chris Mould to Bob Telleen, memo, September 10, 1991, Parent-Child Indian Program.

28. Bob Telleen to YMCA executives, memo, May 17, 1991, Parent-Child Indian Program.

29. Telleen to YMCA executives.

30. Telleen to YMCA executives.

31. National Longhouse conference minutes, January 26, 1993, Parent-Child Indian Program.

32. Rosen, interview.

33. Rosen.

34. "Position on Voyagers Parent/Child Program," statement, Parent-Child Indian Program.

35. "Voyagers Parent/Child Program."

36. "Y-Indian Guide Program," draft 2, 1991 National Advisory Committee Resolutions, April 28, 1991; Telleen to YMCA executives.

37. *Man 2 Man*, film, Disney, 1994, box 1, Ronald Kinnamon Papers, Kautz Archives; "52nd National Longhouse—Akron Metropolitan YMCA," 1991, box 59, Boys Work Records. Later the Y attempted to reconnect with the Smithsonian for help restructuring the program so that parents and children could learn about "Native American Indians the way they want us to learn about them." Parent-Child Indian Program, Kautz Archives.

38. Minutes of Y-Indian Guide National Advisory Council conference call, July 9, 1991, Parent-Child Indian Program. The National Advisory Committee was extremely earnest in its belief that the Smithsonian would want to partner with the Y, passing a committee resolution on April 28, 1991, declaring their collaboration prior to receiving a reply.

39. "Minimum Standards for Local Y-Indian Guide Programs," Parent-Child Indian Program.

40. Debbie J. Garber, "Bringing Y-Indian Guides into the '90s: Reexamining Program Values," *Perspective: Journal of the Association of Professional Directors of YMCAs*, August 1994, 28.

41. Thomas Heck, "Why Y-Indian Guides Should Be Discontinued," *Perspective: Journal of the Association of Professional Directors of YMCAs*, April 1995, 33–34.

42. "Disney Movie May Be in the Works," *Hartford Courant*, August 24, 1993, http://articles.courant.com/1993-08-24/news/0000005594_1_indian-guides-program -fathers-and-sons-parent-child.

43. Taylor, interview; Carmelita Gallo, interview, March 19, 2020.

44. Owen Gleiberman, review of *Man of the House*, dir. James Orr, Entertainment, March 17, 1995, http://ew.com/article/1995/03/17/man-house-3/.

45. Minutes of National Longhouse conference call, November 7, 1992, Parent-Child Indian Program.

46. Barb Shaeffer to Lynne Vaughan, fax, June 17, 1994, p. 4, Man 2 Man— Correspondence and Papers, 1994, Boys Work Records.

47. Man 2 Man—Correspondence and Papers.

48. Letter to Jeff Guzzardo, October 13, 1992, Parent-Child Indian Program.

49. Minutes of National Longhouse conference call, January 26, 1993, Parent-Child Indian Program. Tempe also had issues with alcohol at Guides events, which prompted

the National Longhouse to advocate discussions of alcohol at the beginning of Indian Guides trainings.

50. Minutes of National Longhouse conference call , November 7, 1992, Parent-Child Indian Program.

51. Endres, "American Indian Permission for Mascots."

52. Brayboy, "Toward a Tribal Critical Race Theory."

53. Blue Corn Comics page on Indian Guides, http://www.bluecorncomics.com/indguide.htm, accessed July 18, 2020. The song mentioned in this post is called "Al's Song." The original "tribal" website described it as follows: "You probably thought Al was just making this up as he went along, but here are the actual words for the song we sing at federation gatherings. Tah lay lee mau mau (repeat); Geo lay lee mau mau (repeat); Austin healy (repeat); Sop in solly ollie wollie (repeat); Mol mollie mau mau (repeat). Repeat entire verse softly. Repeat entire verse loudly."

54. Atkins, interview.

55. Gallo, interview.

56. Bonnie Miller Rubin, "Bonding without Beads, Feathers," *Chicago Tribune*, October 19, 2002.

57. Gallo, interview. Before moving to Y-USA, Gallo served for nineteen years in a variety of capacities at the Chicago YMCA. The platinum rule was also discussed in our interview with Barbara Taylor and articulated in the YMCA Parent-Child Programs transition packet that Taylor sent to YMCA CEOs in the spring of 2002 (40; copy provided by Taylor).

58. Bob Eilenfeldt, interview, October 7, 2021.

59. Bruce Klunder, interview, October 4, 2021.

60. Klunder.

61. Peggy Larney, interview, 2 May, 2022.

62. Atkins, interview.

63. Eilenfeldt, interview.

64. Taylor, Parent-Child Programs transition packet, 2.

65. Norris Lineweaver, interview, July 14 and December 19, 2017.

66. Taylor, Parent-Child Programs transition packet, 41–44.

67. Rubin, "Bonding."

68. Stephen Hanpeter, interview, June 27, 2015.

69. Jim Wotruba, interview, June 27, 2015.

70. Gladish is quoted in Barbara Taylor, memo to YMCA Adventure Guide Program Network, "Re: YMCA Adventure Guide Update," November 2, 2003, Word document provided by Pam Atkins.

71. Larney is quoted in an excerpt from James Ragland, "Homage or Cultural Exploitation?," *Dallas Morning News* (no date given), reproduced in Taylor. Remarkably, until we managed to find and interview her, Larney had no idea what influence her comments had back in that meeting room in Dallas in 2001. "Four, five years later I received a phone call. . . . I don't know whether he was a National Board member or whether he was on a committee at the national level, but he said what I had presented to him made him do some thinking . . . and so he wanted me to know that my voice

made a difference in helping him. But he also said he got many, many threatening calls because he was doing that. . . . He wasn't associated with the unit by the position I had known him. But he thanked me, and since then I haven't heard anything from him. . . . I wasn't quite aware of what had happened until you called me." Larney, interview.

EPILOGUE

1. Greg Measor, interview, May 20, 2014.

2. "Brief History of the Programs," National Longhouse, nationallonghouse.org/about-programs/basic-info/brief-history/, accessed August 13, 2021.

3. "Charles Keltner-Shanks Biography," National Longhouse, nationallonghouse.org/about-programs/basic-info/charles-keltner-shanks-bio, accessed August 13, 2021.

4. Measor, interview.

5. Barbara Taylor, interview, July 26, 2021

6. Pam Atkins, interview, July 30, 2021.

7. Dave Lehleitner, interview, June 27, 2015.

8. Stephen Hanpeter, interview, June 27, 2015.

9. Les Neal Jr., interview, June 27, 2015.

10. Larry Rosen, interview, August 20, 2021.

11. American Psychological Association, "Summary of the APA Resolution Recommending Retirement of American Indian Mascots," https://www.apa.org/pi/oema/resources/indian-mascots. See also American Psychological Association, "APA Resolution Recommending the Immediate Retirement of American Indian Mascots, Symbols, Images, and Personalities by Schools, Colleges, Universities, Athletic Teams, and Organizations," https://www.apa.org/about/policy/mascots.pdf, June 2001, accessed July 2, 2019, which includes a full page of scholarly citations.

12. Daniel Yi, "Native American Groups Decry YMCA Program's Use of Cultural Themes," *Los Angeles Times*, April 30, 2001.

INDEX